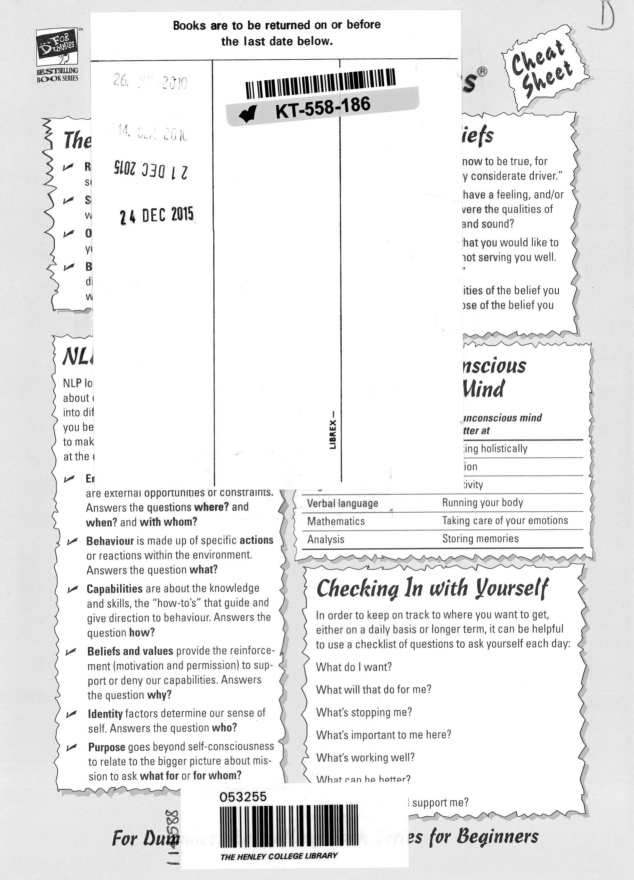

Cheat Sheet

BEST SELLING BOOK SERIES

The ...

- ✔ R...
  s...
- ✔ S...
  w...
- ✔ O...
  y...
- ✔ B...
  di...
  w...

...iefs

...now to be true, for ...y considerate driver."

...have a feeling, and/or ...ere the qualities of ...and sound?

...hat you would like to ...not serving you well.

...ities of the belief you ...ose of the belief you

NL...

NLP lo...
about ...
into dif...
you be...
to mak...
at the ...

- ✔ En...
  are external opportunities or constraints. Answers the questions **where?** and **when?** and **with whom?**

- ✔ **Behaviour** is made up of specific **actions** or reactions within the environment. Answers the question **what?**

- ✔ **Capabilities** are about the knowledge and skills, the "how-to's" that guide and give direction to behaviour. Answers the question **how?**

- ✔ **Beliefs and values** provide the reinforcement (motivation and permission) to support or deny our capabilities. Answers the question **why?**

- ✔ **Identity** factors determine our sense of self. Answers the question **who?**

- ✔ **Purpose** goes beyond self-consciousness to relate to the bigger picture about mission to ask **what for** or **for whom?**

...nscious ...Mind

...unconscious mind ...tter at
...ing holistically
...ion
...tivity
Running your body
Taking care of your emotions
Storing memories

Verbal language	
Mathematics	
Analysis	

Checking In with Yourself

In order to keep on track to where you want to get, either on a daily basis or longer term, it can be helpful to use a checklist of questions to ask yourself each day:

What do I want?

What will that do for me?

What's stopping me?

What's important to me here?

What's working well?

What can be better?

...l support me?

For Dummies... ...k Series for Beginners

Neuro-linguistic Programming For Dummies®

The 4-point Formula for Success

1. **Know your outcome.**

   It is important to specify precisely what it is you want. You can use the outcome frame to fine tune the desired outcome and satisfy the well-formedness conditions.

2. **Take action.**

   Unless you take that first step, and then the following ones, nothing will happen to help you towards you outcome, no matter how clearly they are defined.

3. **Have sensory awareness.**

   If you have the awareness to see, hear, feel what it isn't working, you can modify your behaviour to steer you towards the desired outcome.

4. **Have behavioural flexibility.**

   This ties in beautifully with the NLP presupposition: "In interactions among people, the person with the most flexibility of behaviour can control the interaction." Or you could say…"If it ain't working, do something different."

Altering States with Music

Here are some different ways to think about the music you play. Perhaps you're stuck in a groove with your listening taste:

- **Vary the range of CDs you buy** – from Baroque to classical, jazz and blues, reggae, pop and rock to opera.

- **Change the rhythm** – compare predictable rhythms with varied and unfamiliar ones to encourage your creativity. World music is good for this.

- **Instrumentation or lyrics?** – words can distract – solo instruments tend to encourage relaxation.

- **Intuition** – trust your own tastes. If you dislike a piece of music, don't struggle with it. Turn it off – it's unlikely to make you feel good.

- **Start the day differently** – when you feel good in the morning, you'll get off to a flying start. Try swapping the confrontational news channel on the radio for inspiring and uplifting music.

The NLP Fast Phobia Cure

1. Identify when you have a phobic response to a stimulus or a traumatic or unpleasant memory that you wish to overcome.

2. Remember that you were safe before and after the unpleasant experience.

3. Imagine yourself sitting in the cinema, watching yourself on a small, black-and-white screen.

4. Now imagine floating out of the you that is sitting in the cinema seat, and into the projection booth.

5. You can now see yourself in the projection booth, watching yourself in the seat, watching the film of you on the screen.

6. Run the film in black-and-white, on the very tiny screen, starting before you experienced the memory you wish to overcome and running it through until after the experience when you were safe.

7. Now freeze the film or turn the screen completely white.

8. Float out of the projection booth, out of the seat into the end of the film.

9. Run the film backwards very quickly, in a matter of a second or two, very quickly, in full-colour, as if you are experiencing the film, right back to the beginning, when you were safe.

10. You can repeat steps 8 and 9 until you are comfortable with the experience.

11. Now go into the future and test an imaginary time when you might have experienced the phobic response.

For Dummies: Bestselling Book Series for Beginners

Neuro-linguistic Programming

FOR

DUMMIES®

by **Romilla Ready**
and **Kate Burton**

JOHN WILEY & SONS, LTD

Neuro-linguistic Programming For Dummies®

Published by

John Wiley & Sons, Ltd.

The Atrium

Southern Gate

Chichester

West Sussex

PO19 8SQ

England

E-mail (for orders and customer service enquires): cs-books@wiley.co.uk

Visit our Home Page on www.wiley.co.uk or www.wiley.com

Wiley also publishes its books in a variety of electronic formats. Some content that appears in print may not be available in electronic books.

British Library Cataloguing in Publication Data:

A catalogue record for this book is available from the British Library.

ISBN-13: 978-0-7645-7028-5 (pbk)

Printed and bound in Great Britain by Bell & Bain Ltd., Glasgow

20 19 18 17 16 15 14 13 12

WILEY

About the Authors

Romilla Ready is a Master Practitioner of Neuro-linguistic Programming, and is the director of Ready Solutions, which was founded in 1996. She runs professionally developed workshops across a range of areas and has trained clients in the UK and overseas, using her cross-cultural skills to build rapport between different nationalities. Romilla has been interviewed on local radio and has had articles on stress management and applications of NLP published in the press.

Kate Burton is an NLP coach and trainer who enables individuals and organisations to focus their energy effectively. Her business career began in corporate advertising and marketing with Hewlett-Packard. Since then she has worked with many varied businesses across industries and cultures on how they can be great communicators. What she loves most is delivering custom-built training and coaching programmes. She thrives on supporting people in boosting their motivation, self-awareness and confidence. Her belief is that people all have unique talents, abilities and core values. The skill is about honouring them to the full.

Authors' Acknowledgments

From Romilla: It's strange to think of finding *Neuro-linguistic Programming For Dummies* in the bookshops. The fulfillment of this dream wouldn't have been possible without the help and support of a raft of wonderful people, to all of whom I wish to offer my heartfelt thanks. My 'partner in crime', Kate Burton: I am so glad you agreed to collaborate on this project when I rather nonchalantly asked you if you'd like to write a book on NLP with me. Thank you, mum, for all your love, support and ideas, keep them coming; Angela, my sister, has always been there in times of trouble and celebration and has done a grand job of being the first 'test dummy' for our book and making sure I didn't split my infinitives! Oswyn for being the perfect grandfather to 'brattus' and Derek for keeping me in style while I was busy with the writing; my son, Derwent, who bails me out when I come a cropper with my laptop and his wonderful friends, Ben, Ezra and Matt, to name a few, who have taught me so much about tolerance and laughter; Carol who thankfully keeps us in order; some of my NLP 'playmates' David Staker, Anne-Marie and Rintu who help me learn and stretch; the quadrupeds in my life, both canine and feline, who taught me about unconditional love; my Yoga teacher, Swami Ambikananda Saraswati, for her patience in the face of all my questions; David, my NLP trainer, who gave me another rung in the ladder for personal change. Last but not least, I'd like to thank Jason for taking a blind leap of faith and giving us the opportunity to write this book. Daniel and his terrific editorial team have added an extra dimension to our writing with their incisive questions and brilliant suggestions. Sam and the rest of the support and marketing team are pretty terrific too.

From Kate: When Romilla and I set out to write this book, our intention was to learn and have some fun. So my thanks to Romilla – we did both and developed such a deep understanding and friendship. All my family, especially Bob, Rosy and Jessica have my thanks for your unconditional love and support, especially your unfailing ability to nurture me so I could keep the chapters flowing. To my special friends, thank you for hanging on in there when I've been too busy to come out and play. I thank Ian for getting me hooked on NLP and remain in awe of his skill, and Jan for demonstrating the sheer joy of NLP coaching at its finest. To my clients and colleagues, especially Lynda and Helen, thank you for endless opportunities to learn and practice NLP with you. To Jason, Sam, Dan, Julia, Shaun and the fabulous professionals at Wiley for shaping the idea into reality. You certainly demonstrated the power of belief. And above all it's thanks to you, the reader, that this book sprang to life. May you be intrigued and inspired to learn.

Publisher's Acknowledgments

We're proud of this book; please send us your comments through our Dummies online registration form located at www.dummies.com/register/.

Some of the people who helped bring this book to market include the following:

Acquisitions, Editorial, and Media Development

Executive Editor: Jason Dunne

Executive Project Editor: Caroline Walmsley

Project Editors: Daniel Mersey, Amie Tibble

Technical Reviewer: Anne-Marie Halliwell

Editorial Assistant: Samantha Clapp

Cover Photos: bobo / Alamy

Cartoons: Rich Tennant, www.the5thwave.com

Production

Project Coordinator: Bill Ramsey

Layout and Graphics: Denny Hager, Joyce Haughey, Michael Kruzil, Kristin McMullan, Heather Ryan, Jacque Schneider, Mary Gillot Virgin

Proofreaders: Brian H. Walls

Indexer: TECHBOOKS Production Services

Publishing and Editorial for Consumer Dummies

Diane Graves Steele, Vice President and Publisher, Consumer Dummies

Joyce Pepple, Acquisitions Director, Consumer Dummies

Kristin A Cocks, Product Development Director, Consumer Dummies

Michael Spring, Vice President and Publisher, Travel

Brice Gosnell, Publishing Director, Travel

Kelly Regan, Editorial Director, Travel

Publishing for Technology Dummies

Andy Cummings, Vice President and Publisher, Dummies Technology/General User

Composition Services

Gerry Fahey, Vice President of Production Services

Debbie Stailey, Director of Composition Services

Contents at a Glance

Introduction 1

Part I: Welcome to a Brave New World 7

Chapter 1: NLP Explained 9
Chapter 2: Some Basic Assumptions of NLP 17
Chapter 3: Taking Charge of Your Life 31

Part II: The Brain's Highway Code 47

Chapter 4: Who's Steering the Bus? 49
Chapter 5: Pushing the Communication Buttons 69

Part III: Winning Friends . . . Influencing People 83

Chapter 6: Seeing, Hearing, and Feeling Your Way to Better Communication 85
Chapter 7: Creating Rapport 101
Chapter 8: Understanding to Be Understood: Metaprograms 117

Part IV: Opening the Toolkit 135

Chapter 9: Dropping Anchors 137
Chapter 10: Sliding the Controls 153
Chapter 11: Changing with Logical Levels 167
Chapter 12: Driving Habits: Uncovering Your Secret Programs 183
Chapter 13: Time Travel 197
Chapter 14: Smooth Running Below Decks 211

Part V: Words to Entrance 223

Chapter 15: Heart of the Matter: The Meta Model 225
Chapter 16: Hypnotising Your Audience 237
Chapter 17: Stories, Fables, and Metaphors: Telling Tales to Reach
the Subconscious 249
Chapter 18: Asking the Right Questions 263

Part VI: The Part of Tens 275

Chapter 19: Ten Applications of NLP 277
Chapter 20: Ten Books to Add to Your Library 287

Chapter 21: Ten Online NLP Resources 291
Chapter 22: Ten Movies That Include NLP Processes 295

Part VII: Appendixes *299*
Appendix A: Resource List 301
Appendix B: Rapport Building 307
Appendix C: The Well-formed Outcome Checklist 309

Index *311*

Table of Contents

Introduction *1*

About This Book..1

Conventions Used in This Book 2

What You're Not to Read 2

Foolish Assumptions 3

How This Book Is Organised...3

    Part I: Welcome to a Brave New World 3

    Part II: The Brain's Highway Code......................................4

    Part III: Winning Friends . . . Influencing People 4

    Part IV: Opening the Toolkit 4

    Part V: Words to Entrance 4

    Part VI: The Part of Tens 5

    Part VII: Appendixes...5

Icons Used in This Book..5

Where to Go from Here..6

Part 1: Welcome to a Brave New World *7*

Chapter 1: NLP Explained **9**

What Is NLP?...9

    A few quick definitions 10

    Where it all started and where it's going.........................11

    A note on integrity 12

The Pillars of NLP: Straight up and Straightforward 12

Models and Modelling 14

    The NLP Communication Model.......................................14

    Modelling excellence 15

Tips for Using NLP to Greater Effect......................................15

    Attitude comes first 15

    Curiosity and confusion are good for you.......................16

    Change is up to you..16

    Have fun on the way!..16

Chapter 2: Some Basic Assumptions of NLP **17**

NLP Presuppositions 18

    The map is not the territory 18

    People respond according to their map of the world......20

There is no failure, only feedback 20
The meaning of the communication is the response it elicits........22
If what you are doing is not working, do something different........22
You cannot not communicate...24
Individuals have all the resources they need to achieve
their desired outcomes...24
Every behaviour has a positive intent...25
People are much more than their behaviour......................................26
The mind and body are interlinked and affect each other 27
Having choice is better than not having choice...............................28
Modelling successful performance leads to excellence...................29
Final Words on Presuppositions: Suck Them and See............................29

Chapter 3: Taking Charge of Your Life 31

Taking Control of Your Memory 31
You See It Because You Believe It...33
Playing the blame frame...34
Getting stuck in a problem frame..34
Shifting into Outcome Frame...35
The Path to Excellence...35
Knowing what you want 36
Getting smarter than SMART: Creating well-formed outcomes......37
The 4-point Formula for Success...42
Spinning the Wheel of Life 42
Keeping a Dream Diary of Your Goals 44
Just Go for It...45

Part II: The Brain's Highway Code 47

Chapter 4: Who's Steering the Bus? 49

How Our Fears Can Drive Us in the Wrong Direction...............................50
Conscious and unconscious 50
Your quirky unconscious mind...51
The Reticular Activating System (RAS) – Your Tracking System............54
How Memories Are Created 56
Post Traumatic Stress Disorder (PTSD) 56
Phobias 57
The NLP fast phobia cure..58
Beliefs and Values Make a Difference 59
The power of beliefs 60
Values...63
Daydreaming Your Future Reality 68

Chapter 5: Pushing the Communication Buttons 69

The NLP Communication Model 70
    Scenario 1 70
    Scenario 2 71
Understanding the Process of Communication 72
    Seven ± Two 72
    To each his own 75
Giving Effective Communication a Try 81

Part III: Winning Friends . . . Influencing People 83

Chapter 6: Seeing, Hearing, and Feeling
Your Way to Better Communication 85

The Modalities . . . That's VAK Between You and Me 86
    Filtering reality 87
    Hearing how they're thinking 88
Listen to the World of Words 90
    Building rapport through words 90
    Bring in the translators 92
The Eyes Have It 94
Making the VAK System Work for You 98

Chapter 7: Creating Rapport 101

Why Rapport Is Important 102
    Recognising rapport 102
    Identifying with whom you want to build rapport 103
Basic Techniques for Building Rapport 105
    Seven quick ways to sharpen your rapport .106
    The communication wheel and rapport building 106
    Matching and mirroring 108
    Pacing to lead 109
    Building rapport in virtual communication .110
How to Break Rapport and Why 111
    The power of the 'but' word 112
Understanding Other Points of View 114
    Exploring perceptual positions 114
    The NLP meta-mirror 115

Chapter 8: Understanding to Be Understood: Metaprograms 117

Metaprogram Basics 118
    Metaprograms and language patterns 119
    Metaprograms and behaviour 120

Proactive/Reactive 120
Toward/Away From 122
Options/Procedures 125
Internal/External 126
Global/Detail 128
Sameness/Sameness with Difference/Difference 130
Combinations of Metaprograms 132
Developing Your Metaprograms 133

Part IV: Opening the Toolkit 135

Chapter 9: Dropping Anchors 137

Starting Out with NLP Anchors 138
Setting an anchor and building yourself a resourceful state 139
Eliciting and calibrating states 140
Setting your own repertoire of anchors 142
Recognising your own anchors 142
Going through the Emotions: Sequencing States 144
Altering states with anchors 145
Get with the Baroque beat 145
Walking in someone else's shoes 147
Getting Sophisticated with Anchors 147
Changing negative anchors 148
Stage anchors 149
A Final Point about Anchors 151

Chapter 10: Sliding the Controls 153

Submodalities: How We Record Our Experiences 154
Basic Info, or What You Need to Know Before You Begin 154
To associate or to dissociate 155
Defining the details of your memories 156
Getting a little practice 159
Understanding your critical submodalities 160
Making Real-life Changes 161
Taking the sting out of an experience 161
Changing a limiting belief 162
Creating an empowering belief 163
Getting rid of that backache 163
Using the swish 164
Submodalities Worksheet 165

Chapter 11: Changing with Logical Levels **167**

What's Your Perspective? 167
Understanding Logical Levels 168
    Asking the right questions 169
    Taking logical levels step-by-step 170
    Practical uses for logical levels 171
Finding the Right Lever for Change 172
    Environment 172
    Behaviour 173
    Capabilities 175
    Beliefs and values 176
    Identity 178
    Purpose 179
Figuring Out Other People's Levels: Language and Logical Levels 180
Logical Levels Exercise: Teambuilding at Work and Play 180

Chapter 12: Driving Habits: Uncovering Your Secret Programs **183**

The Evolution of Strategies 184
    The S-R model 184
    The TOTE model 184
    NLP strategy = TOTE + rep systems 185
    The NLP strategy model in action 185
The Eyes Have It: Recognising Another's Strategy 187
Flexing Your Strategy Muscles 189
    Acquiring new capabilities 189
    Re-coding your programs 190
    It's all in the 'How' 191
Using NLP Strategies for Love and Success 192
    Deep love strategy 192
    Strategies for influencing people 194
    The NLP spelling strategy 195
    To succeed or not to succeed 196

Chapter 13: Time Travel **197**

How Your Memories Are Organised 198
Discovering Your Time Line 199
Changing Time Lines 200
Travelling Along Your Time Line to a Happier You 203
    Releasing negative emotions and limiting decisions 203
    Finding forgiveness 206
    Comforting the younger you 207
    Getting rid of anxiety 207
    Making a better future 208

Chapter 14: Smooth Running Below Decks **211**

A Hierarchy of Conflict 212
From Wholeness to Parts 213
Part's intentions 214
Getting to the heart of the problem 214
Help! I'm in Conflict With Myself 215
Listening to your unconscious mind 215
Taking sides 216
Becoming Whole: Integrating Your Parts 216
Visual squash 217
Reframing – as if 218
Bigger and Better Conflicts 220

Part V: Words to Entrance *223*

Chapter 15: Heart of the Matter: The Meta Model **225**

Gathering Specific Information with the Meta Model 226
Deletion – you're so vague 229
Generalisation – beware the always, musts, and shoulds 230
Distortion – that touch of fantasy 232
Using the Meta Model 234
Two simple steps 235
A couple of caveats 235

Chapter 16: Hypnotising Your Audience **237**

Language of Trance – The Milton Model 238
Language patterns and the Milton Model 239
Other aspects of the Milton Model 240
The art of vagueness and why it's important 242
You Are Going Deeper 244
Getting comfortable with the idea of hypnosis 245
Everyday trances 246

**Chapter 17: Stories, Fables, and Metaphors: Telling Tales
to Reach the Subconscious** **249**

Stories, Metaphors, and You 250
The Stories of Your Life 250
Storytelling basics 250
Storytelling at work 251
A gift to the next generation 253

Powerful Metaphors 254
   Metaphors in NLP...254
   Using metaphors to find new solutions.....................255
   Direct and indirect metaphors 257
Building Your Own Stories 258
   Using the Personal Story Builder Journal 258
   More ways to flex your storytelling muscles.............259
   And this reminds me of . . . : Adding loops to your story 260

Chapter 18: Asking the Right Questions **263**

Before You Begin: Question-asking Tips and Strategies.........................264
   Cleaning up your language.....................................264
   It's the way you are that counts 265
   Press the pause button..266
   Test your questions 266
   Make positive statements the norm 266
Figuring Out What You Want......................................267
   What do I want? 267
   What will that do for me? 268
Making Decisions 269
Challenging Limiting Beliefs......................................270
Finding the Right Person for the Job: A Question of Motivation 271
   What do you want in your work?.............................272
   Why is that important?...272
   How do you know you have done a good job? 272
   Why did you choose your current work?...................273
Checking In with Yourself...273

Part VI: The Part of Tens................................**275**

Chapter 19: Ten Applications of NLP **277**

Developing Yourself...277
Managing Your Personal and Professional Relationships....................278
Negotiating a Win-Win Solution.................................279
Meeting Those Sales Targets 280
Creating Powerful Presentations...............................280
Managing Your Time and Precious Resources 282
Being Coached to Success 282
Using NLP to Support Your Health.............................283
Connecting to Your Audience: Advice for Trainers and Educators.......284
Getting That Job..285

Chapter 20: Ten Books to Add to Your Library 287

Changing Belief Systems with NLP 287
The User's Manual for the Brain 287
Core Transformation 288
From Frogs to Princes..288
Influencing with Integrity 288
Manage Yourself, Manage Your Life 288
Presenting Magically..289
The Magic of Metaphor 289
Words that Change Minds 289
Awaken the Giant Within 289

Chapter 21: Ten Online NLP Resources 291

Advanced Neuro-dynamics..291
Anchor Point..291
Association for Neuro-linguistic Programming 292
Shelle Rose Charvet 292
Crown House Publishing 292
Design Human Engineering.com 292
Encyclopaedia of Systemic NLP and NLP New Coding 293
Michael Gelb 293
The International Society of Neuro-semantics 293
Quantum Leap, Inc...293

Chapter 22: Ten Movies That Include NLP Processes 295

As Good As It Gets 295
Bend It Like Beckham 295
The Color Purple 296
Field of Dreams..296
Frida..296
Gattaca..296
The Matrix...296
The Shawshank Redemption 297
Stand and Deliver...297
The Three Faces of Eve 297
NLP at the Movies 297

Part VII: Appendixes *299*

Appendix A: Resource List 301

Contact the Authors 301
United Kingdom..301
USA and Canada 304
Denmark 305

Appendix B: Rapport Building 307

Appendix C: The Well-formed Outcome Checklist 309

Index *311*

Introduction

*I*ncreasingly, you will hear the subject of Neuro-linguistic Programming (NLP) mentioned as you go about your daily life – in corporations, colleges, and coffee shops. We wrote this book because our experience of NLP transformed our lives. We wanted to ignite the spark of curiosity in you about what is possible in NLP and with NLP. We also believed it was time for NLP to come away from academic- and business-speak to real-life plain English for all our friends out there. By friends we mean everyone and anyone, especially you the reader.

NLP has grown in popularity because it offers 'aha!' moments. It simply makes sense. Yet the name itself ('Neuro' relates to what's happening in our minds, 'Linguistic' refers to language and how we use it, while 'Programming' tackles the persistent patterns of behaviour that we learn and then repeat) and the jargon associated with it present a barrier to the average person. Some describe NLP as 'the study of the structure of subjective experience'; others call it 'the art and science of communication'. We prefer to say that NLP enables you to understand what makes you tick; how you think, how you feel, how you make sense of everyday life in the world around you. Armed with this understanding, your whole life – work and play – can become magical.

About This Book

This book aims to entrance anyone fascinated by people. By its experiential approach, NLP encourages people to take action to shape their own lives. It attracts those willing to 'have a go' and open their minds to new possibilities.

We've tried to make NLP friendly and pragmatic, accessible, and useful for you. We expect you to be able to dip into the book at any chapter and quickly find practical ideas on how to use NLP to resolve issues or make changes for yourself.

In displaying the NLP 'market stall' our choice of content is selective. We've aimed to offer an enticing menu if you're a newcomer. And for those with more knowledge, we hope this will help you to digest what you already know as well as treat you to some new ideas and applications. To that end, we've aimed to make it easy for you to find information like:

- How to discover what's important to you to pursue your goals with energy and conviction.
- What the main NLP presuppositions are and why they're important to you.
- What the best ways are to understand other people's style, helping you to get your own message heard.
- When to build rapport and when to break it.
- How to get your unconscious mind to work together with your conscious mind as a strong team.

In addition, because the best way to learn NLP is to experience it, take full opportunity of playing with all the exercises we've given you. Some of the ideas and exercises in this book may be quite different from your normal style. The NLP approach is to have a go first, set aside your disbelief, and then realise your learning.

Conventions Used in This Book

To help you navigate through this book, we've set up a few conventions:

- *Italic* is used for emphasis and to highlight new words or terms that are defined.
- **Boldfaced** text is used to indicate the action part of numbered steps.
- Monofont is used for Web addresses.

What You're Not to Read

We've written this book so that you can easily understand what you find out about NLP. And although after all this writing on our part we'd like to believe that you want to hang on our every last word between these two yellow and black covers, we've made it easy for you to identify 'skippable' material. This is the stuff that, although interesting and related to the topic at hand, isn't essential for you to know:

- **Text in sidebars:** The sidebars are the shaded boxes that appear here and there. They share personal stories and observations, but aren't necessary reading.

✔ **The stuff on the copyright page:** No kidding. You'll find nothing here of interest unless you're inexplicably enamoured by legal language and reprint information.

Foolish Assumptions

In writing this book, we made a few assumptions about you. We assumed you're a normal human being who wants to be happy. You're probably interested in learning and ideas. You may have heard the term NLP mentioned, you may already work with the concepts, or maybe it's just new and slightly intriguing for you. You need no prior knowledge of NLP, but essentially NLP is for you if any of the following ring a bell for you:

✔ You're tired or fed-up with the way some things are for you now.

✔ You're interested in how to take your living experience to new levels of achievement, happiness, adventure, and success.

✔ You're curious about how you can influence others ethically and easily.

✔ You're somebody who loves learning and growing.

✔ You're ready to turn your dreams into reality.

How This Book Is Organised

We've divided this book into seven parts, with each part broken into chapters. The table of contents gives you more detail on each chapter, and we've even thrown in a cartoon at the start of each part, just to keep you happy.

Part 1: Welcome to a Brave New World

Someone once said: 'If you always do what you've always done, you'll always get what you always got.' These are great words of wisdom to bear in mind as you begin the journey into NLP territory for yourself. In this part, you'll start to get a feel for what NLP can do for you. As you begin, there's one thing to bear in mind – suspend your disbeliefs or assumptions that may get in the way of your learning.

Part II: The Brain's Highway Code

Do you ever find there are times when you wonder, 'How did that happen to me?' So now you'll be ready to experience some 'aha!' moments that give you the clues to what makes you tick. In this part, we invite you to think about the best NLP question of all time, which is: 'What do I want?' and then to delve into what's happening behind the scenes in your brain and your unconscious thinking. Interesting stuff, we hope you'll agree.

Part III: Winning Friends . . . Influencing People

Ever considered how easy life would be if others would just do what you wanted them to? It's a tough shout. We're not claiming to be magicians, to make your worst enemies smooth putty in your hands, but rapport is such a key theme in NLP that the heart of this book explores it hand in hand with you. In this part, we give you tools for understanding other people's point of view. We'll show you how to take responsibility for making changes in how you connect with the key people in your life and learn how to become more flexible in your own behaviour.

Part IV: Opening the Toolkit

A touch of magic now opens up before you at the heart of NLP. At last, we hear you say, you're ready to be let loose on the core NLP toolkit. Loads of practical stuff here to keep coming back to. You'll learn how you can adapt and manage your own thinking to tackle situations that you find difficult, plus how you can get the resources to change habits that no longer help you, then whiz into the future and work with concepts of time to resolve old issues and create a more compelling path ahead of you.

Part V: Words to Entrance

This part focuses on how the language you use does not just describe an experience, but has the power to create it. Just imagine what it's like to have an audience eating out of your hands. Building on the skills and styles of powerful communicators, we explain the way to get them coming back with an appetite for more, and if you consider that life can be described as a series of stories, you'll find out how to write your own winning story.

Part VI: The Part of Tens

If you're impatient to get your answers about NLP sorted quickly, then stop here first. This part takes you straight to some top ten tips and lists, like applications of NLP, the resources and books to guide you, plus more besides. We designed this part just for those of you who always like to read the end of a book first to understand the meaty stuff inside.

Part VII: Appendixes

In the appendixes we've included an NLP resource list of useful addresses and Web sites, plus the two most important templates to use every day to:

- ✔ Make your outcomes real – explained more in Chapter 3.
- ✔ Build rapport with other people – which is explored in Chapter 7.

Icons Used in This Book

The icons in this book help you find particular kinds of information that may be of use to you:

This icon highlights NLP terminology that may sound like a foreign language but which has a precise meaning in the NLP field.

This icon suggests ideas and activities to give you practice of NLP techniques and food for thought.

This icon highlights practical advice to put NLP to work for you.

This icon is a friendly reminder of important points to take note of.

You'll find this icon beside stories relating real-life experience of NLP in action. Some are real; others have their names changed; while others are composite characters.

This icon marks things to avoid in your enthusiasm to try out NLP skills on your own.

Where to Go from Here

You don't have to read this book from cover to cover, but you will benefit greatly if you capture it all at the pace and in the order that's right for you. Use the table of contents to see what grabs you first. For example, if you're keen to understand someone else, try Chapter 7 first. Or if you'd like to know what makes you tick, turn to Chapter 6 first and discover the power of your senses. Feel free to dip and dive.

Once you've read the book and are keen to discover more, we'd recommend that you experience NLP more fully through workshops and coaching with others. We've included a resource section in the Part of Tens to help you on the journey.

Part I

Welcome to a Brave New World

The 5th Wave — By Rich Tennant

"My thinking has changed a little this year."

In this part . . .

You find out what NLP stands for and why people are talking about it. From seeing how it all started with some smart people in California, to getting you to think about your own assumptions, we help you to start to set off in the right direction to get what you want out of life.

Chapter 1

NLP Explained

In This Chapter

▶ Setting out on a journey together

▶ Exploring the key themes of NLP

▶ Getting the most out of NLP

*H*ere's a little Sufi tale about a man and a tiger:

A man being followed by a hungry tiger, turned in desperation to face it, and cried: 'Why don't you leave me alone?' The tiger answered: 'Why don't you stop being so appetising?'

In any communication between two people, or in this case, between man and beast, there's always more than one perspective. Sometimes we just can't grasp that because we can't see the way forward.

NLP is one of the most sophisticated and effective methodologies currently available to help you do just that. It centres on communication and change. These days we all need the skills to develop personal flexibility to the extreme. Tricks and gimmicks are not enough: we need to get real.

So welcome to the start of the journey and in this chapter you'll get a quick taster of the key themes of NLP.

What Is NLP?

We're all born with the same basic neurology. Our ability to do anything in life, whether it's swimming the length of a pool, cooking a meal, or reading this book, depends on how we control our nervous system. So, much of NLP is devoted to learning how to think more effectively and communicate more effectively with yourself and others.

✔ **Neuro** is about your neurological system. NLP is based on the idea that we experience the world through our senses and translate sensory information into thought processes, both conscious and unconscious. Thought processes activate the neurological system, which affects physiology, emotions, and behaviour.

✔ **Linguistic** refers to the way human beings use language to make sense of the world, capture and conceptualise experience, and communicate that experience to others. In NLP, linguistics is the study of how the words you speak influence your experience.

✔ **Programming** draws heavily from learning theory and addresses how we code or mentally represent experience. Your personal programming consists of your internal processes and strategies (thinking patterns) that you use to make decisions, solve problems, learn, evaluate, and get results. NLP shows people how to recode their experiences and organise their internal programming so they can get the outcomes they want.

To see this process in action, begin to notice how you think. Just imagine that it's a hot summer's day. You go home at the end of the day and stand in your kitchen holding a lemon you have taken from the fridge. Look at the outside of it, its yellow waxy skin with green marks at the ends. Feel how cold it is in your hand. Raise it to your nose and smell it. Mmmm. Press it gently and notice the weight of the lemon in the palm of your hand. Now take a knife and cut it in half. Hear the juices start to run and notice the smell is stronger now. Bite deeply into the lemon and allow the juice to swirl around in your mouth.

Words. Simple words have the power to trigger your saliva glands. Hear one word 'lemon' and your brain kicks into action. The words you read told your brain that you had a lemon in your hand. We may think that words only describe meanings: they actually create your reality. You'll learn much more about this as we travel together.

A few quick definitions

NLP can be described in various ways. The formal definition is that it is 'the study of the structure of our subjective experience.' Here are a few more ways of answering the $64,000 question: 'What is NLP?'

✔ The art and science of communication

✔ The key to learning

✔ It's about what makes you and other people tick

✔ It's the route to get the results you want in all areas of your life

✔ Influencing others with integrity

✔ A manual for your brain

✔ The secret of successful people

✔ The way to creating your own future

✔ NLP helps people make sense of their reality

✔ The toolkit for personal and organisational change

Where it all started and where it's going

NLP began in California in the early 1970s at the University of Santa Cruz. There, Richard Bandler, a master's level student of information sciences and mathematics, enlisted the help of Dr John Grinder, a professor of linguistics, to study people they considered to be excellent communicators and agents of change. They were fascinated by how some people defied the odds to get through to 'difficult' or very ill people where others failed miserably to connect.

So NLP has its roots in a therapeutic setting thanks to three world-renowned psychotherapists that Bandler and Grinder studied: Virginia Satir (developer of Conjoint Family Therapy), Fritz Perls (the founder of Gestalt Psychology), and Milton H Erickson (largely responsible for the advancement of Clinical Hypnotherapy).

In their work, Bandler and Grinder also drew upon the skills of linguists Alfred Korzybski and Noam Chomsky, social anthropologist Gregory Bateson, and psychoanalyst Paul Watzlawick.

From those days, the field of NLP has exploded to encompass many disciplines in many countries around the world. It would be impossible for us to name all the great teachers and practitioners in NLP today, but in Appendix A, you will find more guidance on extending your knowledge.

So what's next for NLP? It's certainly travelled a long way from Santa Cruz in the 1970s. So many more pioneers have picked up the story and taken it forward – made it practical and helped transform the lives of real people like you and me. The literature on NLP is prolific. Today you'll find NLP applications amongst doctors and nurses, taxi drivers, sales people, coaches and accountants, teachers and animal trainers, parents, workers, retired people, and teenagers alike. In 'The Part of Tens' we list just a few.

Each generation will take the ideas that resonate in their field of interest, sift and refine them, chipping in their own experiences. If NLP encourages new thinking and new choices and acknowledges the positive intention underlying all action, all we can say is the future is bright with possibilities. The rest is up to you.

A note on integrity

You may hear the words integrity and manipulation associated with NLP, so we'd like to put the record straight now. You influence others all the time. When you do it consciously to get what you want, the question of integrity arises. Are you manipulating others to get what you want at their expense? The question that we, the authors, ask ourselves when we are in a selling situation is simple. What is our positive intention for the other person – be it an individual or a company? If it's good and our intention is to benefit the other side, then we have integrity – a *win/win*. And if not, it's manipulation. When you head for win/win, you're on track for success. And as you know, what goes around comes around.

The Pillars of NLP: Straight up and Straightforward

The first thing to understand is that NLP is about four things, known as the pillars of NLP (see Figure 1-1). These four chunks of the subject are explained in the following sections.

- ✔ **Rapport:** How you build a relationship with others and with yourself is probably the most important gift that NLP gives most readers. Given the pace at which most of us live and work, one big lesson in rapport is how you can say 'no' to all the requests for your time and still retain friendships or professional relationships. To find out more about rapport – how to build it and when to break it off – head to Chapter 7.

- ✔ **Sensory awareness:** Have you noticed how when you walk in someone else's home the colours, sounds, and smells are subtly different to yours? Or that colleague looks worried when they talk about their job. Maybe you notice the colour of a night sky or the fresh green leaves as spring unfolds. Like the famous detective Sherlock Holmes you will begin to notice how your world is so much richer when you pay attention with all the senses you have. Chapter 6 tells you all you need to know about how powerful your sensory perceptions are and how you can use your natural sight, sound, touch, feelings, taste, and smell capabilities to your benefit.

- ✔ **Outcome thinking:** You'll hear the word 'outcome' mentioned throughout this book. What this means is beginning to think about what it is you want rather than getting stuck in a negative problem mode. The principles of an outcome approach can help you make the best decisions and choices – whether it's about what you're going to do at the weekend, running an important project, or finding out the true purpose of your life. Head to Chapter 3 to get the results you deserve.

✔ **Behavioural flexibility:** This means how to do something different when what you are currently doing is not working. Being flexible is key to practising NLP; you'll find tools and ideas for this in every chapter. We'll help you find fresh perspectives and build these into your repertoire. You might like to head to Chapter 5 for starters on how you can maximise your own flexibility.

Let's just give an example here of what this might mean every day. Suppose you have ordered some goods by mail. It could be a software package to store all your names, addresses, and phone number of friends or clients. You load it on your computer, use it a few times, and then mysteriously it stops working. There's a bug in the system, but you've already invested many hours in the installation and entering all your contacts. You phone up the supplier and the customer service people are unhelpful to the point of rudeness.

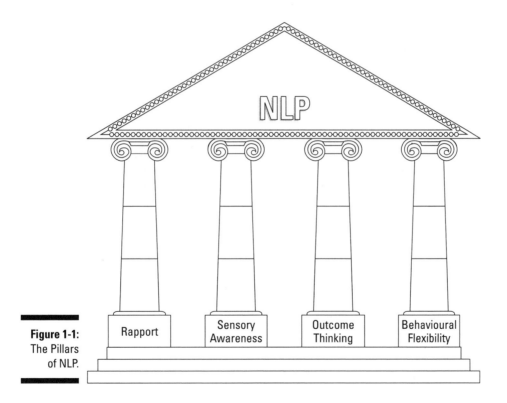

Figure 1-1:
The Pillars
of NLP.

You need to bring out all your skills in building *rapport* with the customer service manager before anyone will listen to your complaint. You'll need to *engage your senses* – particularly your ears as you listen carefully to what the supplier is saying, and notice how to control your feelings and decide on your best response. You will need to be very clear about your *outcome* – what do you want to happen after you make your complaint? For example, do you want a full refund or replacement software? And finally you may need to be *flexible in your behaviour* and consider different options if you don't achieve what you want the first time.

Models and Modelling

Neuro-linguistic Programming (NLP) began as a model of how we communicate to ourselves and others and was developed by Bandler and Grinder based on their study of great communicators. So NLP says a lot about models and modelling.

NLP works by modelling excellence in every field. The premise begins like this: If you can find someone who's good at something, then you can model how they do that and learn from them. This means that you can learn to model whoever you admire – top business leaders or sports personalities, the waiter at your favourite restaurant, or your hugely energetic aerobics teacher.

The NLP Communication Model

The NLP model explains how we process the information that comes into us from the outside. According to NLP, you move through life not by responding to the world around you, but by responding to your model or map of that world.

A fundamental assumption of NLP is that 'the map is not the territory'. What this means is that you and I may experience the same event but we do so differently. Let's imagine that you come to the next *Dummies'* party – we would both have a good time, meet lots of friendly people, enjoy good food and drinks, maybe watch some entertainment. Yet, if we were each asked the next day to recount what happened, we'd each have a different story to tell. And so the internal representations that we make about an outside event are different to the event itself.

NLP does not change the world – it simply helps you change the way that you observe/perceive your world. NLP helps you build a different map that helps you to be more effective.

John is an architect who rents expensive office space in a central city location. He used to moan frequently that the offices were not cleaned to a high enough standard, the staff were lazy, and he never got any satisfaction from the office manager. On meeting John in his office we discovered that he worked in chaos, leaving the office with plans and design ideas on every available surface and not tidying anything away. He frequently worked late into the evening and was grumpy if interrupted, so the cleaners came and went without daring to disturb him. He'd clearly not considered anyone else's point of view and had not noticed what a difficult task it was to clean his office around him. His 'map' of reality was completely different to that of the office management team.

Modelling excellence

Modelling excellence is another theme you'll hear discussed. The NLP approach is that anything somebody else can do is learnable if you break the learning into small enough component parts. It's an empowering perspective and also an encouragement to convert large overwhelming projects into lots of small ones – like eating an elephant.

Tips for Using NLP to Greater Effect

As you'll discover, the practical application of NLP is about increasing choices when it's so easy to fall in the trap of being restricted by your experience and saying: 'This is the way we do things, and this is how it has to be.' In order to get the benefit of NLP, you need to be open and give yourself and others the benefit of questioning and challenging the norms in a supportive way. Here are a few tips to remind you how.

Attitude comes first

At its essence NLP is an attitude about life and a technology which empowers you with the tools and abilities to change anything about your life which does not reflect who you are today. Anything and everything is possible if you have the mind set and attitudes that support your success. If your attitudes don't support you in living a richly rewarding life then you may want to consider changing. Changing your mind and attitude *does* change your life.

Many people spend a lot of time looking at the negatives in their lives – how they hate their jobs, or don't want to smoke or be fat. By conditioning yourself to concentrate on what you *do* want, positive results can be achieved very quickly.

Curiosity and confusion are good for you

There are two helpful attributes to bring with you: *curiosity* – accepting that you don't know all the answers, and a *willingness to be confused* – because that precedes new understanding. As the great hypnotherapist, Milton H Erickson (more on him later too), said: 'Enlightenment is always preceded by confusion.'

If you find that ideas in this book make you feel confused, thank your unconscious mind as this is the first step to understanding. Take the confusion as a sign that you actually know more than you realised.

Change is up to you

Gone are the days when you need to stay stuck in a downward spiral of repetitive behaviours and responses that are tedious and ineffective. Today NLP is all about producing measurable results that enhance the quality of people's lives without a lengthy and painful journey into the past.

Once you move into the chapters ahead, you'll discover the experiential nature of NLP – that it's about trying things out, having a go. Test out the ideas for yourself – don't take our word for it.

The responsibility for change lies with *you*: this book is the facilitator. If you are not open to change, then you have thrown away your money. So we'd encourage you to do the exercises, note your new learning, then teach and share with others, because to teach is to learn twice.

Have fun on the way!

When Clint Eastwood was interviewed on TV by Michael Parkinson he offered sound advice: 'Let's take the work seriously, and not ourselves seriously.' NLP involves much fun and laughter. If you set yourself up to become perfect, you put enormous and unrealistic pressure on yourself too. So pack in a sense of your own playfulness as you travel and try to make sense of a changing world. Learning is serious work that is serious fun.

Chapter 2

Some Basic Assumptions of NLP

In This Chapter

▶ Understanding the presuppositions of NLP

▶ Testing the NLP presuppositions

▶ Walking in someone else's shoes

▶ Learning flexibility in order to take 100 per cent responsibility in any interaction

*B*renda is a friend of mine (Romilla) and has a much loved, only daughter, Mary. At the age of ten Mary was a little spoiled as she had arrived after Brenda and Jim had given up hope of ever having a child. Mary was prone to throwing tantrums the likes of which you are extremely fortunate not to experience. Mary would thrash about on the floor, screaming and flailing her arms and legs. Brenda made no progress with Mary's tantrums until one day . . . Mary was on the floor exercising her lungs with wonderful abandonment when the long-suffering Brenda took some metal pans out of a cupboard and joined Mary on the floor. Brenda banged the pots on the wooden floor and kicked and screamed even better than Mary. Guess what? Mary lay there in stunned astonishment, staring at her mother. She decided there and then her mother was the more expert 'tantrumer' and Mary would lose the tantrum contest every time so it was futile to pursue this particular course of action and the tantrums stopped from that moment. Brenda took control of her interaction with Mary by having the greater flexibility of behaviour.

This little anecdote illustrates how ***the person with the most flexibility in a system influences the system***. This statement is not the result of some experiment conducted in a laboratory. It is an NLP presupposition or assumption; an assumption which, if you were to practise and adopt, could help to ease your journey through life. The story above shows just one of several of these 'convenient beliefs' or presuppositions which form the basis of NLP.

NLP Presuppositions

NLP presuppositions are no more than generalisations about the world. In this chapter, we explain some of the presuppositions that we consider to be most influential out of several that have been developed by the founders of NLP and offer them for your consideration.

The map is not the territory

One of the first presuppositions is that *the map is not the territory*. This statement was published in 'Science and Sanity' in 1933 by Korzybski, a Polish count and mathematician. Korzybski was referring to the fact that you experience the world through your senses (sight, hearing, touch, smell, and taste) – the territory. You then take this external phenomenon and make an internal representation of it within your brain – the map.

This internal map you create of the external world, shaped by your perceptions, is never an exact replica. In other words, what is outside can never be the same as what is inside your brain.

Take one analogy; as I (Romilla) sit in my conservatory, writing, I am looking out at the oak tree in the garden. The representation that I make of it, when I close my eyes, is completely different from the actual tree in the garden. Not being a botanist I may not notice features a botanist would observe. Just because I cannot see those features, and therefore they do not exist in my internal representation, does not mean they do not actually exist. Or try another analogy; if you were driving in London, with your London street map, the 'roads' shown in the map book are completely different to the roads you are actually driving along; for a start the tube stations you drive past are in three dimensions and colour, whereas they are shown as a blue circle with a red line through it on the map.

Putting perceptions through your own personal filter

Your senses bombard you with two billion bits of information per second but your conscious mind can only deal with between five and nine pieces of information at any given moment so there is an awful lot of information that is filtered out. This filtration process is influenced by your values and beliefs, memories, decisions, experiences, and your cultural and social background to allow in only what your filters are tuned in to receive.

A friend of mine (Romilla) believes passionately in animal welfare and has a very special bond with animals. When driving, she will spot animals behind trees, on the side of the road or on fences long before her passengers who are more likely to be looking around.

Some Europeans and North Americans may experience a major culture shock when visiting countries like India or Mexico. Because of their cultural background they may well be shocked by the level of poverty in some areas whereas local people accept the poverty as part of life.

Unfamiliar territory: Travelling down another person's map

What this means is that each of us has a very individual map of our world and to make communication easy it is a really useful exercise to at least attempt to understand the internal reality or map of the person with whom you are communicating.

I (Romilla) was buying some fish and chips and was asked to fill in a short form about the quality, service, and value-for-money of the food. The women serving behind the counter were very upset because the man who had just left had declined, quite rudely, to fill in the form. I asked the ladies if they had considered how the poor man might have felt if he was illiterate and was rude because he was embarrassed. The change in the two ladies was phenomenal. 'Oh, I never even thought about that', gasped one. Their demeanour changed immediately from one of anger and resentment to one of deep sympathy. They also felt much better in themselves and were able to let go of all the negative feelings they had been holding onto.

You can use the same strategy that I did whenever you find yourself in a situation where another person's response surprises you, irritates you, or just leaves you puzzled. When you find yourself face-to-face with a person you think is just a pain, follow these steps to change how you think about that person. (If all is right with your world right now, you can still practise this technique. Just think of someone whose behaviour really gets up your nose.)

1. **Count all the blessings in your life.**

2. **With examples of your own good rattling around in your brain, put on your most generous hat.**

3. **Ask yourself what could possibly be going on in this other person's world that would warrant his or her behaviour.**

Once you have begun to master this process, you may find not only are you happier with your lot, but you can accept people and their idiosyncrasies with ease.

People respond according to their map of the world

You respond according to the map of the world you hold in your head. The map is based on what you believe about your identity and on your values and beliefs as well as your attitudes, memories, and cultural background.

Sometimes the map of the world someone operates from may not make sense to you. However, a little understanding and tolerance could help enrich your life.

When my (Romilla) mother was a junior doctor she used to visit a psychiatric hospital. One of the patients was a very well-spoken, highly educated professor of English. One of the little foibles the professor exhibited was to walk around in the night with an open umbrella. He was convinced that the rays of the moon would give him 'moon madness'. However, the professor took great delight in sharing his passion for English literature with members of the staff whose lives were certainly enriched by their daily interactions with the professor. If the staff had been intolerant of the 'mad professor' and ignored or sidelined him, they may not have realised it but their lives would have been impoverished without the richness of his literary stories and his sense of humour – he often referred to himself as the 'impatient patient'.

There is no failure, only feedback

This is a very powerful assumption to live your life by. Everyone makes mistakes and experiences setbacks. You have a choice between allowing yourself to be waylaid by your undesirable results or learning the lessons that have presented themselves, dust yourself off and have another shot at jumping the hurdle.

A child's map of the world

A child's map of the world can sometimes make an adult think again! This is neatly illustrated by a delightful snippet in an email that was going around.

A policeman was sitting in his police van with his canine partner when he noticed a little boy staring in at them. The boy asked if that was a dog in the van. The policeman confirmed that the other occupant of the van was indeed a dog. The little boy got extremely puzzled and asked, 'What's he done to get arrested?'

I (Romilla) attended a course run by a wonderful Hawaiian Kahuna, Serge Kahili King, during which he said that he never made mistakes. This caused a few chuckles as none of us believed him and also because the twinkle in his eyes belied the deadpan expression on his face. He then added that he may not always get the results he wants, but he never makes mistakes.

Think of a sailor navigating a boat from Southampton to Sydney. Does he throw up his hands in horror and sob into his hanky if he goes slightly off course or does he work out the adjustments he needs to make and then turn the helm and keep an eye on the compass?

Normal 'feedback' is associated with receiving input or getting a response from another person. The meaning of feedback has been expanded in the context of this presupposition to include the result or outcome you may get from a particular situation.

Thomas Alva Edison is the person to learn from about feedback. Although he is famous for inventing the light bulb, he was a prolific inventor. His genius lay in trying out his ideas, *learning from 'unexpected' results* and recycling concepts from an experiment that did not work in other inventions. Where other people saw Edison's thousands of attempts at inventing the light bulb as failures, Edison simply saw each trial as yet another way of learning how not to make a light bulb.

Worrying about 'failure' keeps you focused on the past and the problems. If you examine the results you have already got, even if they are unwanted, you can then shift your focus onto possibilities and move forward.

When you're faced with 'failure', you can use this NLP presupposition to find the opportunities for growth by asking yourself the following questions.

Think of something you 'failed' at and ask yourself:

- ✔ What am I aiming to achieve?
- ✔ What have I achieved so far?
- ✔ What feedback have I had?
- ✔ What lessons have I learned?
- ✔ How can I put the lessons to positive use?
- ✔ How will I measure my success?
- ✔ Then pick yourself up and have another go!

Can you imagine a world where you gave up learning to walk simply because you fell over the first time you stood up to walk? What do you think Waterloo Station in London would look like during the rush hour if only a few people mastered the art of walking?

The meaning of the communication is the response it elicits

No matter how honourable the intentions of your communications, the success of the interaction depends on how the message is received by the listener not by what you intended. In other words, the meaning of the communication is the response it elicits.

This is yet another very powerful assumption about communication. It places the onus of responsibility to get your message across squarely at your door. Once you adopt this presupposition you are no longer able to blame the other person for any misunderstandings. If the response you get is not what you expected then you, as a student of NLP, will have the tools to use your senses to realise that the other person is missing the point. You will also have the flexibility to do things differently, through your behaviour and your words.

So start with the end in mind and think of what the outcome is that you want from your communication. What would happen if a builder started by slapping bricks on one another without a plan? You certainly wouldn't get your cathedral! In order to build something with strong foundations you need to start with an architect's vision of the end product. This is also a very good way of keeping your emotions out of the way when you are involved in a situation that could get tough.

If you want to find out more about sensory awareness please have a look at Chapter 7. Chapter 5 will show you more ways of practising flexibility of behaviour and gives a few more tips on dealing with emotions when the going gets tough.

If what you are doing is not working, do something different

So simple and yet you don't always modify your behaviour. After all, it's a lot easier wandering through life wishing change on other people and . . . you can enjoy all the angst you get from thinking those horrible thoughts about someone else. (This is the author being facetious.)

Not everyone has your internal resources and the very fact you are reading this book means you are showing initiative in making changes in your life. So we would suggest that it may take a lot less energy to change yourself than to have someone conform to your ideals.

If you accept this NLP presupposition then you recognise that it's better to change tactics than to continue to beat your head against a wall or spend your time lamenting your misfortune. Still, before you can actually change your tactics or do something different, you need to understand why what you're doing now isn't working.

So why is what you are doing not working? Could it be that you haven't communicated exactly what it is you want? Perhaps the other person has not discovered the resources they need to help you achieve your outcome. So what do you do differently to get the desired results?

For instance, if you are not getting all the hugs you feel you want perhaps you should come right out and tell your partner. Remember that positive feedback works brilliantly, so if your partner does make physical overtures make sure they know how much you appreciate the contact.

Consider this example. Patricia was a student who learned best through feeling and touch. This meant she had difficulty in following standard 'chalk-and-talk' lessons which are more suited to people who are visual or auditory oriented. As a result Patricia was finding it hard to stay on top of her class work and was failing to reach her potential. A less talented teacher might have placed the blame on Patricia and branded her as either stupid or having a bad attitude to her studies. Fortunately her teacher recognised that Patricia needed to be shown how to study and how to apply the lessons in a more practical way. She was lucky that her teacher recognised the reason for her problems and took the responsibility to do something different by adjusting her teaching methods to help Patricia do well. Patricia's teacher was a good one: she was flexible and took responsibility for the effectiveness of her teaching. Rather than blaming Patricia for her inability to learn, Patricia's teacher found another way to reach her.

Your lead or primary representation system

You experience your world through your five senses – visual (eyes), auditory (ears), kinaesthetic (feelings and touch), olfactory (smell), and gustatory (taste). More than likely you use one sense in preference to the others to collect data about your world, particularly at times of stress.

This is called your *lead* or *primary representational system*. It influences how you learn and the way you represent your external world inside your head. We'll be telling you more about this in Chapter 6.

You cannot not communicate

Have you ever smiled at someone, said something really polite but been thinking, 'Oh! Just drop dead'? No? Just as well, because we, the authors, would bet the way you held your body or gritted your teeth wouldn't have fooled anyone. We are sure that if the person on the receiving end of the message has learned NLP, or has even some sensory acuity, they would detect the lack of warmth in your eyes, the grimace in your smile, or the snarl in your voice. So even though you don't say 'Drop dead', you're still communicating that message.

This is also shown in a fascinating study, pioneered by Professor Albert Mehrabian, which established that, when talking about feelings and attitudes, what you say has a very small impact compared to the tone you use and how you hold your body. The influences, in percentage terms, are as follows:

- Verbal 7%
- Tonality 38%
- Physiology 55%

Individuals have all the resources they need to achieve their desired outcomes

We love this one! It's so positive. What this phrase means is that everyone has the potential to develop and grow. The important point to make here is you may not have *all* the internal resources you need but that you do have the internal resources to acquire new internal and external resources.

Tom, a little eight-year-old boy, was being bullied at school. He was resourceful enough to ask his father for help in dealing with the bullies. His father asked him to behave more assertively and with more confidence. Tom had no idea how to do that. Tom loved the Terminator films and his hero was Arnold Schwarzenegger. Tom's father taught him the *circle of excellence* exercise and asked Tom to imagine he was Arnie as he stepped into the circle. Tom's new found confidence affected his behaviour, his body language, and his attitude. As a result Tom's tormentors faded away and his street cred went through the roof with other little victims begging to learn his technique. The circle of excellence is a brilliant technique for psyching yourself up by building a powerful resource state and you can find out more about it in Chapter 9.

Every behaviour has a positive intent

Unfortunately this also applies to bad or non-productive behaviour. With bad behaviour the positive intention behind it, called *secondary gain*, is obscured.

Secondary gain is the benefit someone gets unconsciously from a particular behaviour that is normally considered to be disempowering or bad.

For instance a child may play the clown in class in order to gain acceptance by his peers, although his teachers and parents will find this quite destructive.

Take, for example, Janet. The youngest of five children, Janet had suffered from a bad back for as long as she could remember but the doctors could not find a reason. Janet's mother was a flighty, self-centred woman who was more interested in partying than her family. As a child, Janet's siblings would help her by carrying her books and making sure Janet was taken care of. Things became really bad after Janet's daughter was born so her husband did all the shopping and carrying of, and looking after, the baby. The little girl grew up to become 'mummy's little helper' and was always at her mother's beck and call. When Janet finally agreed to see a therapist, she was able to acknowledge that her bad back was psychosomatic. She realised that it was her way to get the love and attention she had craved from her mother but never got.

Janet's behaviour is a brilliant demonstration of this presupposition, as the secondary gain for her was to have her family run around after her, and what she really wanted was to have her craving for love and attention satisfied. Once Janet realised her need she was also able to recognise that she was getting massive amounts of love and attention from her husband and daughter. One of the 'side effects' of the therapy was that Janet was able to understand that her own mother's behaviour was based on problems her mother had and were not Janet's fault.

If you can understand the positive intention that is causing a person to behave in a particular, un-resourceful way, you can increase your flexibility and thereby your ability to communicate. You can then help to change the unwanted behaviour by satisfying the intention of the behaviour in a more positive way.

When one of the authors worked for a multinational company, a sales manager, Patrick, would occupy one of the free desks in her corner of the building when he visited. Some of the kinder terms people used for Patrick were obnoxious and inconsiderate. Patrick would spread out. He sprawled in his chair which meant it was pushed out, away from his desk and people in the author's corner would have to squeeze past. He was loud, made demands on everyone around him, and was extremely unpleasant to his secretary. An office gossip told the rest of us that poor Patrick's behaviour was the product of a domineering mother and even more masterful wife. Unfortunately his need for acceptance, and especially respect, made him behave in ways that gave him results that were exactly opposite to those he craved. One of the benefits of finding out about Patrick's background was that most of us were then able to think a little more kindly about him and his presence no longer sent our blood pressures soaring. By showing him a degree of acceptance we were able to satisfy his needs a little and mellow his behaviour.

People are much more than their behaviour

I (Romilla) was watching a television programme on speeches given by important historical figures. The one that made me do a double take was when I heard Martin Luther King Jr. respond to a journalist on how to deal with racists. Martin Luther King could have been quoting the presupposition that people are more than their behaviour when he said: 'I'm talking about a type of love which will cause you to love the person who does the evil deed while hating the deed that the person does.'

The point is that behaving 'badly' doesn't make a person a bad person. It is really important to separate the behaviour from the person. People can behave badly if they do not have the inner resources or ability to behave differently. Perhaps they find themselves in an environment that stops them from being the best they can be. Helping someone develop capabilities and skills or to move to a more conducive environment can often change someone's behaviour dramatically and propel them to new levels of excellence.

I (Romilla) know a very sweet, kind, young man, Bob, who has been diagnosed as being dyslexic. Bob adores animals and is extremely good with any that have been injured or hurt. Unfortunately, due to circumstances, Bob was branded a trouble-maker and had been in trouble with the police over drugs. People in Bob's neighbourhood saw him as a 'bad' person. Once Bob was helped to change his beliefs about his capabilities he became a very valuable contributor to society by working for an animal charity.

Each of us behaves very differently in different areas of our lives. You will read about logical levels in Chapter 11, where you will learn that people have several levels at which they function:

 ✔ Identity
 ✔ Values and beliefs

> ✔ Capabilities and skills
>
> ✔ Behaviour
>
> ✔ Environment

By helping Bob (from the anecdote above) change his capabilities, his beliefs about himself began to change. This allowed him to move into an environment where he could feel valuable and the rest became a self-fulfilling prophecy in that his identity, 'I am a failure', shifted to, 'I can actually make a contribution'. So although Bob's behaviour was bad, it didn't make him a bad person; he is much more than his behaviour, loving and kind, as we saw.

The mind and body are interlinked and affect each other

Holistic medicine works on the premise that the mind affects the body and the body affects the mind. In order to maintain a healthy human being a medical practitioner has to do more than just suppress the symptoms. She has to examine the mind and body and treat both together.

Recent research has shown just how integrated the mind-body connection is. Neurotransmitters are chemicals that transmit impulses along your nerves. They are the means by which your brain communicates with the rest of your body. Each thought you think reaches out to the farthest minuscule cell in your body via neurotransmitters. Further research has discovered that the same neurotransmitters that are found in the brain can also be produced by your internal organs. So the idea that messages are initiated and transmitted in straight lines along the neurons is no longer true; these messages can be initiated and transmitted by your organs too. Dr Pert, of the National Institute of Mental Health, refers to the 'bodymind' – the mind and body working as an integrated whole, because at the level of the neurotransmitter there is no separation between the mind and the body.

To get a better understanding of this connection and to see it in action, follow these steps:

1. **Make a circle with the left finger and thumb.**

2. **Now link your right finger and thumb through the first circle.**

   (The circles are interlinked and will only come apart by pulling on one or other of your hands.)

3. **Think of someone you really like and pull hard to break the circles.**

   Pretty tough, huh?

4. **Think of someone you really dislike and pull hard to break the circles.**

   A bit easier?

Did it require less effort to separate the circles when you were thinking of someone you didn't like? If a simple thought can affect the pressure your muscles can exert, what do you think happens to your body when you subject it to constant stress?

Having choice is better than not having choice

NLP promotes choice for an individual as a healthy way of life. Sometimes you may feel that you do not have the choice to change jobs, shift to another country, or get out of a relationship that is not happy. You may find yourself saying, 'I have no choice', 'I must do this'. Fear of change, lack of confidence in your abilities, or sometimes even unawareness of what your strengths are can hold you back from making much needed change. NLP says, 'What if it was different?' and aims to open up someone's horizons by making you conscious of all the resources you already have and can acquire. NLP helps you explore your reasons for wanting change, even if it is just a little niggle of discontent. Change can be choppy, like riding the rapids, and the people we know who have made it through, having decided on choices that they have made for themselves, are much more content and in control of their lives. You will find help deciding what you may want from your life and how to begin to implement it in Chapter 3.

In a funny way, this rings particularly true for me (Romilla) when I was working for a multinational company that was shedding a lot of people. Many of the employees waited, hoping they would not be forced to go. The IT industry was in the doldrums and jobs were thin on the ground; the general belief was that people had no choice other than to hang onto the job they were in, no matter how far they were pushed by the company. They had no choice. The ones who were relieved to get away from the stress were the ones who knew what they wanted from their jobs and had made provisions to move into alternative careers or were willing to look at all the options that were available to them, no matter how far fetched they seemed.

Modelling successful performance leads to excellence

When watching Paula Radcliffe cross the finishing line, I (Romilla) was filled with admiration. What must it feel like to be at such a peak of fitness? It occurred to me that if you had aspirations to be a Paula Radcliffe and were able bodied, then provided you had her single-minded determination and support network you could develop your beliefs and values to align your environment, capabilities, and behaviour to achieve your aspirations.

NLP gives you the tools to model someone, take what they do well, and repli-cate it. However it does not have to be such a big dream as becoming the next major figure in a sport. It could be something very simple like modelling the skills of a co-worker who always brings projects in on time or a friend who always knows the right thing to say at the right time. You could question the person you want to emulate to find out what inspires them, how they know the time is right to do what they do, and how they keep focused on their goal. In the case of the colleague, they may have a string of strategies to meet their project target which you could learn to reproduce. Modelling someone's suc-cess is a wonderful way to turn potential feelings of envy or jealousy into a constructive process for experiencing their success for yourself.

Final Words on Presuppositions: Suck Them and See

Test them for yourself by behaving as if the generalisations are true. Practise those that you find particularly useful until they become second nature to you. In trying out the NLP presuppositions, make a list and pick one from the list to live by every day. You will find, suddenly, you are living the presupposi-tions and 'the living is easier'!

One great way to increase your understanding of NLP is to explore your basic assumptions, or presuppositions, about life. Whatever you currently think about different people and problems, how you communicate and what's impor-tant, sometimes it helps to take a new perspective. This may trigger some new action or behaviour.

Remember: There is no correct answer. As you get a flavour for each of the presuppositions, consider them carefully. You don't have to agree with every one of them. You can simply try them on for size and see, hear, and feel what that does.

Chapter 3

Taking Charge of Your Life

In This Chapter

▶ Understanding that you can choose to feel good or bad

▶ Influencing how the world treats you

▶ Placing yourself firmly in the driving seat of your life

▶ Working with your brain to achieve your goals easily

▶ Discovering the secret formula for success

*Y*our memories can be a wonderful gift or a terrible scourge. They can cradle you softly in strands of silk or bind you in coils of razor wire. Your memories can propel you to your dreams or keep you trapped in the past. However, with the help of NLP, and by understanding how you can program your mind, *your past need not create your future*.

This chapter is all about making you the driver not the passenger in the story of your life. So let's get rolling. It's time to have fun.

Taking Control of Your Memory

Your memories are recorded as pictures, sounds, and feelings and by adjusting the buttons on these qualities you can enhance positive memories and take the sting out of negative memories. We invite you to read more about adjusting the quality of your memories in Chapter 10 – 'Sliding the Controls'. However, you can start off by flexing your taking-control-of-your-memory muscles with the following very simple exercises.

In the first exercise, you find out how to recall and manipulate a positive memory so that you can feel good, or even better, at will. Follow these steps:

1. **Think of a day when you were truly happy.**

2. **Notice what you see, hear, and feel when you bring back the memory.**

3. **If the memory is a picture adjust its quality by making it bigger, brighter, and bringing it closer. If you're observing yourself, try stepping into the picture to see if this makes you feel even better.**

   You can find out about 'stepping into the picture' in Chapter 10, under the section 'To associate or to dissociate'. You will find that by adjusting the qualities of the picture you can heighten the positive emotions and feel even happier and even better.

4. **Notice any sounds that may have been in the memory at the time. Does making them louder, moving them to inside or outside your head increase the positive feelings?**

5. **Notice the feelings you have, if any. Where in your body are you experiencing them? Do they have a colour, texture, or weight? Does moving the location of the feelings or changing their colour, texture, and weight alter these feelings? Adjust these parameters to enhance the feelings.**

By completing this exercise you have manipulated the qualities of the experiences you have had and more importantly, you have seen that you *can* change the structure of your memories in order to diminish the affect of negative experiences and re-experience and heighten joyful ones.

Of course, not all memories are good ones. This second exercise will show you how you can change the qualities of an unpleasant memory. By changing the attributes of the negative memory, you will be able to release negative emotions which may still be holding you in their grasp. Follow these steps:

1. **Think of a memory that is only marginally unpleasant.** For this exercise, and until you become more practised at NLP techniques, think of a memory that is only marginally unpleasant. Please leave heavy duty memories like traumas to when you are with a trained therapist.

2. **Notice the pictures, sounds, and any feelings that the memory brings up.**

3. **If you are in the picture, step out of it to become an observer.**

   You can find out about stepping in and out of a picture in Chapter 10, under the section 'To associate or to dissociate'. For now, imagine you are behind a film camera, filming yourself acting out the memory with which you are working.

4. **Change any sounds so that they're softer or perhaps make people in the picture speak like Mickey Mouse.**

   So if there are sounds like sirens or crying, you can make them softer or if you hear someone saying something unpleasant, you can have them talk to you in a silly cartoon voice.

5. **Adjust the quality of the picture.**

Make it smaller, darker, and in black and white; move it far away from you until it's a dot and almost invisible. You may want to send it into the sun and watch it disappear in a solar flare. By carrying out this step, you experience destroying the hold the memory previously had on you.

Changing the memory does not mean the event did not occur. It does, however, mean that you have a choice over how the memory affects you today and the impact it has on your tomorrows.

You See It Because You Believe It

If you were in a group of people who witnessed a robbery, chances are that none of you would give the police the same account. This is because everyone receives the data that creates their reality through their five senses (visual – sight, auditory – sound, kinaesthetic – touch, gustatory – taste, and olfactory – smell). However, your senses bombard your brain with so much data at any one time that, in order to maintain your sanity, you only process a very small fraction of the incoming data. What your brain accesses is dictated by filters that are combinations of who you believe you are, your values and beliefs, and your memories. You'll pick up more about these filters in Chapter 5 – 'Pushing the Communication Buttons'.

Just as your filters direct what you perceive, so they affect what you project out into the world. So if you find yourself surrounded by angry people or selfish people, or people who are jealous, it may be because you are harbouring unresolved anger, operating from a scarcity model of the world, or perhaps feeling jealous of someone else's success.

One of my (Romilla) clients, Mary, was extremely unhappy at work because she was being bullied. The supervisor and the departmental secretary had ganged up on Mary and were being very unpleasant and extremely petty. I helped Mary to recognise that the supervisor was a very lonely, older woman who did not have any friends and was very unpopular at work. Whenever Mary looked at the supervisor she imagined that the supervisor was holding a placard which said: 'I feel I am worthless and unlovable.' Mary started to have compassion in place of fear. She realised her own self-esteem needed a prop and began standing her ground – learning to say no. It was not easy in the beginning, but Mary not only raised her own sense of self-worth, but she was no longer affected by the supervisor's behaviour. In Mary's case, she was, perhaps, projecting her own lack of self-esteem and thereby perceiving that she was being bullied. Changing her inner-self by increasing her own confidence resulted in her observing a corresponding change in behaviour in the people around her. One way in which you can change things around you is by examining and changing yourself, and you can achieve this by taking responsibility for your thoughts and actions by overcoming obstacles such as blaming others.

Playing the blame frame

It's a lot easier to blame someone else for your own misfortunes than it is to take responsibility for putting things right for yourself. It is not easy to recognise that by blaming someone else you are handing over your power to them. By blaming someone else, you don the mantle of a victim.

Apart from being bullied, Mary complained, 'My boss won't give me a pay rise.' This was true. However, Mary was over modest of her achievements at work and because her boss wasn't the brightest penny in the purse she was not aware of the good work Mary was doing. I made sure that Mary prepared well for her next appraisal. Mary was able to present a list of her successes since her last appraisal as well as areas for improvement. She talked about her goals for her job and suggested ways of how she could work with her manager to achieve these. In NLP terms, Mary stopped blaming her lack of a raise on her boss and took action herself. When she realised her boss's inability to recognise her strengths, Mary showed the flexibility of a master communicator by changing her behaviour to get the response from her boss that she wanted . . . and yes, she did get a pay rise and a promotion!

In order to affect positive change for yourself, you need to step away from the blame frame and take actions to secure what you want.

Getting stuck in a problem frame

As a gross generalisation, because our culture is focused on solving problems, you tend to look backwards when something goes wrong in order to analyse what it is that hasn't worked. One of the nasty side effects of this is to lay blame. The problem with the 'problem frame' is it stops you from:

✔ Thinking about the real results you want

✔ Examining previous successes and modelling those

✔ Learning from what worked for someone else and emulating their strategies

When you go back to analyse why things haven't worked the way you wanted them to, you tend to focus on the following:

- ✔ What's wrong
- ✔ How long you've had this problem
- ✔ Whose fault it is that you have this problem
- ✔ Why this problem occurred
- ✔ Why you haven't done something about the problem

Asking 'why' forces people to go even deeper into the problem, become defensive, and move further away from finding a positive solution. A more constructive way of asking may be to say, 'What did you hope to achieve by doing X?' or 'What was the purpose behind your doing X?'

Think of a time when you were so stuck in a problem that you could not see a solution. Maybe you're having such a problem right now. Ask yourself: Are you focusing on the result you would like or do you get too tied up in the emotion of the moment to have clarity?

Help is at hand in the form of the Outcome Frame questions in the section 'Creating well-formed outcomes' later in this chapter.

Shifting into Outcome Frame

This smarter and more constructive process suggests a different way of thinking about your problems and issues. We call it the 'Outcome Frame'. It's an approach that helps to identify and keep the mind on what is *positively wanted*. When you add in an efficient goal-setting process and monitor each step along the way, you can correct any deviation from the plan to attain the results easily and on time.

The Path to Excellence

The human brain is a learning machine that needs to be kept occupied. If it isn't, it can dwell on the negative and get its owners into all kinds of trouble. As a human being, you can use all your ingenuity to direct your brain in to helping you achieve your goals. If you can create a compelling, irresistible future your brain will help you to align your behaviour in a way that will get you to your outcome quickly and easily. *The first step is working out what you want.*

Knowing what you want

When Alice (*Alice's Adventures in Wonderland* by Lewis Carroll) asks the Cheshire Cat, 'Would you tell me, please, which way I ought to walk from here?', without any clear idea of where it is she wants to go, she just wants to go somewhere, the Cheshire Cat responds that Alice is sure to get somewhere if she just walks long enough. And like Alice, imagine what would happen next time you go to a train station and ask for a ticket to somewhere.

If you want to move forward and achieve your goals, you need to be very clear about what it is you *do* want. So often in life, you get caught up in what it is you don't want and spend an awful lot of energy, both physical and emotional, in avoiding the undesirable result.

To figure out what you want and put your energies toward achieving it, sit down and write your own obituary. You can then decide on the legacy you want to leave to posterity and the actions you would take to fulfil the legacy. For more information on this technique, head to Chapter 4. There you can discover that your unconscious mind is a wonderful ally in assisting you to achieve the goals you want . . . AND don't want!

A client who came to see me (Romilla) as she was trying to 'escape' from her second marriage said, 'I am bad with relationships.' On working through her issues, we discovered that she had lost her much adored grandfather as a very young child. The trauma of this particular event had gone very deep into her psyche and her fear of loss had been driving her to end her relationships before she could experience the pain of loss again. Because the client was focusing, at a subconscious level, on what she didn't want – pain of loss – her unconscious mind was assisting her in maintaining behaviours that made her avoid the pain. Unfortunately it created other problems. For her to get the relationship she craved, she had to think about and design exactly what she wanted in a relationship and focus on creating it in her life.

One way to discover what you really want is to go way into your future. Imagine you are a grey-haired grandparent. You're sitting on a rock, under the stars, with a roaring campfire in front of you and at your feet are your grandchildren, demanding another story about your life. Would you want to tell them of the time you missed the chance to fulfil a dream because you were too scared, too influenced by someone else's 'you can't'? Or would you want to tell them that, despite all the odds and in keeping with your values, you did something spectacular?

Fast-forward the years and looking back at your life now, make a list of the dreams you would dare to live if you had all the money and influence in the world and you knew you couldn't fail.

So you may decide that you want material things like a huge nest egg, a big house, nice cars, or you may decide you want to be influential in the political arena. Working through the section on 'Creating well-formed outcomes' in this chapter and flicking through to read Chapter 5 will help you to discover the reasons why you want the goals you do and help you to find the hot buttons that drive you.

Getting smarter than SMART: Creating well-formed outcomes

SMART goals were all the rage a few years ago in the corporate world. According to the SMART model, goals need to be Specific, Measurable, Achievable, Realistic, and Timed. Great so far as they go. What NLP does is to add sensory specific information which can help you modify your behaviour or seek help in the form of extra resources, including guides and mentors.

Thanks to NLP we can recommend a better way forward, one that makes SMART goals even smarter by helping you work out what you want using the 'well-formed' outcome process. NLP builds on the SMART approach by making you use all of your senses to design a goal, to fine tune it to being more than just Specific, Measurable, Achievable, Realistic, and Timed. This process requires you to answer a series of questions that really help you explore the hows, whys, and wherefores of your desired outcome. By following the process you will really begin to understand your true motives for wanting your goals and you will be able to weigh up the pros and cons of success versus failure! An fairly common example of a well-formed outcome may be you want a better paid job.

When your desired outcome meets the following criteria, NLP says it satisfies the well-formedness conditions. For every result you want to achieve, we suggest that you ask yourself the following questions:

- Is the goal stated in the positive?
- Is it self-initiated, maintained, and within my control?
- Does it describe the evidence procedure?
- Is the context clearly defined?
- Does it identify the needed resources?
- Have I evaluated whether it is ecological?
- Does it identify the first step I need to take?

The following sections explain these points in more detail.

Stated in the positive?

What do you want? Or . . . what would you rather have?

These are questions that help clarify the desired outcome, as it is important to know what it is you *want* in order to have focus and direction. What you want needs to be very clear. A fluffy goal like I want more money won't do because it will be satisfied by you finding a £5 note on the pavement. A better goal might be 'I want to weigh 12 stone' or 'I want £1,000 in my bank account' or 'I want a gross salary of £35,000 per annum'. Having negative goals like 'I don't want to stay in this job' can have dire consequences. So when you find yourself saying 'I don't want . . . ', ask yourself 'What do I want instead?'

Is it self-initiated and maintained and within my control?

So often we hear of a person wanting to give up smoking who, when questioned, replies 'My wife wants me to stop.' A person has a far better chance of succeeding if the drive to attain a particular outcome comes from within, for example 'I want to enjoy a long and healthy life – for me.' In contrast, if your goal is 'I want two weeks in the sun during March', your boss may not agree and this is therefore not under your control.

So ask yourself these questions:

 ✔ Am I doing this for myself or someone else?

 ✔ Does the outcome rely solely on me?

In my marketing consultancy, I (Kate) realised that several projects involved working closely with corporate business clients who were extremely stressed, very busy, and disorganised. I was spending long meetings sitting with clients at their chaotic desks while they made phone calls or gathered together the project information as I waited. My outcome, for future client assignments, was 'to work in a calm, efficient, and commercial way'. Looking at my goal, it may not initially be apparent that I had control of the outcome because I was also dependent on the clients playing their part too. However, in applying the

---

Dwelling on the negative can damage your health

I (Romilla) know at least two people who have managed to get themselves sacked from jobs by unconsciously adopting behaviours that were out of character. When examining the situation later, they realised that they would have behaved differently had they focused energy on defining the jobs they wanted and finding better employment. Instead, they sapped their energy by just not wanting to be there and fell into destructive, aberrant behaviours.

principles of the NLP well-formed outcome, I set clearer expectations with disorganised clients. My strategies included arranging meetings in quiet offices with no distractions, or holding a video conference rather than visiting the client site. It involved specific boundaries such as defining the start and end times of meetings and distributing the objectives, agenda, and actions and information required in writing. By fully itemising time spent, and billing for every hour wasted – like the legal profession – there was a direct impact on making others more efficient. Initially my goal 'to work in a calm, efficient, and commercial way' did not appear to depend solely on me and therefore, on the face of it, I may not have been able to satisfy it. However, by showing flexibility of behaviour, I was able to take responsibility for getting my goal by influencing my clients with complete integrity.

Does it describe the evidence procedure?

Evidence procedure is another way of asking 'When will I know if I've achieved my goal?' The following are extremely important questions as they can help to identify goals that are too fluffy, or if someone is not clear on the outcome.

- ✔ How will I know that I am getting the outcome?
- ✔ What will I be doing when I get it?
- ✔ What will I see, hear, and feel when I have it?

On one of my (Romilla) workshops, David, an accountant, wanted to become self-employed. His only desire was to earn enough within three months. By answering the above questions he discovered he hadn't really worked out what he truly wanted from working for himself. His initial goal, although stated in the positive, was too fluffy to help him get anywhere. It was as bad as saying, 'I know I don't want to work for someone else' (a negative). By following the well-formed outcome process he was able to work out that what he really wanted to do was to teach other self-employed accountants how to win business by training them in NLP-based sales techniques.

Appropriately contextualised?

Is the context of your goal clearly defined? Where, when, how, and with whom do I want it? This question is very good in helping you fine tune what you want by eliminating what you don't want. For instance if you know you really did not enjoy that holiday on the moon, then your goal of, 'I want my own holiday home' would exclude the Lunar colony, or if Martians aren't your favourite people you will know you don't want to settle on Mars.

By defining *when* you want something, you may identify steps that need to be taken before you can have that something. For instance, 'I want my holiday home when I can afford to have someone else maintain it' may make you realise that you need an income of £50,000 per annum before you can buy your holiday retreat.

When entrepreneur Keith wanted to expand his home-based enterprise, his first desired outcome was to build a separate outbuilding in the grounds of his house. As a result of asking himself the above question, his outcome changed to finding office premises away from the home. The happy result was that his six-person team moved into luxury, purpose-built offices, at a low rent, which provided the space to grow the business. He and his wife regained the use of two main rooms in their house with the bonus of quality leisure time without the hassle of living above the shop.

Does it identify the resources needed?

The questions below can help you to identify what you will need, by way of people, knowledge, and so on to satisfy your outcome. They help you to draw on possible past experiences when you previously made use of resources which can prove useful in the current exercise. Imagine Peter who wants to learn hang gliding but is afraid of heights. What sorts of answers would he give?

- What resources do I have now?

  Peter: 'I have the desire to learn and friends who are hang gliders who can guide me. I am athletic and find it easy to learn new sports. It can't be that different to water skiing!'

- What resources do I need to acquire?

  Peter: 'I need to get over my fear of heights, so I will find a therapist or hypnotherapist who can help me get over my fear. I also need to find a club where I can hire an instructor and a hang glider. I need to adjust my time to make time for my new hobby.'

- Have I evidence of achieving this before?

  Peter: 'Well, I learnt to drive and boy was that scary, the first time that police car seemed to drive at me sirens blaring and lights flashing, but I learnt and am a good driver now.'

- What happens if I act *as if* I have the resources?

  Peter: 'Oh boy, I can feel myself soaring and I don't have those butterflies in my stomach when I look down. I never thought I could leave terra firma without metal below me. Can't wait to get soaring!'

Acting *as if* you have the resources now helps to shift any beliefs that may be holding you back. It also enables you to try the outcome on for size – you may change your mind at this point.

Check if your goal is ecological

The dictionary defines ecology as a 'branch of biology dealing with living organisms' habits, modes of life, and relations to their surroundings'. In NLP, when we talk about *ecology checks,* we're simply asking questions to make sure that the outcome fits within all aspects of your life. Ecology checks shine a very strong beam of light on any hidden agenda or *secondary gain* you may be unaware of when setting your outcomes. A *secondary gain* or *positive by-product* is defined as a behaviour that appears to be negative or causing problems, when in fact it is serving a positive function at some level.

These questions are the laser-guided system that will help you lock on to the nub of your desires. As you ask yourself these questions be aware of any pictures, sounds, and particularly feelings that your unconscious mind raises. Be sympathetic to the response you get and adjust your goal accordingly.

- ✔ What is the *real* purpose why I want this?
- ✔ What will I lose or gain if I have it?
- ✔ What will happen if I get it?
- ✔ What won't happen if I get it?
- ✔ What will happen if I don't get it?
- ✔ What won't happen if I don't get it?

Another of my (Kate) delegates, Keith, was in a quandary. He was an average student and had achieved good enough grades to go to university to study art. His real passion, however, was working with wood. He decided to apply the well-formed outcome process to decide on what to do with his future. He was clear he wanted to work with something creative, so an art degree was fine. He could see himself at exhibitions, talking to people about his work. He knew he was creative and could read around his subject so he had all the resources he needed. However, when it came to checking the ecology of going to university, he realised he didn't want to spend years learning theory. He discovered that what he really wanted to do was apprentice himself to an artisan and learn in a more practical way.

What is the first step?

Lao-Tzu, the ancient Taoist philosopher, is credited with saying that a journey of a thousand miles must begin with a single step. That's a point worth remembering. Often change is not the dramatic breakthrough kind, but a drip, drip, drip effect – slowly getting what you want. A break down of an action plan with the steps that will get you to your goal is a must. So if you have decided that in your desire to be an Oscar-winning script writer, you have to join a class and start writing. BUT . . . if every time you plan on sitting down to write, you allow yourself to be side tracked, your goal will just remain a dream. In order for you to turn your dream into a concrete reality you have to take that first vital step, because without it you may not build up sufficient momentum to take the next step . . . and the next step.

The 4-point Formula for Success

The formula for success consolidates what you have discovered in creating at least one well-formed outcome. This formula can be applied to lifetime goals as effectively as to short-term ones. Remember: It is much easier to hit a target that is clearly defined and visible. Robin Hood would never have won Maid Marion if he didn't aim for the bull's eye!

To hit the target, follow these steps:

1. **Know your outcome.**

   It is important to specify precisely what it is you want. You can use the outcome frame to fine tune the desired outcome and satisfy the well-formedness conditions. See the earlier sections for details.

2. **Take action.**

   Unless you take that first step, and then the following ones, nothing will happen to help you towards your outcome, no matter how clearly they are defined.

3. **Have sensory awareness.**

   If you have the awareness to see, hear, and feel what isn't working, you can modify your behaviour to steer you towards the desired outcome. Chapter 6 will show you how you can develop sensory awareness.

4. **Have behavioural flexibility.**

   This ties in beautifully with the NLP presupposition: 'In interactions among people, the person with the most flexibility of behaviour can control the interaction.' Or you could say . . . 'If it ain't working, do something different.' Head to Chapter 2 for a detailed explanation of this powerful presupposition.

If you always do what you've always done, you'll always get what you always got.

Spinning the Wheel of Life

This section will help you to identify whether you have a balanced life and, if there is scope for improvement, which areas need to be worked on in order to get balance in your life, simply and effectively.

In the diagram of the wheel in Figure 3-1, if you were to label the wedges of the wheel with the words that mean the most to you about areas in your life, those that are important to you, what would you choose? Typically people choose to include work and career (including the home), finances and money, friends and family, relationships, personal growth and learning, fun and recreation, spirituality, and physical environment.

Taking the centre of the wheel as 0 and the outer edge as 10, rank your level of satisfaction with each life area by drawing a straight or curved line to create a new outer edge. The new perimeter of the circle represents your personal wheel of life (see Figure 3-1 for an example). The ideal situation would obviously have all the sections at 10, giving you a beautifully round wheel, like the one in the diagram.

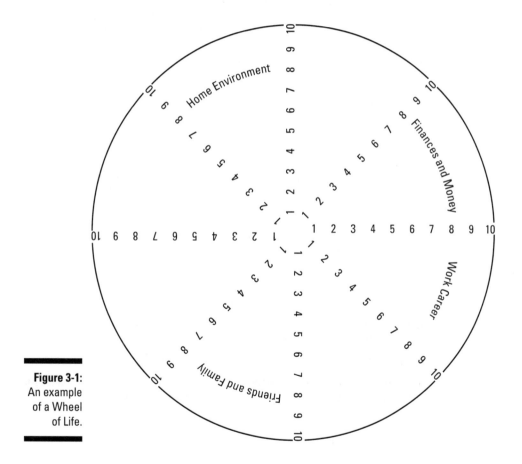

Figure 3-1:
An example
of a Wheel
of Life.

Keeping a Dream Diary of Your Goals

Have you ever agreed to an appointment and forgotten to write it down? What happened? Did you make the appointment? If you did, thank your unconscious mind for its vigilance. If you missed your appointment, did you learn your lesson and now always write down your appointments?

Think of a goal as an appointment with a desired outcome and write it down. If there was only one thought you take from this book to make you more successful, it is to write down your goals, commit to actions to achieve them, and work on your plans every single day.

You'll learn more about your Reticular Activation System, RAS for short, in Chapter 4. Right now, trust that your RAS works like an antenna, honing in on opportunities, people, and other resources that you will need to meet your goals. The act of writing down your goal switches on your RAS. The RAS is a network of nerve cells which operates like a radar, directing your attention to what is important to you. For instance, for survival it'll draw your attention to the car speeding toward you when you are out driving on 'automatic pilot'. Your RAS will also keep you alert to opportunities tied in to your goals.

I (Romilla) run goal-setting workshops called 'Going for Goal'. One of the bonus materials that delegates go away with is a 'dream diary', which is a beautifully textured file in which the delegates can record their dreams and aspirations. The idea is to have something that is good to hold and beautiful to look at so that you pick up your dream diary every day to tick off actions that have been met and add pictures and notes to bring other goals to life.

Pick some areas in your life you would like to have goals in. This may be a little involved and we invite you to take your time and savour each stage because what you are really doing here is *designing the future you will want to live*. Basically, you're going to create your own dream diary and fill it with your own dreams and goals. Follow these steps:

1. **Find yourself a wonderful file that you will enjoy working with every day; get some colourful dividers, too.**

2. **Draw and fill in a Wheel of Life (refer to Figure 3-1).**

3. **Pick each area in your life which you may want to design or re-design and label each divider with the area you want to work at.**

   You may decide to just work on one or two areas to start with.

4. **Think of some goals for each area.**

   Consider both long-term (lifetime, five years, or more) and short-term (six months to a year) goals.

   5. **Apply the *well-formed outcome* process to your goals.**

      Refer to the section 'Getting smarter than SMART' earlier in this chapter.

   6. **Write down your goals and include the date by which you want to have achieved them.**

   7. **Break the goals down into monthly, weekly, and daily goals and write them in your diary along with their dates.**

      You may want some more dividers (best to keep them the same colour).

   8. **Each night before you go to sleep (this only takes a few minutes) look at your dreams and make a list of what you will do the next day in order to meet your goals.**

REMEMBER

Savour the sense of achievement when you come to tick off the goals you have achieved and *count your blessings*.

Just Go for It

We met a new author, Jack, who had put a lot of time, effort, and passion into writing a book. He told us of meeting a man named John, who said, 'Don't be too disappointed when not many people buy the book.' Jack was hurt and stunned before he realised that at least he had done something John hadn't – invested in passion and self-belief. There are an awful lot of people in the world who operate from a position of few or no choices. They hate it when the rest of us are free from limitations, so remembering that 'there is no failure, only feedback', why not *have courage and go and live your dreams*?

Part II
The Brain's Highway Code

The 5th Wave — By Rich Tennant

"How can you not feel confident? You're wearing Versace sunglasses, a Tommy Hilfiger sweater, Calvin Klein jeans and Michael Jordan gym shoes. Now go on out there and just be yourself."

In this part . . .

We delve into what's happening behind the scenes in your brain and your unconscious thinking. Scary subject? Not at all when you realise that your unconscious is the part of you that looks out for your well-being.

Have you ever wondered what makes you tick but not known where to start? Don't worry: this part should help many things become clearer to you. And we want you to begin to master the skills of great communicators, so if you read the next few chapters you're well on your way.

Chapter 4

Who's Steering the Bus?

In This Chapter

▶ Understanding the unconscious mind

▶ Learning how the brain works

▶ Overcoming fears

▶ Discovering motivators

*U*ntil we ask you to become aware of your breathing you don't notice each breath, the air going in through your nose or the movement of your chest with each inhalation and exhalation. By following this simple request you have brought your breathing into your conscious awareness. As you continue reading and forget to notice your breathing, it will slip back out of your awareness along with the other processes which run your body.

Do you consciously know when it's time for you to feel thirsty? We challenge you to consciously activate each muscle in your arm in order to pick up a glass of water and get it to your mouth. Impossible? Do you need a degree in anatomy and physiology before you can attempt to raise your arm consciously? This just goes to show that your unconscious mind runs your body, outside of your conscious awareness.

If you still have any doubts at all about the power of your unconscious mind on the running of your body just consider an experiment conducted by researcher, Paul Thorsen, who hypnotised a man and told him that the pen which Paul was holding was a hot skewer. Paul then touched the arm of the subject with the pen and . . . lo and behold a blister formed on the subject's arm where he had been touched by the pen.

In this chapter you will get to meet your unconscious mind and learn how to use your brain to focus on and help you achieve your goals more easily and quickly. You will understand the psychology of Post Traumatic Stress Disorder and phobias and discover how you may overcome them. Most importantly, you will learn about your values – the buttons that motivate you. Once you find out that your beliefs have a structure and that you can change this structure, you will be well on your way to taking charge of your emotions, your memories, and the way you choose to respond to people and events in your life, without the baggage of the past weighing you down.

How Our Fears Can Drive Us in the Wrong Direction

Not only does your unconscious mind control the running of your body, it can also have a tremendous impact on the results you get in your life. Have you ever wanted to do something consciously but ended up doing something totally different?

You may decide consciously that you want to get a goal. If your unconscious mind is not on board, it will assist you by fulfilling its own agenda – which may be contrary to what you consciously think you want. Imagine what you could achieve if you were in rapport with your unconscious mind and able to go in the direction that would get you to your goal quickly.

I (Romilla) worked with a client, Roger, who started working for himself. Despite setting goals and having exceptional ability in his chosen field, he was not getting his business off the ground and was in a complete panic as he watched his savings dwindling away. He had a very closely-held belief that 'I can't sing the blues in an air-conditioned room.' The writer of this song discovered he could only sing the blues in poverty and that success and wealth cramped his musical style. Similarly, Roger was afraid that success would stop him experiencing life and extinguish his creativity. Once he realised he could choose to experience life as a millionaire or a tramp, his behaviour changed and his business improved dramatically.

The key to bringing your unconscious mind into sync with your conscious desires and goals is to understand what each controls and how your unconscious mind works. The following sections tell you what you need to know.

Conscious and unconscious

In NLP terms, your conscious mind is that part of your mind which has awareness of things around and within you at any given moment in time, which, according to research conducted by George Miller in 1956, is a meagre 7±2 chunks of information. (For more information on Miller's findings head to Chapter 5.) This is your short-term memory which can hold thoughts from minutes to hours. You use this part of your brain when you hold a telephone number in memory long enough to make that call. The rest is your unconscious or subconscious mind. The conscious mind can be compared to the tip of an iceberg and the unconscious mind to the nine-tenths of the iceberg which is submerged underwater.

Your conscious and unconscious mind excel at different things (see Table 4-1). Knowing what each is best suited for can help you to recognise if you are better at using your logical left brain more or your creative right brain more. You may then decide to focus on aspects of your mental development, for instance learning to draw, if you are more left brained, or learning applied mathematics, if you are more right brained. Certainly learning to meditate will develop the traits of both and get them communicating better.

Table 4-1	Comparing the Conscious and Unconscious Mind
The conscious mind excels at	*The unconscious mind is better at*
Working linearly	Working holistically
Processing sequentially	Intuition
Logic	Creativity
Verbal language	Running your body
Mathematics	Taking care of your emotions
Analysis	Storing memories

Your quirky unconscious mind

As with any friend and their little foibles, your unconscious mind has some interesting quirks with which it would be useful for you to become acquainted so you can get on with it better. The ideal would be to have your conscious and unconscious minds working as one.

This is not a sexist thing

Did you know that your brain has a left and a right half which are joined together by the corpus collosum? Generally, women have a thicker corpus collosum than men, which enables them to multitask better.

Oh! And by the way, if someone calls you thick . . . thank them. They're simply complimenting you on the density of the network connecting your brain cells which makes you more intelligent.

By getting your unconscious mind on board, working with you instead of against you, you will be able to achieve much more in life, like setting and achieving compelling goals seemingly effortlessly.

Your unconscious cannot process negatives

Your unconscious can't process negatives. It interprets everything you think as a positive thought. So if you think, 'I don't want to be poor', your unconscious mind focuses on the 'poor' and, because it doesn't do negatives, the thought becomes 'I want to be poor'. Being poor then becomes the goal in your unconscious mind and like a young child, desperate to please, it helps you behave in a way that will keep you poor. Obviously not what you wanted!

That's why stating your goals in the positive is so important. In this instance, instead of thinking 'I don't want to be poor', you'd think 'I want to be wealthy'. For more information on the importance of stating goals in a positive way, head to Chapter 3.

Your unconscious needs direction

Yogis liken the unconscious mind to a mischievous monkey, always leaping from tree to tree. The way to keep the monkey occupied and out of mischief is to stick a pole in the ground and direct the monkey to climb up and down the pole. If your conscious mind does not provide a direction for your unconscious mind, it will look to find it wherever it can. A young, directionless boy, for example, may find that joining a street gang provides a structure to his life and he will then find that he gets his direction from the leader of the gang and the gang laws. Your unconscious mind will do the same thing, and no one wants his or her unconscious mind sporting street colours and spray-painting graffiti.

In order to direct the unconscious mind, you need to open up communication channels between your conscious and your unconscious mind. This rapport is developed by finding a quiet time for meditation or relaxation and examining the memories presented to you by your unconscious mind. For more information on how you can open up communication channels, head to Chapter 7.

Your unconscious – the preserver of memories

In 1957, the Penfield study indicated that all your experiences are recorded faithfully in memory. While she was awake, a woman's brain was stimulated with an electrode and Penfield discovered that the woman was able to vividly recall the details of a childhood party, in minute detail. The storage and organisation of these memories is the responsibility of the unconscious mind.

A part of the function of the unconscious mind is to repress memories with unresolved negative emotions.

Diane's relationship with Tom broke up and she started having severe stomach cramps for which the doctors could find no physical cause. In therapy, Diane remembered the day her mother left the family for another man. She got a picture of her mother driving away and Diane sobbing 'Come back mummy, my tummy hurts.' Diane realised that her stomach ache which she used as a child as a ploy to get her mother to come back had been recreated by her unconscious mind as a ploy to get Tom back. The memory had lain dormant all these years.

Another function of the unconscious mind is to present repressed memories for examination in order to release trapped emotions. Unfortunately, like a very young child embarrassing its parents in public, it does not always pick the most appropriate time to present a memory that needs to be examined. So you could be at a family gathering, basking in feelings of love and contentment, when your unconscious mind says to you, 'Deal with the memory when dad smacked you on your birthday . . . *now!*' and suddenly you are blubbing into your trifle in front of your highly embarrassed relatives.

Your unconscious is a lean, mean learning machine

Your unconscious thrives on new experiences and is always on the lookout for something new. It needs to be fed with new experiences and, like a mischievous monkey, it will get you into trouble if you do not keep it from getting bored. The authors know of a very kind, generous, extremely clever person who got very bored at work. Instead of finding constructive ways to alleviate his boredom he got hooked on playing computer games. This addiction had some very severe repercussions in his life. Luckily, a new job brought new challenges and he is now very successful in his chosen profession.

You can find constructive ways of keeping your mind occupied such as reading, doing puzzles, or taking up a hobby. Activities like these will make your brain cells grow more physical dendrites (the branches of a brain cell) and keep you mentally fitter. For calming your mind, keeping stress levels at bay, and increasing your creativity, there is nothing better than meditation.

Your unconscious behaves like a highly moral being

The unconscious mind will keep you on the straight and narrow path of whatever morality it has learned by enforcing its morality on you, even if society judges that morality wrong. A terrorist will kill and destroy without qualms because her moral code teaches her that she is a freedom fighter. She therefore believes that she is actually being a moral person in fighting against a criminal society. A gang member may kill to protect the honour of his gang, without feeling any guilt because he has learned that gang honour is more important than the Christian commandment 'thou shalt not kill' or the law of the land which makes murder illegal. If, however, *your* unconscious decides that you deserve to be punished then you will be wracked with guilt and exhibit behaviours designed to punish yourself, even though there are no laws to say that what your unconscious mind sees as bad is actually so.

I (Romilla) had a coaching client, Jane, who had had several, unsatisfactory relationships and was in one at the time she came to see me. During a series of breakthrough sessions Jane admitted to feeling that she manipulated men and discarded them when she felt they were looking for commitment. Investigations revealed a memory of when she was five years old and had 'manipulated' her father, who was verbally violent, into apologising to her. When I suggested that Jane's father really loved her although he could not show it and that he had found the resources within himself to express his love by apologising to her, Jane was really shocked. One of the consequences of identifying the negative feelings of guilt that Jane had felt all her life was to allow her to move on and leave a relationship that was not fulfilling her needs and modify the behaviours that drew her into unrewarding relationships.

The Reticular Activating System (RAS) – Your Tracking System

There are approximately 2,000,000 pieces of data coming in through your five senses every second. To maintain your sanity, this deluge is filtered through a network of cells in your brain so that only a very minute proportion of the information gets through to the rest of the brain. This network is called the Reticular Activating System or RAS for short. The RAS works like an antenna, noticing stimuli and alerting your brain to pay attention. The RAS lets in only data that meets at least one of the following criteria:

✔ It is important to your *survival*.

  For example when you are in a deep sleep but wake up because you hear a strange noise in the house or if you are jay walking and in a daydream you will be alerted to traffic bearing down on you.

✔ It has *novelty* value.

  Remember the last time you decorated a room? Initially you had this feeling of real pleasure each time you walked into the room as you saw the wallpaper with fresh eyes. Then after a few weeks you might have noticed that a painting was askew or an ornament not quite central and not necessarily the pattern on the wallpaper or the colour of the paint. That is because the novelty had worn off.

✔ It has a high emotional content.

The survival aspect also applies to others than yourself and you will be alert instantly if your baby's breathing changes but sleep through your husband's snoring or mumbling in his sleep.

Can you remember the last time you misplaced a loved one in a shopping centre and you were searching high and low, promising to do all kind of horrible things to him for getting lost? And then it's as if the crowd fades into obscurity as you catch a glimpse of your loved one in the distance and you zero in on them with nothing but relief. If no emotional connection with the misplaced person existed, he would just be another body in the crush. But because he is a loved one, he stands out like a beacon.

Effectively the RAS operates on stimuli that are above its threshold of observation. Mundane and daily routines slip below this threshold. It helps you to notice things that are relevant to your current goals.

Can you remember making a list and sticking it on the wall. You may have noticed it for a while and then no longer seen it even though you may have walked past it several times a day. This is because the list no longer had novelty value and was allowed to slip below the threshold for observation.

We're sure you know of chronically unlucky people, those who say things like, 'I never win anything' or 'Lucky breaks don't come my way'. These are the people whose belief systems stop them from seeing opportunities. If an opportunity was to jump up and slap them in the face, they would say, 'That's too good to be true' as they skirted the opportunity. Then there are those who always land on their feet. The lucky people are the ones who are open to possibilities. This way of thinking will have them seeking success out of failure because their belief systems dictate they deserve to win.

Your beliefs will affect the threshold level of the RAS. Someone who believes that he is a poor speller may not 'see' an advertisement for a reporter's job, even though this shortcoming can be helped with spelling technology and he may be much better at investigating stories than someone who may not have a hang-up over their spelling ability and who applies for the job.

By being aware of your beliefs, you can identify how these beliefs may be stopping you from achieving your goals. Think of a time when you really wanted to do something but, for whatever reason, couldn't find the opportunity to achieve your goal. Now examine your beliefs. You may discover that these beliefs were stopping you from noticing openings that could have enabled you to achieve your goal.

How Memories Are Created

Memories are normally created when information from the RAS is sent to the part of the brain called the amygdala, where it is given an emotional weighting before being passed on to the hippocampus. The hippocampus evaluates the data against that held in long-term memory and presents it to the cortex for analysis and re-filing back into long-term memory. Figure 4-1 shows you where these strangely named brain parts are located.

Post Traumatic Stress Disorder (PTSD)

The general public first became aware of Post Traumatic Stress Disorder (PTSD) when films about veterans from the Vietnam War started to be made. Today the news coverage has made us much more aware that PTSD is common among people who work in the emergency services as well as people who are the unfortunate victims of war and crime.

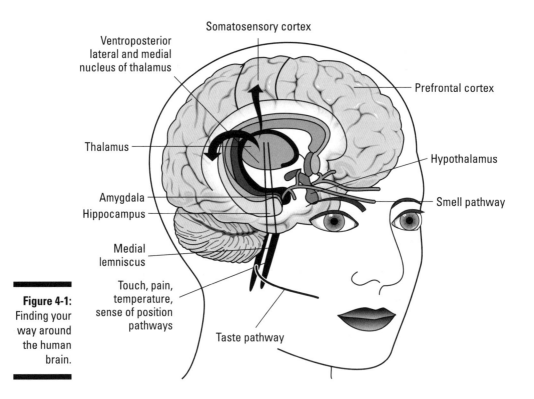

Figure 4-1: Finding your way around the human brain.

Hippos and pyramids

Oh! And did you know . . . the hippocampus is made up of banks and banks of pyramid-like structures that get filled up during the day and emptied out at night? This means that you are able to make connections more quickly when you first wake up, so do your hardest thinking before the pyramids fill up.

PTSD occurs when the amygdala receives input with a very high emotional value, gets in a panic and cannot send the information to the hippocampus. Because of this, the traumatic event gets trapped within the amygdala and the hippocampus is not able to present the memory to the neocortex for evaluation, which means the brain cannot make sense of the event. As the amygdala is the organ primarily involved with your survival, in PTSD sufferers it stays in the constant state of arousal, causing flashbacks and high levels of anxiety.

Virginia Woolf wrote *Mrs Dalloway* in the early 1920s and her portrayal of Septimus Smith clearly identifies him as suffering from post traumatic stress after the horrors of World War I. Unfortunately, at the time, conventional medicine was relatively inexperienced at dealing with psychological problems. Patients like Septimus Smith were advised to have plenty of rest in order to recuperate and were given advice such as 'pull yourself together, man'.

Phobias and PTSD are part of a group of *anxiety disorders*. Both have a similar structure, in that a memory stays trapped in the amygdala. Fortunately these days we have the NLP fast phobia cure which can be very useful in helping people recover from both anxieties. Head to the section 'The NLP Fast Phobia Cure' later in this chapter for details.

Phobias

The experts have differing opinions about the origins of phobias. Some psychologists say phobias are the result of a trauma, such as having a frog dropped down your back, others that phobias are a learned response, when a two-year-old is confronted by a cobra and becomes phobic as a result of the reactions of the adults around her. Flick through to 'The NLP fast phobia cure' later in this chapter for help in overcoming phobias.

I (Romilla) was an ophidiophobic and I do not mind admitting it. If I say a more meaningful word might be snakephobic you might be more sympathetic. The phobia was so severe that if I dreamt of snakes, as I did with painful frequency, I would wake up with my limbs locked and in a cramp and would have to consciously relax each part of my body. In fact, I let myself down rather badly when I walked into a friend's living room in Holland and freaked out in front of a group of complete strangers. The cause of my out-of-character behaviour? . . . A stuffed cobra she had on display.

I am no longer afflicted by my terror of snakes. Unfortunately, at the time I overcame my phobia I did not know about NLP and consequently my desensitisation process took place very dramatically in a small zoo in Mombasa, Kenya. I was wandering through the zoo with my husband, chatting to exotic fauna like the turtle from Madagascar, when we were approached by one of the keepers who asked if we were interested in handling the python he had draped around his neck. By the time my husband and the keeper had persuaded me to handle the python we had an audience of about 30 local people, although I was unaware of them at the time. The keeper attempted to put the python around my neck, at which point I ran out screaming. This is when I discovered the audience, all of whom were laughing, some so uproariously they were crying. The second attempt proved to be a success even though I screamed until the python was around my neck. By the way, snakes are not slimy!

Had I known NLP at the time the process of overcoming my phobia would have been much less traumatic, using the fast phobia cure.

The NLP fast phobia cure

The fast phobia cure allows you to re-experience a trauma or phobia without experiencing the emotional content of the event or having to face the trigger that would normally set off the phobic response. You should ensure that you work in an environment where you know yourself to be completely safe, in the presence of another person who can help to keep you grounded.

Fun with phobias

Below are some words to have fun with at the dining table. A word of caution . . . please do not accuse members of the opposite sex of having phronemophobia (fear of thinking) and you may wish to sit someone suffering from ablutophobia (fear of bathing) near your mother-in-law if you suffer from pentheraphobia (fear of mother-in-law).

✔ Peladophobia – fear of bald people

✔ Philophobia – fear of falling in love or being in love

✔ Phobophobia – fear of phobias

✔ Xyrophobia – fear of razors

✔ Galeophobia – fear of cats

✔ Triskadekaphobia – fear of the number 13

✔ Otophobia – fear of the number 8

This means that you examine an experience while you are doubly dissociated from the memory, creating a separation between you (in the now) and the emotions of a trauma or a phobic response. In the following list, the double dissociation is done through having you watch yourself in a cinema theatre (dissociation), while watching yourself on a cinema screen (double dissociation). You can find more on dissociation in Chapter 10 in the section, 'To associate or to dissociate'.

1. Identify when you have a phobic response to a stimulus or a traumatic or unpleasant memory that you wish to overcome.

2. Remember that you were safe before and are safe after the unpleasant experience.

3. Imagine yourself sitting in the cinema, watching yourself on a small, black-and-white screen.

4. Now imagine floating out of the you that is sitting in the cinema seat and into the projection booth.

5. You can now see yourself in the projection booth, watching yourself in the seat, watching the film of you on the screen.

6. Run the film in black and white, on the very tiny screen, starting before you experienced the memory you wish to overcome and running it through until after the experience when you were safe.

7. Now freeze the film or turn the screen completely white.

8. Float out of the projection booth, out of the seat, and into the end of the film.

9. Run the film backwards very quickly, in a matter of a second or two, in full colour, as if you are experiencing the film, right back to the beginning, when you were safe.

10. You can repeat steps 8 and 9 until you are comfortable with the experience.

11. Now go into the future and test an imaginary time when you might have experienced the phobic response.

Beliefs and Values Make a Difference

You may have heard someone say, 'Those teenagers today, they have no values.' Everyone has values; they are just different for different people and different groups of people. Your values and beliefs are unconscious filters that you use to decide what bits of data coming in through your senses you will allow in and what bits of data you will keep out. You know what that means, don't you? That the unconscious nine-tenths of your brain has been sitting there on the quiet, building up all sorts of beliefs and making all sorts of decisions about you and your environment and . . . you aren't even aware of them.

The power of beliefs

Your beliefs can, when allowed to go to the extreme, have the power of life and death over you. Your beliefs can help you to health, wealth, and happiness or keep you unwell, poor, and miserable.

The beliefs we are talking about here are distinct from religious beliefs – these beliefs are the generalisations you make about your life experiences. These generalisations go on to form the basis of your reality which then directs your behaviour. You can use one empowering belief, for example, to help you to develop another belief to the next level of achievement. So 'I am a really good speller' can help you develop the belief that you enjoy words and are really quite articulate. This might lead you to believe that you can tell stories and suddenly you find that you have the courage to submit a short story to a magazine and . . . all of a sudden you are a published author.

Just as you have positive, empowering beliefs, you can also have negative, disempowering beliefs. If you had the misfortune of being bullied at school, you may have developed a belief that people, in general, are not very nice. This might make you behave quite aggressively toward people when you first meet them. If some people then respond in a similarly aggressive way their behaviour could well reinforce your belief that 'people aren't very nice'. You may not even notice when someone responds in a friendly manner because your belief filters are not geared to notice nice people.

Be aware that a limiting belief may be lurking if you find yourself using words or hearing words like can't, should, shouldn't, could, couldn't, would, ought, and ought not. As Henry Ford said, 'He can who thinks he can, and he can't who thinks he can't. This is an inexorable, indisputable law.'

Being impacted by others' beliefs

The really scary thought is that other people's preconceptions can place false limitations on you, especially if the other people are teachers, bosses, family, and friends.

A very interesting study conducted with a group of children who had been tested and found to be of average intelligence illustrates how a teacher's belief can enhance or hinder a child's learning ability.

The students were split into two groups at random. The teacher for one group was told that the students in the group were gifted, whereas the teacher for the other group was told that these students were slow learners. Both groups of children were retested for intelligence a year later. The intelligence score for the group where the teacher thought the students were gifted was higher than when previously tested; whereas the group where the teacher had been told the students were slow learners scored lower on the intelligence test than they had done before.

Sadly these limitations are not just the domain of overcrowded schools but exist in homes where parents shoehorn their children into an 'acceptable' position. Other examples include when your friends remind you to be careful of changing a secure job to pursue a dream, or if a boss whose communication style is different to yours has a detrimental affect on your career progression. Not only are some of these people perceived to know more than you, you may even have placed them on a pedestal.

It may be difficult for a child to overcome the shortcomings of a teacher without parental assistance and even more so the restrictions of a parent or family environment. As an adult, you can weigh up the pros and cons of the advice you are being given by seeing it from the other person's point of view. There is more on this in Chapter 7 on creating rapport, in the section 'Exploring perceptual positions'. Once you understand the reasons for the other person's opinion, you can choose to follow their advice or not and, last but not least, you can always learn to utilise your boss's communication style in order to get your message across and so progress your career.

Changing beliefs

Some beliefs you hold may empower you. Other beliefs can limit the way you think and hold you back. The good news is that beliefs can and do change. Take the example of the four-minute mile. For years sportsmen did not believe it was possible to run a mile in four minutes. Roger Bannister achieved this in May 1954. Soon after, even this record was broken several times over.

Do I hear you say, 'Why would I want to change something that glues my world together?' Yes, beliefs do hold your world together, but . . . is it for better or for worse? If a belief is holding you back, change it. If you find you need the security blanket of the old belief, you can always change it back.

If I ask you to think of a belief you have, you may make a picture, have a feeling, hear something, or experience some or all of the three. From this we can conclude that your beliefs have certain qualities. These qualities – visual (pictures), auditory (sound), and kinaesthetic (feelings) – are called *modalities*. Modalities can be fine-tuned using submodalities – qualities like brightness, size, and distance for pictures, loudness and tone for sounds, and pressure, heat, and location for feelings.

One way of changing a belief is to adjust its submodalities. This is a really useful process as it can help you loosen the hold a limiting belief can have on you and reinforce the effects of a positive belief to develop a more empowering belief about which you are less confident. Suppose you can't help but be drawn to people and have long been told that being subjective is bad – changing your belief to 'I'm good with people' can make a huge difference to your confidence when dealing with others. Similarly, if you know you are good at art, this belief can help you branch into a more technical, art-based career like computer graphics.

To practise manipulating or changing your beliefs, follow these steps:

1. **Think of a limiting belief you have and make a note of the picture that comes to mind.**

2. **Think of a belief that you no longer find true.**

   This can go along the lines of, 'I used to believe in Santa'. Look at the picture presented by the belief that is no longer true.

3. **Think of a belief that, for you, is an absolute certainty.**

   Need help? Think of the stars when you're sitting in a brightly lit metropolis. Even though you can't see them close to, you know the stars exist and you know the sun will rise in the morning.

4. **Think of a belief you would rather have than the limiting belief you picture in Step 1.**

   This may be the opposite of your limiting belief, stated in the positive. 'I can be fit, healthy, and weigh 140 pounds again.' And then notice the picture that accompanies your new belief.

5. **Change the submodalities of the limiting belief from Step 1 into those of the belief that is no longer true for you in Step 2.**

6. **Change the submodalities of the belief you would rather have from Step 4 into those of the belief of which you are absolutely certain from Step 3.**

As a member of the human race what beliefs are holding your 'isms' (sexism, ageism, racism) in place and whose 'isms' are you allowing to keep yourself boxed in?

A cluster of beliefs is called a belief system. A belief or belief system can support a particular value. Values are the _why_ you do something. Beliefs direct your behaviour which then helps you fulfil a value – provided of course there are no conflicts created by your unconscious mind. To find out more about values, head to the next section, 'Values'.

Values

Values are the 'hot buttons' that drive all your behaviours and are your unconscious motivators and de-motivators. It is because of your values that you do something. After you have done it, you use these values to judge whether the deed is either good or bad. For instance, if you value honesty you may decide to pick up a wallet you find in the street for safe-keeping and feel good about handing it over to the police.

Values affect the choice of your friends and partners, the types of goods you purchase, the interests you pursue, and how you spend your free time. Just like your beliefs, your values also influence the filters that the RAS operates (see the section earlier in this chapter 'The Reticular Activating System (RAS) – Your Tracking System' for more information about RAS and how it works).

Your life has many facets. You are probably a member of a family, a team at work, and maybe you belong to a club in your pursuit of a hobby, just to name a few. Each of these areas of your life, family, work, leisure, and so on will have its own values hierarchy, with the most important value at the top. The values at the top of the hierarchy are usually more abstract than those further down and exert the most influence in your life. For example in Figure 4-2, family and friends is fairly concrete, whereas happiness is more intangible.

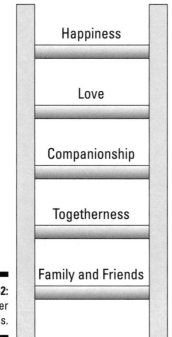

Figure 4-2:
A ladder
of values.

Means to an end values

Values can either be *ends* values or *means* values, with means values occurring further down the hierarchy, acting as the rungs in a ladder that enable you to reach your ends value. Freedom is an ends value and all the other values are means values in Figure 4-3. Means values are those which need to be fulfilled in order to get you to your final, ends value. Freedom is harder to quantify than, say, money. In the example you can have money without having freedom, but to have freedom you need money. So freedom – ends value – is dependent on money – means value.

Your values can either drive you toward pleasure or away from pain.

Toward Values	Away from Values
Love	Guilt
Freedom	Sadness
Health	Loneliness
Happiness	Anger
Wealth	Poverty

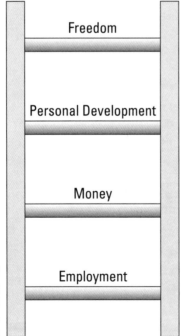

Figure 4-3:
A ladder of happiness.

Freedom

Personal Development

Money

Employment

Values with *away from* tendencies are indicative of negative emotions, negative decisions, or emotional traumas that may be exerting an influence on your life. These can be released using techniques such as Time Line Therapy. The main purpose of any such technique is to learn the lessons that may be of value from the negative events in order for the unconscious mind to release the trapped emotions. Essentially Time Line Therapy works on the principle that your memories are arranged along a time line, and by changing a memory along this time line you can release the hold of some memories, which in turn will help you gain more control over your reactions to events and have more choices in your life. For more information on this technique, please refer to Chapter 13.

Creation of values

Your values are essentially formed over three periods in your life.

- The **imprint** period occurs from the time of your birth to when you are approximately seven years old. During this time you learn largely unconsciously from your parents.

- The **modelling** period occurs between the ages of eight and 13 when you learn by consciously and unconsciously copying friends. Some of your most important values, core values, are formed when you are around ten years old.

- The **socialisation** period occurs between the ages of 14 and 21 years. It is during this time that you learn values that affect your relationships.

Eliciting your values

If there are areas in your life that you think could do with some improvement, you can examine your values to get a clue that may enable you to make positive change. By following the suggestions in these steps, you may discover what's holding you back from getting what you want.

1. **Pick an area (or context) in your life that you're not happy with or want to improve.**

   For instance, are you living or working in an environment that you don't like and want to make more enriching?

2. **Make a list of what is important to you in this context.**

   You will notice that the first few values will come to mind very quickly. Stay with it and you will notice another batch of values will surface.

3. **Put these values in order of importance to you, with the most important appearing at the top.**

If you have trouble rearranging the list, just ask yourself, 'If I could have A but not B, would this be OK?' If the answer is yes, A is of greater importance than B; if the answer is no, then B needs to be moved above A. For example, in the list of values below, which may relate to your job, you may decide that security is much more important to you than adventure:

Success

Power

Achievement

Adventure

Security

Once you put all of these into an order of importance you will probably find the ones that surfaced later have greater significance for you.

4. **After you arrange your values, ask yourself if there is a value that would be useful for you to have in this area of your life but which is missing. Where would you slot it in the list of existing values?**

For instance, if you value your job but you cannot get the level of success you want, it may be because you don't have fulfilment in your hierarchy. In fact by going through the above process you may decide it is more important to you to have:

Success

Fulfilment

Achievement

Adventure

Security

Conflict of values

When your means values are aligned (see the preceding section), it is much easier to achieve your end value. Unfortunately your values can end up in conflict. You think you want to move towards an outcome but your unconscious mind has other ideas that actually move you away from your objective.

You may have had a very financially poor childhood and have a strong *away from poverty* value which is in direct conflict with a *towards wealth* value. So you want to be wealthy but keep thinking 'I don't want to be poor' which is what your unconscious mind helps you create in your life.

Another conflict can occur when you want to move toward two outcomes simultaneously and you think you can only have either one or the other. An example of this conflict could be if you want to be thinner but you also want to be able to enjoy your food.

Is there an overriding value in your life which is stopping you from getting satisfaction in other areas of your life? For instance, having money as your number one value may make you incredibly rich. However, it may detract from your having a fulfilling relationship.

Make sure you don't spend so long fulfilling your means values that you miss achieving your end value!

Changing values

When you think of your values you create an image, just as you do when you think of your beliefs (see the earlier section 'The power of beliefs' for more information about beliefs). You can change the hierarchy of your values by changing the characteristics of the image that the value creates. Say, for example, that your values for living are the following:

Freedom

Achievement

Financial security

Fun

Family

Health

However, you find yourself let down by poor health. You may decide that it is more important for you to have health than fun and decide to make a swap in your hierarchy. You can do so by using the following technique.

1. When you think of fun, notice the picture you make in terms of the following:

   Size

   Colour/black and white

   Position

   Still or movie

   Focused or hazy

2. Notice the picture you make when you think of health.

3. Swap the qualities of the images.

   As with changing the picture qualities of a belief, changing the qualities of the picture you have for health so that it is the same as the one you have for fun will move health up and place it at the same level as fun. Now change the picture for fun so that it has the same qualities as the one you had for health. This will move fun down to the level of health.

Daydreaming Your Future Reality

Contrary to what your teachers may have told you when they saw you gazing out the classroom window, allowing your mind to wander can be a powerful first step in achieving your goals. By using the techniques described in earlier sections of this chapter, you can discover what your heart's desire is and take the first steps toward achieving it – all by daydreaming.

So give yourself permission to dream and play. What would you want to succeed at if Cinderella's fairy godmother came to you and gave you one wish? She would make sure you had all the influence, contacts, and resources you need to fulfil your heart's desire. Got your goal? Now follow these steps:

1. **Make a list of what is important to you about your goal, all the reasons why you want it, and put them in order of importance.**

   Are you surprised by your values? Did you realise something you thought important wasn't that important after all and did you think of a value that may have been missing in the beginning?

   If you're not sure how to do this, refer to the section 'Eliciting your values' earlier in this chapter.

2. **Now, while still daydreaming, imagine floating out of your body and into the future, to a time when you might have achieved this goal.**

3. **Notice the pictures, sounds, and feelings and manipulate them.**

   Can you make these stronger, more vibrant, and then even more so?

4. **From the place in the future, turn and look back to now and let your unconscious mind notice what it needs to know about and help you do in order for you to achieve your goal.**

   Remember to notice what the first step would be!

5. **When you've savoured the dream fully, come back and *take that first step*!**

You may surprise yourself!

Chapter 5

Pushing the Communication Buttons

. . . .

In This Chapter

▶ Learning the NLP communication model

▶ Taking total responsibility for any interaction

▶ Understanding how others communicate

▶ Finding out how to communicate effectively

▶ Discovering techniques to disengage your emotions and focus on your results

. . . .

*I*f I were to ask you, 'When engaged in a dialogue, what percentage of the communication are you responsible for?' would you reply 50 per cent? After all, there are two of you involved in a dialogue, so logically each of you has half the responsibility to make and elicit responses. If you're familiar with the following NLP presuppositions (explained in detail in Chapter 2), you'd reply 100 per cent:

✔ The meaning of the communication is the response you get.

✔ If what you are doing isn't working, do something different.

✔ The person with the most flexibility within a system controls the system.

This chapter shows you how to take total responsibility for any communication in which you are involved. You will be given tools to recognise when the person you are talking to isn't getting the message so that you can change your words, deeds, and actions to get the response you want.

The NLP Communication Model

The NLP communication model is based on cognitive psychology and was developed by Richard Bandler and John Grinder.

According to the NLP communication model, when someone behaves in a certain way (their *external behaviour*), a chain reaction is set up within you (your *internal response*), which in turn causes you to respond in some way (your *external behaviour*), which then creates a chain reaction within the other person (their *internal response*), and the cycle continues. Figure 5-1 shows this chain reaction.

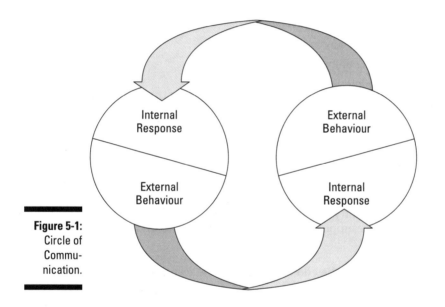

Figure 5-1:
Circle of
Commu-
nication.

The *internal response* is made up of an *internal process* and an *internal state*. The internal process consists of self-talk, pictures, and sounds and the internal state is the feelings that are experienced.

The following sections present two scenarios, showing the NLP communication model in practice.

Scenario 1

For some, it's been a lovely, hot summer's day. But the air-conditioning in the office wasn't working and Dan has had an awful day. He gets in the car and with a sigh of relief puts on the air-conditioning to battle his weary way home. His son, Drew, had promised he would cut the grass. Dan is looking forward to sitting out on a tidy, freshly mown lawn with a glass of chilled lager. As he drives up he notices the grass is *uncut*.

Dan storms into the house, so caught up in his emotions that all he can feel is the bitter resentment welling up. He starts ranting at Drew, who retreats into his sullen teenage shell muttering about the broken lawnmower which Dan doesn't hear. Finally Drew yells 'Cut the damn grass yourself', as he storms off. Neither is willing to communicate any more and both slide down the spiral of shouting, slammed doors, and finally silence.

In this example, when Dan explodes, the uncut grass would be the trigger for setting up an *internal state* of anger, resentment, and frustration in him. The *internal process* may be a monologue something like . . . 'He promised. I knew I shouldn't expect anything from him. We always give him the best and he always lets us down . . . ' along with pictures from the past when Drew did not live up to Dan's expectations.

Dan's *external behaviour* of ranting at Drew, in that tone of voice or with that look on his face provoked an *internal state* in Drew. Drew may experience feelings of anger, resentment, and frustration very similar to those felt by Dan. He may make pictures of previous altercations with his father and know he won't be heard, just like all those other times. Drew's *external behaviour* of adopting his usual, sulking manner and muttering may then further inflame his father . . . and so it continues.

Scenario 2

Now imagine scenario 2. Dan drives up and sees the uncut grass. Instead of exploding, he takes a deep breath and asks Drew why the grass hasn't been cut. Drew, expecting recriminations, gets defensive as he explains that the mower broke down. From past experience, Dan realises Drew is likely to retreat into his shell and offers to show Drew how to mend the mower. He chills out with a glass of lager before helping Drew carry out the repairs. Drew mows the lawn before the family sits down to a companionable meal.

In this scenario the father may change his internal process and make a conscious effort to remember when he was a teenager himself, in need of guidance and a firm hand. He decides on the result he wants from his interaction with the teenager and, having disengaged his emotions, is able to proceed down the path which keeps communication channels open in order to achieve the desired outcome . . . get Drew to mow the lawn.

This scenario illustrates how, by putting the presuppositions into practice, Dan is able to achieve his outcome of having Drew mow the lawn. The male bonding is an added bonus. The response he gets from Drew when the teenager starts to become defensive is obviously not the one Dan wants. Dan has the flexibility to recognise Drew's behaviour patterns and modify his own responses in order to get his outcome, thereby controlling the system.

Understanding the Process of Communication

John Grinder and Richard Bandler discovered that people who are master communicators have three sets of capabilities:

- They know what they want.
- They are very good at noticing the responses they get.
- They have the flexibility to modify their behaviour until they get what they want.

I (Kate) have a friend, Simon, who has taught me some valuable lessons about dealing with people. Simon always manages to keep his cool and usually achieves his outcome even in the most difficult situations. He does this by distancing himself from his emotions and keeping his focus on the result he wants. He also attempts to understand the other person's point of view in order to come to a win-win result.

Each of us processes information differently and so reacts to situations differently. Wouldn't it be really useful to understand *how* someone ticks? Read on for some clues.

Seven ± Two

Professor George Miller conducted research into how many bits of data people can hold in their short-term memory at any given time. He came to the conclusion that a person can hold 7 ± 2 pieces of information; nine bits if they are feeling good or have an interest in a subject and only as few as five if they're feeling a bit low or are not particularly interested in what it is they are trying to remember. If you are not into multi-tasking you may have trouble coping with more than one!

Persecuted by the number seven

My problem is that I have been persecuted by an integer. For seven years this number has followed me around, has intruded in my most private data, and has assaulted me from the pages of our most public journals. This number assumes a variety of disguises, being sometimes a little larger and sometimes a little smaller than usual, but never changing so much as to be unrecognisable. The persistence with which this number plagues me is far more than a random accident. There is, to quote a famous senator, a design behind it, some pattern governing its appearances. Either there really is something unusual about the number or else I am suffering from delusions of persecution.

The Magical Number Seven Plus or Minus Two (Professor George Miller, Psychological Review, 1956).

Your five senses (sight, sound, touch, smell, and taste) bombard you with around 2 billion bits of information every second. If you were to try and deal with this vast array of input, you would go mad. In order to preserve your sanity you filter the incoming information before your brain processes it and makes internal representations from this information.

This is because the processes by which you make internal representations of the external events you perceive through your senses are influenced by your many different experiences and filters.

The way the external stimuli of your world are converted into internal representations in your brain involves three fundamental processes: deletions, distortions, and generalisations. The following sections give you a brief overview of these processes. For more in-depth information, head to Chapter 15.

Deletion

Deletions happen when you pay attention to some information coming in through your senses but are completely oblivious to other stimuli. Think of a nutty professor, so caught up in his work that he leaves home wearing his bedroom slippers.

I (Kate) have a story about my mother-in-law which really illustrates how our unconscious mind makes deletions. My mother-in-law used to travel by bus to Kennington in London to work for the Children's Society, a British charity. Normally she would put her rubbish out before returning for her handbag and briefcase. Because she was running a little late one morning, she grabbed all three bags – handbag, briefcase, and rubbish bag. It was only when she found herself sitting on the bus, thinking the bus was really 'whiffy' that morning that she realised she had taken her rubbish bag onto the bus with her!

Distortion

A distortion occurs when you misinterpret information coming in through your senses.

A cynic might say that being in love is a form of distortion, where you go all starry-eyed behind your rose-tinted glasses, completely oblivious to the faults of your 'perfect' partner.

I (Romilla) was driving home from Bristol late one night, stone-cold sober, and found myself driving down a dual carriageway, when it started to rain. It was a very fine, misty drizzle. I could see a white, ethereal figure in the distance, on the pavement. With pounding heart, the conversation with myself went something like . . .

'Oh my goodness, it's a ghost. I'm the first person in my family to see a ghost.'

'Don't be stupid, there's no such thing as ghosts.'

'Road's empty. Can I do a U-turn without getting caught in an accident?'

'You know you're being idiotic. It isn't a ghost.'

'Yes it is. What if it's a ghost?'

'But it isn't.'

'Yes it is.' And so on . . .

To my extreme relief but, I must confess, also to my bitter disappointment, it turned out to be a tramp in white plastic sheeting looking really spooky in the misty rain. I think I'd have given up the ghost had he been a real ghost!

You can distort the meaning of another person's actions.

My (Kate) friend Jacqui had a male boss, Tom, who, because of his cultural background, found it very hard to deal with women at work and was very abrupt in his interactions with female employees. Jacqui misunderstood Tom's behaviour and decided Tom didn't like her. The situation could have spiralled out of control if Jacqui hadn't confided her misgivings to another colleague. Once Jacqui understood that it was Tom's upbringing that was responsible for his behaviour she did not react emotionally anymore. As a result her behaviour changed to reflect her confidence in herself which resulted in an improvement in the way Tom treated her.

Generalisation

You make a generalisation when you transfer the conclusions you came to from one experience to fit other similar situations or occurrences. Generalisations can be good; they help you to build a cognitive map of the world. If you didn't generalise, you would have to re-learn the alphabet and learn to put together individual letters like 'a+n+d' every time you came to read a book. Generalisations allow you to build on what you already know, without re-inventing the wheel.

The beliefs you hold about your world are generalisations and, if you are anything like the authors, you will delete and distort to the best of your ability to hold them in place. So in other words, your generalisations can become restrictive in that they may make you less likely to accept or trust actions and events that don't fit with your preconceived notion. Do you experience a slight disappointment when someone or a situation fails to meet your worst expectations? And do you feel a little triumphant when you are duly disappointed?

To each his own

The reason people who are exposed to the same external stimuli do not remember and react the same way as each other is because everyone deletes, distorts, and generalises differently based on their own metaprograms, values, beliefs, attitudes, memories, and decisions.

Metaprograms

Metaprograms, discussed in more detail in Chapter 8, are your most unconscious filters. They are the way you reveal your patterns of behaviour through your language. For instance, someone who is inclined to take charge and get things done (meaning that they are proactive) may be heard saying, 'Don't give me excuses, just give me results'. Whereas someone who is likely to take her time to think things over before acting (reactive) is likely to be heard saying, 'Don't rush, think about all the factors and make sure the results are right'. If abused and combined with a tendency to generalise you may pigeonhole people. For example, 'You mean Tom, that really geeky introvert?' (distortion) or 'Yeh, typical salesman, always in your face' (generalisation). However, it is important to remember that people can change their behaviour patterns, depending on the environment and situation that they find themselves in.

Here is a little taster about introvert/extrovert tendencies and how they affect your filtration process. Both of these tendencies are basic metaprograms.

Introvert	*Extrovert*
Will want to be alone to recharge their battery	Needs to have people around when in need of rest and relaxation
Will have a few friends with whom they have a deep connection	Have a lot of friends with whom they connect at a more superficial level
May take a real or imagined slight to heart	May not notice the slight and if they do may attribute it to the other person having an off day
Are interested in a few topics which they know in great detail	Know about a lot of things, but not in as much detail as an introvert
Tend to be more solitary	Are more gregarious

An introvert is not superior to an extrovert and an extrovert can be as good as an introvert.

Metaprograms work along a sliding scale and are not an either/or choice (see Figure 5-2). So at work, where you are confident and enjoy the environment, you may find yourself behaving like an extrovert. This would allow your antennae to pick up a broader band of information and have you noticing contacts and opportunities that will help you in your job. However, meeting your colleagues in a social setting may make you feel very uncomfortable and you may slide down the scale to show more introverted tendencies. As a result, you may delete subtle messages that would have been very obvious to you in your familiar office environment.

Figure 5-2:
Meta-
programs
work along
a sliding
scale.

Introvert   Extrovert

| 0 | 1 | 2 | 3 | 4 | 5 | 6 | 7 | 8 | 9 | 10 |

We are very conscious that extroverts can really annoy their more introverted friends and acquaintances. So extroverts, please take care to tone it down when you meet someone who is perhaps not as responsive as you are and be careful not to encroach on their body space!

An extrovert NLP 'dweeb' (one who plays at NLPing with everyone and everything, all the time) danced a poor introvert he met at a party all around the room by invading the body space of the introvert who kept moving away only to have his body space encroached upon again.

Remembering that people can show different tendencies in different settings, can you think of which side of the scale you favour? Can you make a guess at assessing your friends and family? Here's a tip: The answer to the question 'Do you prefer company or to be alone when you need to recharge your batteries?' will give you a very strong clue to someone's tendencies.

Some extroverts may have a very strong bond with their pets and will seek out the company of their four-legged friends instead of other humans when recharging!

Values

Values are another set of filters that are unconscious, although less so than metaprograms. You learn your values, almost by osmosis, from your parents and close family up to about the age of seven, and then from your peers and friends. Values are what motivate you to do something, but they can also work as brakes stopping you from achieving your ends. These are the factors that are important to you and let you assess whether something that you have done is either good or bad. These influence how you delete, distort, or generalise data from incoming stimuli. Values are arranged in a hierarchy, with the most important at the top of the ladder. Examples of values are health, wealth, happiness, honesty, friendships, job satisfaction, and so on. You can find out more about values in Chapter 4.

James worked for a charity helping to organise an education programme in Africa. He had a young family and loved the work he was doing. Although he was poor as a church mouse, all his day-to-day living needs were taken care of by the charity he worked for. His values hierarchy was satisfied by his work and looked something like:

1. Happiness

2. Enriching lives

3. Being with my family

4. Freedom

5. Variety

6. Support network

These values were obtained by asking James, 'What is important to you about your work?'

Because James's values were being satisfied he did not pay attention (deletion) to any job advertisements that would offer him greater monetary reward, thinking they would detract from the other aspects of his work that he valued. He admits that he bought into the distortion that *all* (generalisation) Western interests in Africa were aimed at exploiting the local people. Although, later, he did realise that in some cases this was simply an excuse by some moaning Minnies not to take responsibility for their own fate.

Values are very contextual. This means some of your values only apply in certain areas of your life and their importance in the hierarchy also changes depending on which aspect of your life you are examining. James's values, above, were only relevant in the area of his work.

To work out what values are important to you in an area of your life, you have to stop, get off life's treadmill, and start thinking! To do that, follow these steps:

1. **Choose an aspect of your life that you may not be as successful in as you would like.**

   You can use work, as James did (see the anecdote earlier in this section), or you may want to think about relationships, education, the environment in which you live, and so on. Chapter 3 has further suggestions.

2. **Make a list of what is important to you in this context.**

3. **Look at the list and think again. Do you need to add something that may be missing that's important to you?**

4. **Arrange the list in order of importance.**

   Is your second value really more important than your third value or should your fifth value move up to position two?

5. **For each value can you identify how you may be making a deletion, a distortion, or a generalisation that is stopping you from fulfilling a desire?**

   This is the $64,000 question!

6. **Also note whether there are any limiting decisions lurking that are having an impact on your values.**

During a deep relaxation, James remembered, when he was about six, his parents having a discussion about their landlord increasing the rent on their house. He recalled how worried his parents sounded. He realised he had formed a belief then that rich people were greedy and bad.

Beliefs

Beliefs are really scary; they can propel you to the heights of success or drag you to the depths of failure because, to paraphrase Henry Ford, 'Whether you believe you can or whether you believe you can't . . . you're right.'

Your beliefs are formed in all kinds of unconscious ways. You learn you are gifted from your parents, that you can't draw from your teacher, you must support your friends from your peers, and so on. In some cases, as with the teacher, when you're told, 'You can't draw', you delete any opportunities you may have had to learn to draw. After all, one teacher told you that you couldn't draw.

Beliefs can start off like a 'splinter in your mind' (remember Morpheus talking to Neo in the film *Matrix*?) and, as it irritates and niggles, you begin to find instances which validate the 'splinter' and over a period of time you develop a concrete belief.

Choose your beliefs very carefully because they have a tendency to become self-fulfilling prophecies!

Attitudes

Your attitude is your way of thinking about a topic or perhaps a group of people. Your attitude tells others how you are feeling or your state of mind about someone or something. It is a filter of which you are much more conscious and is formed by a collection of values, beliefs, and opinions around a particular subject. It is much harder to change an attitude because your conscious mind is actively involved in building and holding on to an attitude.

You can get some awareness of another person's attitude from what they say and how they behave. At work, someone who goes the extra mile and has a positive frame of mind is considered to have a good attitude to his work, whereas a dodger or malingerer may be seen as having a bad attitude to work.

Because your attitude is based on your values and beliefs, it affects your abilities by making you behave in certain ways. Someone who has a positive attitude may always expect to get a positive outcome. By demonstrating a pleasant and helpful demeanour, they influence others to behave in a similar vein.

Next time you're with a moaning Minnie, experiment with getting them to catch your positive attitude virus. If you find someone moaning about the rain, ask them to look forward to the rainbow when the sun shines again. Or if you hear someone backbiting another person say something positive about the victim. Tell them how people who have a positive attitude to life are less stressed. You might even see your moaning Minnie doing something good and decide to praise them!

Memories

Your memories determine what you anticipate and how you behave and communicate with other people. Memories from your past can affect your present and your future. The problem occurs when your memories don't stay in the order in which they were recorded. When the memories get jumbled up, they bring along all the emotions of when they actually happened. By this we mean that your current experience invokes old memories and you find yourself responding to memories and emotions of the past rather than to the experience you're currently having.

My (Kate) friend, Tamara, worked with a woman called Sheila. The relationship between Tamara and Sheila was unsuccessful, to put it mildly. Sheila was a class-A bully who focused her attentions on Tamara. It didn't help that Sheila was Tamara's supervisor. When a very relieved Tamara found a new job, she found that she was working, in a similar relationship, with another Sheila. Because her new colleague was also called Sheila and was senior to her, it took Tamara a lot of convincing that the second Sheila was in fact a lovely person and, until she was able to accept this, she was very wary of the second Sheila. If her memories had stayed in the correct order Tamara would not have re-experienced the negative memories and emotions from the past. She made generalisations and distortions about the second Shelia from her experiences with the first.

Decisions

Your decisions are closely linked to your memories and affect all areas of your life. This is especially important when it comes to decisions that actually limit the choices you feel you have in life – what NLP calls *limiting decisions*. Examples of limiting decisions include: 'I can't spell', 'Money is the root of all evil, so to be good I mustn't be rich', and 'If I go on a diet I won't be able to enjoy my food'.

Many of your limiting decisions would have been made unconsciously, some when you were very young, and may have been forgotten. As you grow and develop, your values may change and you need to recognise and reassess any decisions that may be hindering you.

When James returned to England, after several years in Africa, he was even poorer than a church mouse as he now had to provide for his family, without the help of the charity for whom he had worked. On thinking about their circumstances he drew up a new set of values which went like this:

Happiness

Enriching lives

Being with my family

Security

Financial freedom

Variety

It was when he decided that he needed financial freedom that it dawned on him that the decision he had made (rich people = greedy = bad) when he was little was hampering him from providing for his family. He thought about how he could be rich, help people, and stay close to his family. Today, James is extremely happy, very wealthy, and enriching lives. How? He topped up his MSc in Business Management with a PhD in Psychology. He runs workshops around the world, travelling with his wife.

Giving Effective Communication a Try

As the preceding sections show, much of the way you think and behave is unconscious; your responses are formed and impacted by your values, beliefs, memories, and so on. Fortunately, you don't have to be at the mercy of your unconscious.

With awareness, you can actually take control of how you communicate with people, and that is a liberating and empowering thought indeed! Just keep these pointers in mind:

- ✔ **Engage your brain before your mouth.** Think of the result you want when you are interacting with people and speak and behave bearing that outcome in mind.

- ✔ **Tread softly.** Having this knowledge does give you power and power as we all know can corrupt. On the other hand, power can also free you from fear. It can allow you to work with generosity and kindness, so that with knowledge of someone else's model of the world you can come to a win-win conclusion.

Part III
Winning Friends . . . Influencing People

The 5th Wave — By Rich Tennant

"Well that's just great! We're this close to landing 'Godzilla—The Mini-Series,' and you lose your emotional distance over syndication rights!"

In this part . . .

You see that life's all about people connecting with one another. You find out about two key subjects of NLP known as Sensory Awareness and Rapport – which are all about noticing more of the world around you and how you can engage with it. And without rapport you simply don't get listened to.

We also show you the value of hearing how people use words in different ways, and how to switch perspective so you can see a situation from another point of view.

Chapter 6

Seeing, Hearing, and Feeling Your Way to Better Communication

In This Chapter

▶ Exploring the amazing power of your senses

▶ Getting truly in touch with the world around you

▶ Noticing how people think differently by the language they prefer

▶ Spotting eye movements in other people and what they mean

*T*hink back a moment. At the beginning of this book (if you're those wonderfully organised people who have the discipline to start at the beginning of a book rather than diving straight into the middle) we introduced you briefly to the four main pillars of NLP. One of these upstanding elements is what NLP labels *sensory awareness* or how we make meaning of the world and create our own reality by using our senses.

Just for a minute, imagine a special creature with highly developed personal antennae. Well, actually that's you. You come tumbling into the world as a new human baby with amazingly well-developed senses, all geared up to discover the secrets of the universe. Unless you were born with difficulties in some way, you arrive as a perfect mini learning machine with eyes, ears, a sense of smell, taste, and touch, plus that most distinctly human quality – the ability to experience an emotional connection with others.

Of course, life all starts very well and then around the age of nine or ten it begins to go downhill. Ever heard the term 'Use it or lose it'? Often, as human beings, we get a bit lazy about learning or stuck in a rut. Once we find we're good at one way of doing things, that's the way things can stay. We take the easy option, narrowing down the possibilities. This is what can happen with our sensory awareness. We get very good at one style of thinking and processing information and let the rest of our senses lie dormant in a rusty heap.

Leonardo da Vinci mused that the average human 'looks without seeing, listens without hearing, touches without feeling, eats without tasting, moves without physical awareness, inhales without awareness of odour or fragrance, and talks without thinking'.

What an invitation for personal improvement!

So as you move on, dear reader, let us encourage you to try out some new ways of engaging with the world, fine tuning those incredible senses, and notice what a difference it can make. Guess what? You can look forward to serious fun and learning along the way.

The Modalities . . . That's VAK Between You and Me

The NLP model describes the way that you experience the external world – and, by the way, it's called real life – through your five senses or modalities of sight, sound, touch, smell, and taste.

Notice what happens inside your head and body, for example, when I say: 'Think about a delicious meal you've enjoyed.' You might see a picture of the table spread with colourful dishes, hear the sound of knives and forks, a waiter telling you about today's specials, or a friend chatting in the kitchen. Perhaps you notice a warm and pleasant anticipation inside as the aromas of food drift your way, you hear the uncorking of a bottle of wine or feel a cool glass of water in your hand, and then there's the taste of the first mouthful. Mmm . . . a multi-sensory experience. And this is just thinking about it in your armchair.

Until now you might not have thought about *how* you think (the process), only *what* you think about (the content). However, the quality of your thinking determines the quality of your experience. So the *how* is just as important, if not more important, than the *what.* This section introduces you to some dimensions of your thought processes that you may never have considered before. As you open up your own awareness as to how you think and make sense of the world, some interesting things happen. You begin to notice that you can control how you think about a person or situation. You also realise that not everybody thinks like you do about even the everyday events that seem so clear and obvious to you. And in the process you may decide that life can be more rewarding if you begin to think differently by paying attention to different senses.

Filtering reality

As you experience reality, you selectively filter information from your environment in three broad ways known in NLP as visual, auditory, and kinaesthetic (VAK for short, and VAKOG if you include the olfactory and gustatory bits).

- ✔ Some see the *sights* and *pictures* – you'll have a clear picture of the *visual* dimension.

- ✔ Others of you *hear* the *sounds* – you'll be tuned into the *auditory* dimension.

- ✔ A third group *grasp* the *emotional* aspects or *touch* – you'll feel the *kinaesthetic* dimension as *body awareness*, and in this grouping we also include the sense of taste (gustatory) and of smell (olfactory).

Let's think for a moment about the way you experience using this *Dummies* book. Everybody who picks it up will notice the look, sound, and feel in different ways. Take three individual *Dummies* readers. The first one chooses the book because of the friendly pictures, layout, and cartoons. The second likes the sound of what is said and discussed in the print. The third enjoys the feel or smell of the paper or has a gut feeling that this is an interesting book to get hold of. Perhaps for you, as a sophisticated *Dummies* reader, it's a mix of all three! Check it out. As you use this book, start to notice how you prefer to take in information. Begin to notice which pages make you sit up and pay attention. What works best for you? Are you most influenced by the words, the pictures, or the feel of it?

In everyday life, you will naturally access all of your VAK senses. However, in any one context, one sense may currently dominate for you. As you become more sensitive to the three broad groupings of visual, auditory, and kinaesthetic at work and play, we promise it'll pay dividends for you. Let's imagine, for example, that you want to change a room in your home. You may have been thinking about this in purely *visual* terms – what paint colours to choose or patterns for the fabrics. If you began to engage in the *auditory* dimension, you may think about the sounds of objects in the room, those squeaky floorboards, how to cut the noise of the external traffic or let the birdsong in, the music or conversations you'd like to take place there. Or what would happen if you considered this space in terms of textures and smells – the *kinaesthetic* or *olfactory* dimensions? Perhaps then you'd choose a plush, velvety carpet or perhaps rush matting. You might expose some brickwork or prefer a new smooth plaster finish on the walls, depending on the feel that appeals to you.

In the context of learning, when you know about VAK, you may start to play around with different ways of taking in information. Perhaps when you've studied a language in the past, you've done it by playing auditory tapes in your car. You may find it faster to learn by watching foreign films or plays instead, or by playing sport, sharing a meal, or learning a dance routine with native speakers of that language. Once people learn to develop their abilities to access pictures, words, and feelings, they often discover talents that they were unaware of before.

In 'NLP-speak' the different channels through which we represent or code information internally using our senses are described as the *representational systems*. You'll hear NLPers talk about rep systems for short, VAK preferences or preferred thinking styles. Visual, auditory, and kinaesthetic make up the main rep systems. The actual sensory-specific words (such as 'picture', 'word', 'feeling', 'smell', or 'taste') we employ – whether nouns, verbs, or adjectives are called the *predicates*. More examples of these are given in Table 6-1, under the heading 'Building rapport through words' further on in this chapter.

Hearing how they're thinking

As human beings we naturally blend a rich and heady mix of these three main dimensions, yet we tend to have a preference for one mode over the others.

So how do you decide whether you or others have a preference for the visual, auditory, or kinaesthetic dimension? Here's a fun quiz for you – and we don't claim it's scientific. Try it out on yourself and with friends and colleagues to find out more about your primary representation system. It'll take just a couple of minutes.

1. For each of the following statements, circle the option that best describes you.

   1. I make important decisions based on:

   a) Following my gut feelings

   b) The options that sound best

   c) What looks right to me

   2. When you attend a meeting or presentation, it is successful for you when people have:

   a) Illustrated the key points clearly

   b) Articulated a sound argument

   c) Grasped the real issues

   3. People know if I am having a good or bad day by:

   a) The way I dress and look

   b) The thoughts and feelings I share

   c) The tone of my voice

4. If I have a disagreement I am most influenced by:

    a) The sound of the other person's voice

    b) How they look at me

    c) Connecting with their feelings

5. I am very aware of:

    a) The sounds and noises around me

    b) The touch of different clothes on my body

    c) The colours and shapes in my surroundings

2. Copy your scores from the question onto the grid below:

1a	K	4a	A
1b	A	4b	V
1c	V	4c	K
2a	V	5a	A
2b	A	5b	K
2c	K	5c	V
3a	V		
3b	K		
3c	A		

3. Add up how many Vs, As, and Ks you got.

4. See how you did!

Did you get mainly V, A, or K or was it evenly mixed? Check your preferences below and see whether what we say here makes any sense for you.

✔ **V – visual –** A visual preference may mean you will be able to see your way clearly, keep an eye on things, and take a long-term view. You may enjoy visual images, symbols, design, watching sport, physics, maths, and chemistry. You may need to have an attractively designed environment.

✔ **A – auditory –** An auditory preference may mean you will be able to tune into new ideas, maintain harmonious relationships, and sound people out. You may enjoy music, drama, writing, speaking, and literature. You may need to manage the sound levels in your environment.

✔ **K – kinaesthetic –** A kinaesthetic preference may mean you will be able to get to grips with new trends, keep a balance, hold tight onto reality. You may enjoy contact sports, athletics, climbing, working with materials – electronics or manufacturing. You may need to have a comfortable environment.

Within Britain and America it's estimated that visual is the dominant style for approximately 60 per cent of the population. This is hardly surprising given the bombardment of our visual senses.

Beware of labelling people as visuals, auditories, or kinaesthetics – a gross generalisation. Instead, think of them as preferences or behaviours rather than identities. Be mindful, too, that no one system is better or worse than any other. (You can't help but operate in the different modes, even if this happens unconsciously.) It's simply a different way of taking in and storing information as you experience the world about you. After all, everyone's unique.

Listen to the World of Words

In the early days of NLP, the founders, Richard Bandler and John Grinder, became fascinated by how people used language in different ways. The whole NLP notion of *representational systems* came out of their seminars and study groups when they identified patterns of speech linked to the VAK senses. We represent our experience through our senses, and NLP calls the senses representational systems.

The everyday language you use provides clues to your preferred representational system. In enhancing your own communication skills, listen to the types of words people use. You'll find clever clues as to what's going on inside their heads, whether they will be more responsive to pictures, words, or sounds.

Building rapport through words

In our own training sessions, we often test this out and observe how easy it can be for groups with the same preferences to build rapport quickly. They find it naturally easy to speak to those who 'speak their language'.

So what can you do when you feel you're speaking a 'different' language and the conversation is harder? Begin by listening more carefully and identifying other people's language preference. Then you're in a great position to adjust your language pattern so it aligns with theirs and thus build rapport through the similarity of your language pattern.

Table 6-1 lists some of the sensory-specific words and phrases – those VAK predicates – you'll hear people say. You can start to build up your own lists and notice which words you say or write frequently. If you're finding it hard to get through to some people, check whether you are stuck in a rut with your own language.

Table 6-1	VAK Words and Phrases	
Visual	*Auditory*	*Kinaesthetic*
Bright, blank, clear, colour, dim, focus, graphics, illuminate, insight, luminous, perspective, vision	Argue, ask, deaf, discuss, loud, harmony, melody, outspoken, question, resonate, say, shout, shrill, sing, tell, tone, utter, vocal, yell	Cold, bounce, exciting, feel, firm, flow, grasp, movement, pushy, solid, snap, touch, trample, weight
It appears that	The important question we are all asking is . . .	Driving an organisation
A glimpse of reality	So you say	We reshaped the work
We looked after our interests	I heard it from his own lips	Moving through
This is a new way of seeing the world	Who's calling the tune?	It hit home
Now look here	Clear as a bell	Get a feel for it
This is clear cut		Get to grips with
Sight for sore eyes	Word for word	Pain-in-the-neck
Show me what you mean	We're on the same wavelength	Solid as a rock
Tunnel vision	Tune into this	Take it one step at a time
	Music to my ears	
	That strikes a chord	

There are also a few olfactory and gustatory words. These include the following: bitter, fragrant, fresh, juicy, odour, pungent, salty, smell, smoky, sour, spicy, sweet, and whiff.

Many words in your vocabulary don't actually have any link to the senses. They are non-sensory and because they are 'neutral' you will neither connect nor disconnect with somebody else's representational system. Neutral words include the following: analyse, answer, ask, choose, communicate, complex, educate, experience, favourite, imagine, learn, question, remember, transform, think, understand, use, and wonder.

ANECDOTE

Rich or digital?

In any walk of life, people develop their own shorthand style of language with co-workers, friends, and family. Listen to a group of doctors, teenagers, or builders and they'll have their own way of getting the message across quickly and efficiently.

Speaking from personal experience, we can safely generalise that many business people, and especially those who work in the IT industry, stay highly tuned into their own digital style of language. Surrounded by logical technology they forget how to put any sensory-specific language into their communication (until they learn about NLP, of course!).

Communication issues arise for any bunch of people when they step outside their peer group.

All too often, corporate-speak sends people to sleep. Just contrast the average script of a *Death by Powerpoint* presentation in corporations across the globe with the inspired 'I Have a Dream' speech of a leader like Martin Luther King and you'll soon see why so many executives power nap in front of their laptops in the afternoons.

The answer lies in passion. When people live their passion and want to share it with the world, they naturally engage all their senses and this is reflected in the words they speak. If you were to analyse the famous speeches of Martin Luther King or the TV series of world-renowned naturalists like David Attenborough or David Bellamy, you'd notice the richness and use of sensory-specific words in their speech.

When people's thoughts and words are highly logical and conceptual and devoid of sensory language, NLP calls this digital processing. Documents from insurance companies are typical of digital language, as in the following example: 'The obligation to provide this information continues up to the time that there is a completed contract of insurance. Failure to do so entitles the Underwriters, if they so wish, to avoid the contact of insurance from inception and so enables them to repudiate liability.'

Bring in the translators

Sometimes two people struggle to communicate because they speak with different language styles, even if they have similar viewpoints. One may use an auditory style, for example, and another a visual or kinaesthetic style. To be an effective communicator, you need to be able to do two things: know your own preferred style or representational system, and also practise using other ones.

Have you ever heard a dispute that goes something like this one between a manager and a member of their team in the office? To demonstrate the different language styles, we've shown the predicates (the actual sensory-specific words and expressions) in italics.

Manager: (Betty) 'I can't *see* your point of *view* about your appraisal' (visual).

Employee: (Bill) 'Well, can we *talk* about it further?' (auditory).

Betty: 'It's perfectly *clear* to me – just *black and white*' (visual).

Bill: 'If you would *discuss* it, it might be more *harmonious* around here' (auditory).

Betty: 'Just have a closer *look*. I'm sure you'll get a better *perspective*' (visual).

Bill: 'You never *listen*, do you? End of *conversation*' (auditory).

Did you notice how Betty, the manager, stays with visual language, and the employee, Bill, is stuck in auditory mode? They are disconnecting and not making progress.

Here's how a third person – maybe Bob from human resources or another department – can help to shift the dispute.

1. Bob sums up the situation in *visual* mode to Betty and *auditory* mode to Bill. This conversation goes something like:

'So, Betty, it looks like you have a *clear picture* of the situation (visual). And Bill, you've still got some important questions to *talk through* (auditory).' (Heads nod in agreement.)

2. Then Bob shifts into the third system (kinaesthetic) which is neutral ground for both arguing parties.

'You both want to *get this moving* and *off the agenda*. So how about we all *kick around the stumbling blocks* for an hour in my office, *re-shape* it and finally *put it to bed*.'

One of our colleagues, Helen, was a touch sceptical about the language differences when she first became curious about NLP. Yet she experienced one of those wonderful light-bulb moments when she first discovered her own representational systems and decided to play with them at home before trying them out in her business life. She'd noticed how her husband, Peter, some-times switched off and seemed disinterested when she wanted to talk about important decisions at home. She was curious as to whether changing the words she used would have any effect.

'I'd be ready to talk to him about pretty major issues such as which schools the girls should go to or whether we should go ahead and spend thousands of pounds on re-designing the kitchen, and all I'd get was a cursory 'Yup, fine,' or 'No, not now.' I realised that having a strong kinaesthetic preference, I'd often begin a conversation with: 'Peter, how do you *feel* about XYZ . . . ?' I also noticed that he used plenty of visual language. So I thought I'd give it a go and ask him: 'Peter, how do you *see* XYZ?' The difference, once I began play-ing with it and slipping more visual words into the conversation, was quite staggering. It was such an easy change to make and, hey presto, I could get his attention. This was magical.'

The Eyes Have It

Body language offers wonderful clues to people's preferred representational systems. How we breathe, our posture, body type, and voice tone and tempo tends to vary according to visual, auditory, and kinaesthetic styles. In the early days of NLP, Bandler and Grinder observed that people move their eyes in systematic directions depending on which representational system they are accessing. These movements are called *eye accessing cues*.

What this means is that when people move their eyes in response to a ques-tion, you can pretty much guess whether they are accessing pictures, sounds, or feelings. Why is this helpful, you may wonder? The answer is that you have a great chance of knowing, even without them uttering a word, which system they will use and how you can talk to them in a way that will make them respond positively to you. Table 6-2 outlines what eye movements are associ-ated with which representational system.

Table 6-2		Accessing Cues	
Pattern	*Eyes move to the subject's*	*What's happening inside*	*Sample of language*
Visual constructed	Top right	Seeing new or different images	Think of an elephant covered in pink icing
Visual remembered	Top left	Seeing images seen before	Think of your partner's face

Pattern	Eyes move to the subject's	What's happening inside	Sample of language
Visual	Blank stare ahead	Seeing either new or old images	See what's important
Auditory constructed	Centre right	Hearing new or different sounds	Listen to the sound of your name backwards
Auditory remembered	Centre left	Remembering sounds heard before	Hear your own doorbell ring
Auditory internal dialogue	Bottom left	Talking to oneself	Ask yourself what you want
Kinaesthetic	Bottom right	Feelings, emotions, sense of touch	Notice the temperature of your toes

The following picture shows the kind of processing most people do when they move their eyes in a particular direction. A small percentage of the population, including about half of all left-handers, are reversed – their eye movements are the mirror image of those shown.

The picture in Figure 6-1 is drawn as if you are looking at someone else's face and shows how you would see their eyes move. So, for example, if they are moving up and to your right into the *visual remembered* position, your own eyes would be shifting up and to your left if you're trying it out on yourself as in a mirror.

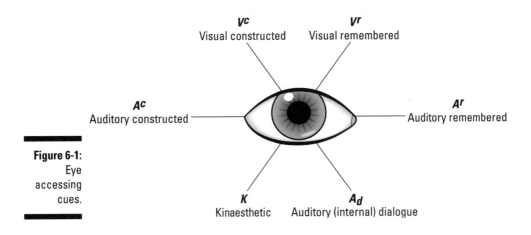

Figure 6-1:
Eye
accessing
cues.

The telltale signs of a liar

How well do you think you can spot a liar? You may believe you're totally clued up and can see instinctively when someone's fibbing, but numerous scientific studies over the last 30 years show that most of us can only guess when someone tells little white lies. We can even be duped by the most outrageous untruths.

Years of research by Paul Ekman, world-respected for his studies of emotions, reveal that the secret lies hidden in our micro-expressions. Some 42 different muscles move in a person's face to create thousands of different micro-expressions. These change all the time in all sorts of subtle ways. So subtle, in fact, that if you can learn to focus and catch these super-fast movements you have all the information you need to read the liars.

The trouble is that with so many possibilities, any human being finds it hard to register the discrepancies that show a false emotion – a lie. Even the latest generation of machines can't get it right all the time. So who can accurately pick out the naughty tricksters? Ekman's research (*New Scientist* 29 March, 2003) rates the star performers as members of the US Secret Service, prison inmates, and a Tibetan Buddhist monk.

It's probably no surprise that that Secret Service agents would be highly trained to select out dangerous suspects. Prisoners live in an environment of people experienced in crime and deception and need to learn who to trust in order to survive. Meanwhile, Ekman's Buddhist subject had none of these life experiences, but had spent thousands of hours meditating, and appeared to have the sensitivity to read other people's emotions very accurately from their fleeting facial expressions.

By developing your sensory awareness, spotting the details, you can become more attuned to how people may be thinking at different times. Once you know this, you can select your words so they will listen to you. In this exercise, your aim is to notice how people's eyes move so you can calibrate them and decide if they are thinking in pictures, sounds, or feelings. Find a willing friend; then use the questions and diagrams on the Eye Movements Game sheet, shown in Figure 6-2. Each question on this game sheet is phrased to engage with the senses – either in the past or future. Follow these steps:

1. **Get your friend to think about something neutral so that you can check what their face looks like in neutral.**

   Washing up or sock-sorting may be a pretty safe and mundane subject to suggest.

2. **Ask one question at a time from the Eye Movements Game list. As you do so, pay full attention to their eyes.**

3. **Pencil in arrows on the diagram to record the direction in which your partner's eyes move.**

Your arrow marks should match up to the positions on the eye accessing cues picture (refer to Figure 6-1, earlier in this chapter), so they will move to top, centre, or lower positions and to the left or the right. Once you've recorded your friend's eye movements, see if your partner's eyes go to the position that you'd expect based on the eye accessing cue pattern outlined in Table 6-2.

Eye Movements Game

1.   What does the Queen of England look like on TV?

2.   What do you see when you wake up in the morning?

3.   Picture a pink elephant.

4.   A circle fills a triangle; how many shapes are there?

5.   Remember the sound of a car horn.

6.   What are the first words you said today?

7.   Imagine Donald Duck saying your name and address.

8.   What do you say to yourself when you've made a silly mistake?

9.   How hot do you like the water when you take a shower?

10.   What is the sensation of crumbs of food in your bed?

Figure 6-2:
The Eye
Movements
Game sheet.

Making the VAK System Work for You

Once you become aware of VAK, then life gets more interesting. Here are some ideas on how you can pull it out of your new toolkit and use it to your advantage.

- ✔ **Influence a business meeting, training session, or presentation.** Remember that when you speak to a room full of people they will all have a preference for how they take in information and you don't know what that is. Unfortunately, people don't have a label on their foreheads to inform you about what they want to know and how they want to receive it – give me the picture, tell me the words, share your feelings about this subject. So what you need to do is ensure you connect with each and every person in the room by presenting your ideas with a variety of media. Vary your presenting style and aids to help the visuals see it with pictures, the auditories to hear it loud and clear, and the kinaesthetics to experience it with feeling.

- ✔ **Make home projects fun for all.** Recognise that each family member has a different way of thinking about a major project. Perhaps you'd like to extend the house, re-decorate a room, or re-design the garden. Not everybody wants to spend hours talking it through, with discussions that stretch late into the night. Your partner may want to pore over the drawings, while your kids will be motivated by the chance to just get in there and get their hands dirty with paint or earth.

- ✔ **Develop your goals so they're more real for yourself.** When you set goals in your personal or professional life, they will come alive if you really use all your senses. Think of what they will really look, sound, and feel like when you've achieved them and at every step along the way. NLPers get proficient at imagining all the fine details of their future experience – you'll hear the phrase 'putting up a movie screen' to describe how people can create their own dream. So if you want to motivate someone (or yourself) to push themselves out of their comfort zones, help them to explore what it will be like when the task is complete and the hard work is done.

- ✔ **Help children to learn better.** Thank goodness education has changed dramatically since we were at school and teachers now recognise that pupils all learn in different ways. As both parents and teachers, you need to support children to understand how they learn at their best – and appreciate that it may be different to the way you were taught or would like to learn. Visual learners will benefit from pictures, wall displays, and diagrams. Auditory learners need to hear what they are learning – through discussions, lectures, and music. Kinaesthetic learners benefit from practical sessions and role playing. They like a 'hands-on' approach. Teachers of groups of pupils need to provide a multi-sensory approach that caters for all styles. Children may be labelled as 'slow' when in fact the dominant teaching style does not fit with their preferred way to learn. All these principles apply to adult learners, too.

✔ **Increase the impact of the written word.** When you put pen to paper, words to screen – from a job description, to customer proposal, charity letter, product advertisement, or article for your local community newsletter – you'll need to broaden your vocabulary to cover all the modalities. To appeal to every reader, select words that include all three.

✔ **Connect with clients and colleagues on the phone.** Nowadays more and more business happens on the phone and with email rather than face-to-face. You may never get to even meet some of your clients or colleagues. Keep a pad by the phone and make a note of the kind of language they use – can you hear visual, auditory, or kinaesthetic language? As you listen, and then reply, phrase your sentence to match their preference.

One a day

As you read this chapter, you may have become more curious about yourself and those you spend time with – how you think and experience life around you. To enhance your skills further, you can explore your senses in different ways. Pick a sense theme for each day.

This could be an *olfactory* day, when you pay attention to every fragrance, smell, and aroma. Or a *visual* day, when you switch off the music and focus on the sights, shapes, and pictures – see what's around you. A *touch* day can be fun, when you feel the textures around you or get in touch with your feelings at regular points in the day.

If you're a creature of habit who takes the dog for a walk every morning or drives the same route every day, notice what changes for you when you pay attention to just one sense at a time.

Chapter 7

Creating Rapport

. . . .

In This Chapter

▶ Learning how to get people to listen to you in challenging situations

▶ Getting on with difficult people

▶ Improving your ability to say 'no'

▶ Increasing your choices in how you respond

▶ Gaining insights into what it's like for the other person

. . . .

Rapport is like money. You only realise you have a problem when you haven't got enough of it. Rapport is not a technique that you turn on and off at will. It should flow constantly between people. Rule one of communication: establish rapport before expecting anyone to listen to you. And this is the case with anybody and any situation, whether with a teacher, pupil, spouse, friend, waitress, taxi-driver, coach, doctor, therapist, or business executive.

Rapport sits at the heart of NLP as another central pillar, or essential ingredient, that leads to successful communication between two individuals or groups of people. You do not need to like someone to build rapport with him or her. It is a mutually respectful way of being with others and a way of doing business at all times.

Don't kid yourself that you can pull it instantly out of the bag for a meeting or problem-solving session. True rapport is based on an instinctive sense of trust and integrity. This chapter will help you to spot situations when you do and don't have rapport with another person. We'll encourage you to focus on building rapport with people whom it might be valuable for you to have it, and we'll share with you some special NLP tools and ideas to enable you to build rapport.

Why Rapport Is Important

The word rapport derives from the French verb *rapporter*, translated as 'to return or bring back'. The English dictionary definition is 'a sympathetic relationship or understanding'. It's about making a two-way connection. You know you've made such a connection when you experience a genuine sense of trust and respect with another person, when you engage comfortably with someone no matter however different they are to you, and when you know that you are listening and being listened to.

While you may like to spend your time with other people who are just like you, the real world is full of a wonderful variety of different types of people with special skills, opinions, and backgrounds. Rapport is the key to success and influence in both your personal and professional life. It's about appreciating and working with differences. Rapport makes getting things done much easier. It means you can provide good customer service to others and enjoy being on the receiving end of it, too. Ultimately, it preserves your time, money, and energy. What a great stress-free way to live!

Recognising rapport

There's no magic pill to learn rapport. It's something you learn intuitively – otherwise robots and aliens would have the leading edge on us humans. So, in order for you to understand how you personally build rapport and what is important to you in different relationships, let's begin by making some comparisons.

ANECDOTE

Is anyone in?

Do you ever meet a new group of people and then forget their names almost immediately? Your intention is to concentrate; yet you find yourself losing focus. Or perhaps you say good morning to your colleagues and don't have time to look them in the face.

Robert Dilts tells the story of a West African tribe and the way they greet each other:

Person A says: 'I see you . . . (name).'

Person B replies: 'I'm here. I see you . . . (name).'

Person A replies: 'I'm here.'

Try it with a friend who's willing to play! It just takes a few seconds longer than 'Hi there, mate' or 'Morning!' and has the effect of making you concentrate on that other person and really make a connection.

1. First think for a moment about someone you have rapport with. What signals do you send out to them and receive back that allow you to know that you're on the same wavelength? How do you create and maintain that rapport?

2. Now, as a contrast, think for a moment about someone you do not have rapport with, but would like to. What signals do you send out to them and receive back that allow you to know that you're not on the same wavelength? What gets in the way of creating and maintaining rapport with that person?

3. Based on your experience with the first person, what might you do differently in your behaviour with the second person that can help you build a stronger relationship?

You might think that the first person (the one you have rapport with) is naturally easy to get on with and the second (the one you don't yet share any rapport with) is just a difficult person. Yet, by being more flexible in your behaviour or thoughts about the second person, you may well find that you can build rapport with them through some simple stages. It may be that you need to take more time to get to know them and what's important to them rather than expecting them to adapt to you and your style. You'll find more tips on doing so in this chapter.

Identifying with whom you want to build rapport

By now you may be getting curious about people around you – those you work with, share a home with, or spend time socialising with. There may be some key individuals that you'd like to get to know better. It could be the manager of a project or your new partner's family. Perhaps the bank manager is somebody you'd like to influence!

Here's a form to fill out for anyone you'd like to have better rapport with. The reasons we're asking you to write it down are: first, to make you stop and think, and second, so that you can come back to revisit it at a future date. Good relationships take serious investment – time to build and nurture. You'll see that the questions require you to think about your needs and also about the other person. Rapport is a two-way street.

Name: _____

Company/group: _____

What is your relationship to this person?_____

Specifically, how would you like your relationship with this person to change?

_____

_____

What impact would this have on you?_____

_____

_____

What impact would it have on the other person?_____

_____

_____

Is it worth investing time and energy?_____

_____

_____

What pressures does this person face?_____

_____

_____

What is most important to them right now? _____

_____

_____

Who do you know that you could talk to who has successfully built rapport with this person? And what can you learn from them? _____

_____

_____

What other help can you get to build rapport? _____

_____

_____

What ideas do you have now in moving this relationship forward?_____

_____

_____

What is the first step? _____

_____

_____

When rapport really matters

Fast-moving businesses breed stressful working conditions. Take the frenetic world of advertising: highly competitive, new young teams, artistic temperaments, large budgets, and crazy deadlines. When people frequently work all night, it's hardly surprising that mistakes happen.

In advertising agencies from London to Sydney, you can be certain there will be a number of client problems brewing at any time. Media like the *Financial Times* appears on the desks of executives the world over, and what happens when your client's advertisement from last week appears in place of this week's new message? All too often, anxious calls fly back and forth across the airwaves as the wrong ad appears in the newspapers, artwork goes astray, and computers crash mysteriously taking with them the latest version of an important design.

One of our advertising friends once produced a customer magazine for a corporate client where some of the main photographs appeared in black and white: they should have been in colour. In a hurry, he hadn't checked the proofs carefully. When the print was delivered, he called the client, confessed the error, apologised, and took full responsibility for a costly mistake. As this was his own agency he knew that if he had to pay for the reprint, the bill for several thousands of pounds would come straight out of his own profits.

At the other end of the phone, the young corporate marketing executive's first reaction on learning of the error was that she felt the whole job would have to be reprinted; she'd discuss it with her boss and get back to him.

Within an hour, the client called back to say her boss's reaction was that it was a genuine mistake. Because of the good working relationship, they would accept the job and let it go out. They had remembered the times when he had gone beyond the call of duty to respond at the weekend and late evenings so the client could achieve a product launch on time. They also valued the time he had taken to understand their business, plus the advice and experience he had shared to use budgets wisely.

And what's the moral of the story? Simply that it's worth investing time in building the right relationships as well as getting the job done.

Basic Techniques for Building Rapport

Having rapport as the foundation for any relationship means that when there are tough issues to discuss, you can more easily find solutions and move on. Fortunately, you can learn how to build rapport. Rapport happens at many levels. You can build rapport all the time through:

- The places and people you spend time with
- The way you look, sound, and behave
- The skills you have learned
- The values that you live by

    ✔ Your beliefs

    ✔ Your purpose in life

    ✔ Being yourself

Seven quick ways to sharpen your rapport

For starters, try some immediate ways to begin building rapport; for more advanced rapport-building techniques keep reading:

    ✔ Take a genuine interest in getting to know what's important to the other person. Start to understand them rather than expecting them to understand you first.

    ✔ Pick up on the key words, favourite phrases, and way of speaking that someone uses and build these subtly into your own conversation.

    ✔ Notice how someone likes to handle information. Do they like lots of details or just the big picture? As you speak, feed back information in this same portion size.

    ✔ Breathe in unison with them.

    ✔ Look out for the other person's intention – their underlying aim – rather than what they do or say. They may not always get it right, but expect their heart to lie in the right place.

    ✔ Adopt a similar stance to them in terms of your body language, gestures, voice tone, and speed.

    ✔ Respect the other person's time, energy, favourite people, and money. They will be important resources for them.

The communication wheel and rapport building

Classic research by Professor Mehrabian of the University of California at Los Angeles (UCLA) looked at how live communication was received and responded to. His figures suggested that your impact depends on three factors – how you look, how you sound, and what you say. His research broke it down as illustrated in the communication wheel here: 55 per cent body language, 38 per cent quality of the voice, and 7 per cent actual words spoken (see Figure 7-1).

Clearly, first impressions count. Do you arrive for meetings and appointments hot and harassed or cool and collected? When you begin to talk, do you mumble your words in a low whisper to the floor or gaze directly and confidently at your audience before speaking out loud and clear?

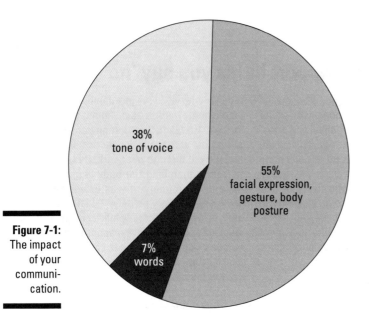

55%
facial expression,
gesture, body
posture

38%
tone of voice

7%
words

Figure 7-1:
The impact
of your
communi-
cation.

In terms of building rapport – *you* are the message. And you need all parts of you working in harmony: words, pictures, and sounds. If you don't look confident – as if you believe in your message – people will not listen to what you are saying.

Rapport involves being able to see eye-to-eye with other people, connecting on their wavelength. So much (93 per cent) of the perception of your sincerity comes not from what you say but how you say it and how you show an appreciation for the other person's thoughts and feelings.

When you are in rapport with someone, you can disagree with what they say and still relate respectfully with him or her. The important point to remember is to acknowledge other people for the unique individuals that they are. For example, you may well have different political or religious views to your colleagues or clients, but there's no need to fall out about it. It's also likely that there are several choices about what's favourite to eat for supper and you can agree to differ with your family on that one, too.

Hold on to the fact that you simply wish to differ with their opinion and this is no reflection on the person. If you flick through to read about logical levels in Chapter 11, you will see that NLP makes a distinction between beliefs and values at one level, and identity at a higher level. A person is more than what they say, do, or believe.

When rapport helps you say 'no'

You may have a teddy bear style of behaviour. Perhaps you're one of those people who prefer to say 'yes' to everything, to be helpful and pleasing to the boss, clients, and family. You'll be the first person to put your hand up in committee meetings, the one who organises the school jumble sale or charity dinner, who drives the kids around, and you're always the one who ends up having to do the tasks. Learning to say 'no' sometimes is essential learning if you're to protect yourself from overload. Consider James's story:

At work, how tempting it is for a manager to ask the willing worker to take on more. As a maths teacher who loves his job, James was finding it increasingly hard to say: 'I'm not going to take that on.' He felt he was letting people down by saying 'no' and was in danger of making himself seriously ill through overwork. He learned that by simply matching the body language of his head of department, it was easier for him to smile and say very politely: 'I'd love to do that, and yet my time is already fully committed. If you want me to take on extra responsibility you must decide what you'd like me to stop doing to make time for this.' In this way he refused to take on a greater load than he could possibly handle.

Matching and mirroring

When you are out and about in bars and restaurants, even the staff cafeteria (if you're lucky enough to get meals at work), have you noticed how two people look when there's rapport between them? Without hearing the details of the conversation you can see it's like a dance. People naturally move in step with each other. There's a sense of unison in their body language and the way they talk – elegantly dovetailing their movements and speech. NLP calls this *matching and mirroring*.

Matching and mirroring is when you take on someone else's style of behaviour and their skills, values, or beliefs in order to create rapport with them.

By contrast, think of a time when you've been the unwilling witness to an embarrassingly public argument between a couple, or a parent and child in the street or supermarket. Not quite a punch-up, but almost. Even with the volume turned off, you soon feel what it's like when people are totally out of synchronisation with each other just from their body posture and gestures. NLP calls this *mismatching*.

Matching and mirroring are ways of becoming highly tuned in to how someone else is thinking and experiencing the world. It's a way of listening with your whole body. Simple mirroring happens naturally when you have rapport.

What NLP suggests is that you can also deliberately match and mirror someone to build rapport until it becomes natural. To do this, you will need to match:

  ✔ Voice tonality (how you sound) or speed

  ✔ Breathing rates

  ✔ Rhythm of movement and energy levels

  ✔ Body postures and gestures

Beware the fine line between mimicry and moving in rhythm with someone. People instinctively know if you are making fun of them or being insincere. If you decide you'd like to check out mirroring for yourself, do it gradually in no-risk situations or with foreigners who you'll never see again. Don't be surprised though if it works and the strangers want to become your friends!

Pacing to lead

Building great relationships requires that you pace other people. As a metaphor, NLP compares pacing people to running alongside a train. If you tried to jump straight on to a moving train, it's likely you'd fall off. In order to jump on a moving train you would have to gather speed by racing alongside it until you were moving at the same speed before you could jump on. (And please, never actually try jumping on to a moving train!)

In order to lead somebody, to influence them with your point of view, remember to pace them first. This means really listening to them, fully acknowledging them, truly understanding where they have come from – and being patient about it.

Additional important advice from NLP to build rapport is to: Pace . . . pace . . . and pace again before you . . . lead. Pacing is how NLP describes the your flexibility to respectfully pick up and match other people's behaviours and vocabulary, where you are actively listening to the other person. Leading is when you are attempting to get the other person to change by subtly taking them in a new direction.

In business, companies that succeed in introducing major change programmes do so in measured steps. This allows changes to gradually become accepted by employees. People are unwilling to be led to new ways of working until they have first been paced – listened to and acknowledged. The most effective leaders are those who pace their people's reality first.

Watch effective salespeople in action and you'll see how they master the art of pacing the customer and demonstrate genuine interest. (By effective, we're thinking of those who sell a genuine product with integrity rather than the shark approach.) They listen, listen, and listen some more about what the customer's needs are, what they really want, before trying to sell them anything. People resent being sold to, but they love to be listened to and to talk about what's important to them. An antiques dealer friend has perfected this art over many years, gently guiding his customers by his genuine affection for the articles he sells from his own home, and sharing his expertise.

When I (Kate) last bought a car, I went to six different showrooms where salespeople were hasty to sell the virtues of their car without showing any interest in how it fitted in with my lifestyle. The successful salesperson had superb interpersonal skills as well as the right product. He paced me well, listening carefully, treating me with respect (unlike those who assumed the buying decision would be made by my husband), and trusted me to take the keys and take it for a spin immediately. As I drove along, he gently gathered the information he needed to match the right model of car to my buying criteria, realising I wasn't going to accept a hard direct sell.

Building rapport in virtual communication

Fifteen years ago, the Internet and e-mail tools were confined to the research labs and those nerdy types. Regular business transactions involved lots of letters and faxes, mostly filed in hard copy: it was OK to jump in the car to drive and visit suppliers and colleagues in other offices. Today life's different. Of course, we still write and phone, the paperless office remains elusive, and the percentage of electronic transactions has shot through the roof. If the computer goes down and we can't email for an hour, we feel lost and helpless.

Virtual teams who hold virtual meetings have entered the workplace. We have also the phenomenon of virtual management, of multi-cultural project teams that sit across global networks and work remotely thanks to the technology – conference calls, email and video-conferencing. In fact, a recent survey of 371 managers by British business management school, Roffey Park, showed that 46 per cent of managers currently work in virtual teams and 80 per cent said that virtual management arrangements were increasing.

In this environment of reduced face-to-face contact, you lose the nuances of facial expressions, the body language, and subtlety of getting to know the colleague at the next desk as you work closely with others. At its best, the virtual team spells freedom and flexibility of working practices, diversity, and a richness of skills. At its worst, it's lonely, isolated, and ineffective.

For all, the challenge of virtual working to build rapport is greater than before. Little wonder that people are being recruited more for soft skills – the ability to influence and negotiate – than for technical competence. Following are ten ways to develop rapport over the phone and teleconferences.

- Make sure that all the locations are connected and can hear each other on the phone. Introduce and welcome people with a roll call.

- Work to a clear agenda. Set outcomes for the call and agree these with all participants.

✔ Check you've had input from a mix of people. If necessary, encourage the quieter individuals to take part. Say, for example: 'Mike, what are your thoughts on this?'

✔ Discourage small talk or separate chats at different sites. One discussion, one meeting, one agenda.

✔ Speak more slowly and precisely than in face-to-face meetings. Remember you can't get clues from the body language.

✔ Listen for the style of language – check if people have visual, auditory, or kinaesthetic preferences and match your language style to theirs as we suggest in Chapter 6 – Seeing, Hearing, and Feeling Your Way to Better Communication.

✔ Get attention before making your point (otherwise the first part of the message gets lost). Begin with phrases like: 'I have something I'd like to mention here . . . it's about . . . '.

✔ Use people's names more than in face-to-face meetings. Address questions to people by name and thank them for their contribution by name.

✔ As you listen to the conversation, visualise the person at the other end of the phone line (you may even like to have a photo of them in front of you).

✔ Continually summarise and check understanding of points and decisions.

How to Break Rapport and Why

There will be times when you choose to *mismatch* people for a while and break rapport. Mismatching is the opposite of matching or mirroring. To mismatch somebody you aim to do something dissimilar to them. This might be to dress very differently, speak in a different tone or at a different speed, adopt a different physical posture, or behave quite differently to them.

Three changes enable you to break rapport in the short term:

✔ **How you look and move physically.** You may want to physically move away from someone, break eye contact, or use a facial expression to communicate your message. Raised eyebrows say a lot. Turning your back is even more powerful. So, beware of doing this inadvertently!

✔ **How you sound.** Change your voice intonation or volume. Take it louder or softer, high or low. Remember the power of silence.

✔ **The words you say.** Remember that useful little phrase: 'No, thank you.' Sometimes it's the hardest to say, so practise it for when you need it. In multi-cultural settings, switching to your native language when you've been working in a common language is another clear way of saying, 'I need a break now.'

There are plenty of times when you may want to say 'thank you' and 'good-bye for now'. Notice which come easily to you and where you could use some practice.

- **You are closing a deal.** Salespeople momentarily break connection with a customer at the point of signing a contract. They'll walk away and leave the customer to look at the paperwork alone rather than becoming connected to that final signing in the customer's eyes. This helps maintain rapport for the long term if buyer's remorse sets in.

- **You have enough information.** Maybe your brain has filled up for the moment and you're heading into sensory overload. You want time to think and digest what you have heard and to come back for the next instalment later.

- **You see someone else you'd like to talk to.** Perhaps you're at a drinks party and you've got stuck with the ultimate bore and there's someone much more attractive at the other side of the room.

- **You're tired.** All good things come to an end and it's good to know when it's time for the party to end and head home.

- **You're busy.** At any one time there will be a number of demands on your energy. Hold onto your own outcome rather than satisfying someone else's for them.

- **You're getting into tricky subjects.** Sex, politics, and religion are all good subjects to avoid in a business negotiation. They also cause lively dinner-party conversations where you may want to blow the whistle, call time out, and agree to differ as discussions get heated.

It's a skill to learn to break rapport and end a conversation, particularly if your best friend or mother wants to chat. Do it with consideration. Give clear feedback that you'd love to talk so long as it's contained to the right time of day, place, and length of time. You care about them as a person, so try and arrange a time to talk that suits you when work's over for the day.

The power of the 'but' word

There are times when something as small as a tiny word makes a huge difference between your ability to keep rapport and break it. NLP pays attention to such details in the pattern of conversation and so offers some useful clues for your influential communication. Work by NLP leaders like Robert Dilts has demonstrated that simple words like 'and' or 'but' make you focus your attention in different ways. When you adopt the 'but' word, people will remember what you said afterwards. With the 'and' word, people remember what you said before and afterwards.

ANECDOTE

Enough is enough

Ralph was a very competent engineer and a great storyteller. He'd travelled widely, met all the senior people in the corporation where he worked as they were climbing the ranks, and had had interesting jobs. All the newcomers in the team loved to hear his anecdotes and exploits at the coffee machine – for a while.

Unfortunately Ralph didn't recognise the signs when people had heard enough. As colleagues were politely edging back to their desks or desperately trying to leave the building at night, Ralph would corner them and carry on with his stories oblivious to the bored stares or attempts to end the conversation. The more they tried to get away, the more he would become entrenched

in the next episode: 'And let me just tell you about . . . .' You had the feeling that if you walked away and came back next year, he would just pick up where he had left off.

In the end, team members began to avoid him. They'd joke about him behind his back because he refused to pick up the cues that he'd taken more than his allowed slot. They stopped inviting him to meetings for fear he would dominate. His career progress suffered. Colleagues deliberately broke rapport to protect their own time.

As Ralph became more and more ostracised from the team, he became more desperate to tell his stories and gather an audience around him.

Be aware that if you are making a comment to someone, they may only notice part of what you say. Consider the following example: 'The company has returned £5 million profit this financial year, but we're closing the San Francisco operation.' If you say it like this, people may only remember what you said after the 'but' word. Now consider the following: 'The company has returned £5 million profit this financial year, and we're closing the San Francisco operation.' If you say it like this, people remember what you said *before* and *after* the word 'and'.

Find out just how much little words make a difference in your daily communication with the 'Yes, but . . . ' game for three or more players.

1. **Get your friends into a circle.**

2. **Person A begins *round one* with offering 'a good idea'.** (For example, 'It's a sunny day, how about if we take the afternoon off and head out to the beach?')

3. **Person B replies 'Yes, but . . . ' and offers their own 'good idea'.**

4. **Person C and all other team members offer their ideas in turn, always starting with 'Yes, but . . . '.**

5. ***Round two* continues with Person A offering a good idea.**

6. **Person B replies 'Yes, and . . . ' and offers their own 'good idea'.**

7. **Person C and all other team members offer their ideas in turn, always starting with 'Yes, and . . . '.**

Notice the difference?

Understanding Other Points of View

Successful people enjoy the flexibility of being able to see the world in different ways. They take multiple perspectives, enabling themselves to explore new ideas. NLP offers various techniques to help people build rapport in very challenging relationships, especially where there is some kind of emotional conflict happening. These techniques are also used to explore new ways of building rapport, even in relationships that are only mildly troublesome or confusing.

Exploring perceptual positions

One of the ways that NLP helps you to build rapport with others is by distinguishing at least three different points of view. NLP calls these *perceptual positions*. It's rather like looking at a building from all angles – coming in at the front entrance, moving round to the back door, and then looking down with a bird's eye view from a helicopter overhead.

- **First position** is your own natural perspective, where you are fully aware of what you think and feel regardless of those around you. This can be a position of strength – when you're really clear about what you want and your own beliefs and values. It can also be incredibly selfish until you consciously become aware of what other people want.

- **Second position** is about shifting into someone else's shoes – imagining what it's like for them. You may already be really good at always considering others' needs. Mothers rapidly develop this skill in caring for new offspring. You put someone else's view first.

- **Third position** involves taking an independent position where you act as a detached observer noticing what is happening in the relationship. At its best, this is a mature position where you appreciate a situation from both sides. Sometimes it means you're reluctant to engage fully in a situation – you merely sit on the fence.

Mastery of all three perspectives puts you in a wise place to enjoy life to the full.

The NLP meta-mirror

The meta-mirror is an exercise developed by Robert Dilts in 1988 to bring together a number of different perspectives or perceptual positions. The basis of the meta-mirror is the idea that the problem you face is more a reflection of you, and how you relate to yourself, than about the other person. It's a way of allowing you to step back and see a problem you are facing in a new light – hence the idea of the mirror.

The meta-mirror will help you to prepare for, or review, a number of possible scenarios you face:

- A difficult conversation with a teenager or family member
- A presentation at work
- A meeting
- A contract negotiation
- Sensitive discussion with a partner or friend
- How you relate to your boss or a colleague at work
- Dealing with difficult clients

This exercise is based on the work of Robert Dilts and takes four perceptual positions. You may like to try this exercise with the help of a coach or friend to help you concentrate on the process so that you just work with your issue.

First choose a relationship you'd like to explore. Perhaps you'd like some insight into a difficult conversation or confrontation in the past or the future. Then lay out four spaces on the floor to denote four positions (see Figure 7-2). Pieces of paper or Post-it notes are fine. Notice that it's important to 'break state' between each position by physically moving between each move. Just shake your body a little!

1. Stand in *first position*, your point of view, imagining that you're looking at the other person in second position. Ask yourself: 'What am I experiencing, thinking, and feeling as I look at this person?'

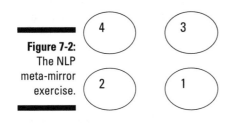

Figure 7-2:
The NLP meta-mirror exercise.

2. Now shake that off and go to stand in *second position,* imagining you're that person looking back at yourself in first position. Ask yourself: 'What am I experiencing, thinking, and feeling as I look at this person?'

3. Now shake that off and stand in *third position*, that of the independent observer looking at both people in this relationship impartially. Looking at yourself in first position, how do you respond to that 'you' there?

4. Now shake that off and stand in a further external space, the *fourth position*. Think about how your thoughts in third position compared to your reactions in the first position and switch them around. For example, in the first position you may have felt confused, while in the third position you may have felt sadness. Whatever your reactions were, in your mind's eye switch them to the opposite positions.

5. Go back and revisit *second position*. Ask yourself: 'How is this different now? What has changed?'

6. Finish by coming home to *first position*. Ask yourself: 'How is this different now? What has changed?'

ANECDOTE

The 'evil' boss

Rosie Miller, director of London-based consultancy firm *The Success Group,* shared with us the impact of the meta-mirror on an executive coaching session.

'My client was unable to stop thinking about her last manager, who she described as evil. She and her group were spending all their time and energy on how to work with this difficult man and move around his bullying, interfering style. She wanted to move away from this unproductive relationship. We agreed to use the meta-mirror to see what ideas might come out.

In first position, she sat in a chair and thought about her relationship with him.

Next, in second position, she sat in the opposite chair as if she were him looking back at her and realised she probably knew very little about him. She said: "I can't begin to fathom what's driving him".

Then, in third position, she climbed on a chair and looked right down on him and said to herself. "Oh, come on, girl. Don't let that little moron affect you". She likened the relationship to being caught in a spider's web and she decided to pull herself out of it.

In fourth position – she switched the learning. By the time she had come back to the first position, she simply looked once more and dismissed him with a wave of the hand: "Let's just forget it. I've got my life to lead. See you."

What was interesting was how quickly she moved on to the point where she had sidelined this person and, within a few weeks, struggled to remember the relationship. Now he's become almost a storybook character from her career history.'

Reproduced with the permission of Rosie Miller.

Chapter 8

Understanding to Be Understood: Metaprograms

In This Chapter

▶ Learning about metaprograms – your most unconscious mental filters

▶ Eliciting other people's metaprograms

▶ Modelling the personality traits of someone you admire

*R*esearch done by George Miller in 1956 showed that, of the millions of bits of data that bombard your senses every second, your conscious mind can only handle between five and nine pieces of information at any one time. This means that an awful lot of information is filtered out.

Metaprograms are some of these unconscious filters which direct what you pay attention to, the way you process any information you receive, and how you then communicate it.

If you want to build rapport with someone quickly and you are forearmed, you may choose to dress like them, behave like them, or at least speak like them. And by that we don't mean you mimic someone's accent, rather that you use their vocabulary. By beginning to hear people's metaprograms you have the choice to use the same words and phrases as the person with whom you are interacting. Because people's use of metaprograms are mostly unconscious, by matching their metaprograms, what you say will have the added dimension of communicating with someone's unconscious mind at the same time as with their conscious mind.

In this chapter we introduce you to six metaprograms we hope you will find most useful in communicating more effectively, more quickly and . . . as you experience the benefits of better communication we hope you will be motivated to discover more about other metaprograms.

Metaprogram Basics

As children, you pick up metaprograms from your parents, teachers, and the culture you are brought up in. Your life experiences may change these learned programs as you get older. For instance, if you grow up being admonished for being too subjective, you may start practising detachment and learn to suppress your feelings. You could find this affects your choice of career. Instead of entering a caring profession you may decide to become someone who uses their intellect more. Your learning style may be influenced too and you learn to focus more on facts and figures. If you deliver training, you may depend more on drier, chalk-and-talk systems than on getting students more involved with touchy-feely experiments.

Of the many metaprograms that have been written about, we have chosen six that we think are the most useful to get you started. We selected the *global and detail* metaprogram as we believe that this is one that has great potential for conflict and by recognising another's capacity for operating at the global or detail end of the scale you may be able to avoid possible problems. By understanding the other five metaprograms you will be able to learn how you can motivate not only yourself but other people with whom you come in contact.

In Chapter 5 you will find a discussion on the Introvert and Extrovert metaprograms. The metaprograms discussed in this chapter are:

- ✔ Proactive/Reactive
- ✔ Options/Procedures
- ✔ Toward/Away From
- ✔ Internal/External
- ✔ Global/Detail
- ✔ Sameness/Difference

As you think about metaprograms, keep these things in mind:

- ✔ Metaprograms are not an either/or choice as they operate along a sliding scale ranging from one preference to the other.
- ✔ Metaprograms are not a means to pigeonhole people.

There is no right or wrong metaprogram. It is simply that you run various combinations of metaprograms depending on the context of the communication and the environment in which you find yourself.

A short history of metaprograms

We have been trying to understand personality types since time immemorial. Hippocrates defined four 'temperaments' based on his observations of fluids in the human body as long ago as 400 BC. He called these temperaments melancholic, sanguine, choleric, and phlegmatic. Although the Hippocratic classifications fell by the wayside, others are used a great deal.

In 1921, Carl Jung published *Psychological Types*. This book was based on his work with several hundred psychiatric patients and was his attempt to categorise his patients in order to be able to predict their behaviour from their personality. Jung defined three pairs of categories in which one of the pair would be used in preference to the other.

✔ An **Extrovert** is energised by interacting with the outside world, whereas an **Introvert** recharges his batteries by taking time to be on his own.

✔ A **Sensor** takes in information through the five senses, whereas an **Intuitor** will rely more on instincts and intuition to collect the information.

✔ A **Thinker** will make decisions based on logic and objective thinking, while a **Feeler** will make decisions based on subjective values.

Jung's personality types formed the basis of the *Myers-Briggs Type Indicator* which is one of the most widely-used profiling tools today. In the early 1940s, a mother (Katherine Briggs) and daughter (Isabel Briggs Myers) team added a fourth category: A **Judger** will attempt to make his environment adapt to suit him, whereas a **Perceiver** will try to gain an understanding of the external world and adapt to fit into the world.

As George Bernard Shaw said, 'Reasonable people adapt themselves to the world. Unreasonable people attempt to adapt the world to themselves. All progress, therefore, depends on unreasonable people.'

Metaprograms and language patterns

Everyone has patterns of behaviour which can be picked up from their language, long before the behaviour becomes apparent. Leslie Cameron-Bandler, among others, has conducted further research into the metaprograms developed by Richard Bandler. She and her student, Rodger Bailey, established that people who use similar language patterns portray similar patterns of behaviour. For example, people with an entrepreneurial flare may have similar patterns – outgoing, good at persuading people, strong belief in themselves, and so on – even though they may work in very different fields.

Imagine a gathering of the heads of the United Nations without any translators. There would be very little communication. A similar break down in communication can occur if you are unaware of the metaprograms the person you are trying to communicate with is operating. Learning about metaprograms allows you to become proficient in translating the mental maps people use to navigate their way around their experiences.

Bandler and Grinder realised that people who used similar language patterns developed deeper rapport more quickly than people who used dissimilar ones. I am sure you have heard some English people who are non-French speakers complain that the French are unfriendly. Others who can speak French refute this. Metaprograms are a powerful way to establish rapport verbally by hearing the patterns someone is running and then responding with language that they can understand easily.

To help you understand the type of language that is characteristic of the various metaprograms, we've included in the following sections phrases that you're likely to hear with each metaprogram.

Metaprograms and behaviour

In the *Encyclopaedia of NLP and NLP New Coding*, Robert Dilts and Judith DeLozier explain metaprograms in terms of two people with the same decision-making strategies getting different results when presented with the same information. For example, although both people might make a picture of the data in their head, one person might become completely overwhelmed with the amount of information while the other reaches a quick decision based on the feelings the pictures produce. The difference lies in the metaprograms each person is running which impacts their decision-making strategy.

Suppose you want to emulate Richard Branson, the founder of the Virgin group of companies. You could do it the hard way by trying to implement the processes you think he uses. Or, with his help, you could do it more quickly and easily by modelling him. Part of the modelling process would require you to understand and use his metaprograms.

The later sections in this chapter describe the behaviours and preferences associated with the different metaprograms. By being able to recognise which metaprogram a person is prone to operating in a given setting, you can begin to match their metaprograms in order to become more like them and get your message heard more easily. By trying on someone else's model of the world you may actually gain a different perspective and add to the choices available to you – an added bonus.

Proactive/Reactive

If you are more inclined to take action and get things moving you operate at the proactive end of the scale. If, however, you are inclined to take stock and wait for things to happen, you are probably more reactive. Following are more in-depth descriptions:

✔ **Proactive:** If you are proactive you will take charge and get things done. You are good at spotting solutions to situations which require constant fire-fighting. You may find yourself drawn to jobs in sales or working for yourself. You find yourself upsetting some people, especially if they are more reactive, as they will liken you to a bulldozer.

✔ **Reactive:** If you are more reactive you may be quite fatalistic. You will wait for others to take the lead or take action only when you consider the time to be right. You may need to be careful not to analyse yourself into a paralysis.

You can exhibit proactive or reactive tendencies, depending on the context within which you are working. For example, I (Romilla) know someone who, although very good at his job, is quite reactive about asserting himself when it comes to requesting promotions and pay rises. He waits for his boss to offer these, rather than ask for them. He prefers to wait for instructions before working on projects, rather than initiating work. However, he loves his holidays and is extremely proactive in visiting travel agents, talking to people, and surfing the Web in his search for the next break.

You can spot the difference between a proactive and reactive person by the body language. A proactive person is likely to have quicker movements, showing signs of impatience. These people are likely to hold themselves erect in a 'shoulders back, chest out' posture that is ready to take on the world. A reactive person will have slower movements and may keep their head down and shoulders slouched.

Proactive Reaction to a Reactive Department

The Information Technology (IT) department at a university in South-East England was always fire-fighting, trying to provide a service for the bursar's and registrar's departments. There was no communication between the two departments who used the systems and the IT department did not trust the users enough to train them in the use of their systems. There was no documentation for which programs needed to be run and when. This situation had existed for several years and was accepted as the norm. Guess what preference the staff in the IT department had? If you guessed reactive, you're right. Then a relative newcomer, with a more proactive bent, came to the department and instigated three simple steps:

✔ Created and maintained a list of tasks, with the operating instructions and when they were needed

✔ Organised regular meetings between the registrar's and bursar's departments

✔ Trained the administrative staff to produce their own reports

This reduced the considerable stress the staff of all three departments experienced, especially at peak times. It opened communication channels between the two departments using the computer systems. The self-esteem of the administrative staff really soared as they took some responsibility for running their own systems.

According to Shelle Rose Charvet, in her book *Words that Change Minds*, when advertising for a person who you want to be proactive, you should ask the candidate to telephone instead of sending a CV. As a general rule, a reactive person will not call.

To discover whether someone is proactive or reactive, you can ask, 'Do you find it easy to take action when you find yourself in a new situation, or do you need to study and understand what is going on first?'

- ✔ A proactive person uses phrases such as 'Just do it', 'Jump to it', 'Go for it', 'Run with it', 'Take control', and 'Hit the tarmac running'.

- ✔ You're more likely to hear these phrases from a reactive person: 'Mull it over', 'Take your time', 'Study the data', 'You may want to weigh the pros and cons', and 'Look before you leap'.

Toward/Away From

People either invest time, energy, and resources moving 'toward' or 'away from' something they find enjoyable or something they wish to avoid. The something is their values which they use to judge whether an action is either good or bad.

Can you remember the last time you started an exercise regime or began a new diet? Were you all fired up and eager to start? Consequently you made terrific progress. Your weight began to come down. You felt so much better because of the exercise. Suddenly you lost your momentum, the weight stopped going down, or worse still, started creeping up. The visits to the gym became more sporadic. As things started to go downhill you got all fired up again until. . . . You were caught in a roller coaster of being motivated and losing your focus. 'What happened?' you cry in despair. Chances are that where your health is concerned you have an *away from* metaprogram. This means that you were propelled to take action to get away from something, in this case weight or perhaps lethargy. Figure 8-1 illustrates how someone whose motivation to health is primarily *away from* might have their weight loss yo-yo over a period of time.

On the other hand, if you are drawn toward a goal, in a particular context, and are able to keep your eye on the ball, you are running a *toward* metaprogram.

As a general rule you either move *away from* or *toward* something. According to Sigmund Freud, your id, which represents your instinctive urges, either moves you towards pleasure or away from pain.

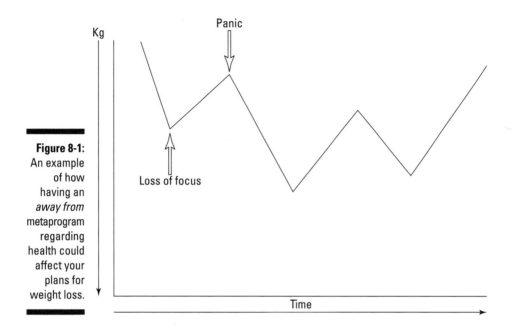

Figure 8-1:
An example of how having an *away from* metaprogram regarding health could affect your plans for weight loss.

It is interesting to note that professions and cultures can exhibit a bias for running either *toward* or *away from* metaprograms. Take the example of conventional medicine as opposed to alternative practices. Which preference do you think practitioners from the two camps might have? To give you a hint, conventional doctors refer to holistic medicine as 'preventative medicine'. In my (Romilla's) assessment, conventional medicine is more prone to having an *away from* tendency with regards to health, the emphasis being more on curing the illness after it has happened rather than on focusing on creating and maintaining good health.

People with *away from* patterns will appear quite negative to those who run *toward* patterns.

The *away from* people have a tendency to notice what could go wrong and are very useful to employ for maintaining production plants and aircrafts, managing crises, or in conducting critical analysis. These are the people who are motivated by the 'stick'. You can motivate *away from* people by threats of job losses and the negative consequences of not meeting financial targets.

People with *toward* metaprograms may be seen as naïve by the *away from* people because the former do not always think about and cater for potential problems in the pursuit of their goals.

Toward people are motivated by the 'carrot'. Tell them about the benefits of improving revenue and receiving a bonus and watch their eyes light up. This is not necessarily because they are greedy, rather that they are excited by positive benefits.

You can find out whether a person has a preference for moving toward or away from something by a series of questions, as in the following example.

Person A: 'What is important to you about your work?'

Person B: 'I know I have security.'

Person A: 'So what is important to you about security?'

Person B: 'I don't have to worry about paying my bills.'

Person A: 'And what is important to you about paying your bills?'

Person B: 'It means I'm not in debt.'

It is useful to go to at least three levels of questions as initially people may have a tendency to respond with something positive which can hide *away from* patterns. In the example above, the initial answer is *toward* security, although subsequent answers reveal an *away from* preference.

When selling a product, research the customers' language patterns. You will then elicit whether they want to buy the product in order to gain a benefit, such as when buying investments, or to avoid a problem, for example when buying insurance. Modify your language accordingly to save time and get results.

We move *away from* or *toward* our values. If *moving away* from values are not serving you, you may decide to change them. If sports at school were a painful experience and consequently sports days a humiliation, you may have problems keeping up an exercise routine. One way of releasing the emotions invested in negative memories is through *Time Line Therapy*™.

You may hear a person with more of a *toward* metaprogram using words like 'accomplish', 'get', 'obtain', 'have', 'achieve', 'attain', and 'include'.

A person who operates a more *away from* metaprogram may use words like 'avoid', 'remove', 'prevent', 'get rid of', and 'solution'.

Options/Procedures

If you are more of an *options* person, you enjoy trying out new ways of doing things. As a *procedures* person, you will display a preference for following set methodologies.

An *options* person loves variety. The analogy that springs to mind is that of offering a gourmet a smorgasbord or dim sum and letting him pick and savour the myriad delicacies on offer.

If you are a person with a preference for an *options* metaprogram you will be good at starting projects, although you may not always see them through.

You are good at setting up procedures, just as long as you are not the one who is expected to follow them.

Because of your penchant for testing new ways, you will be unable to resist improving the most rigorously tried and tested methods or of finding some way to bend that company rule.

Do not ask an *options* person to drive unless you want to see the sights. They like to take a different route each time. I (Romilla) always allow plenty of time to get somewhere new as I have a tendency for getting lost. Once, when I got to my destination without losing my way, I felt cheated.

Heaven help the person asking an *options* man or woman to get married! Even if the *options* person loves you to bits, you may have a hard time getting commitment from them because they will worry about getting hemmed in, missing out on experiences, and so on. The way to get an *options* person to say 'yes' is to show them all the opportunities that will open up for them if they do say 'yes'.

If you have a *procedures* preference, you like to follow set rules and procedures, although you may prefer to have these created for you rather than design them yourself.

Once you have a working procedure you will follow it repeatedly, without modification. You may feel compelled to follow each step of a procedure to the end and feel cheated if circumstances prevent you from getting there.

You will stick to speed limits and take personal affront when other drivers drive along using a mobile phone or with only one hand on the steering wheel.

I (Romilla) really understood the difference between the two preferences when I was learning *Huna* in Hawaii. Two of my group of three wanted to sit out under the trees, by a large pond, overlooking the ocean, to work on an exercise and experiment. Richard, the third person, got extremely distressed and was ready to storm off and find another group to work with because he needed to be in the same environment where the exercise had been demonstrated and to conduct it in exactly the way we had been shown.

You can find out which of the two preferences a person has in a given context by asking, 'Why did you choose this job?' or 'Why did you choose to come to this party?', or 'Why did you choose your particular car?'

An *options* person may give you a list of their values which were satisfied by choosing the job, attending the party, or buying the car. You may hear their reasons for making the choice and the possibilities that the choice opens up for them.

A *procedures* person will launch into a story or list the steps that got them the job, how they got to the party, or chose the car. For instance, 'My Ford Puma was seven years old and I needed to change it. I bought car magazines for a few months and studied the pros and cons of comparative makes but in the end it was knowing that I'd only need to have the car serviced every 10,000 miles that made me decide on . . .'.

If your cat is experiencing an insulin shock on a Sunday afternoon and needs to be rushed to the vet's, do not ask a *procedures* person to drive you. They will stick to the speed limit even though the roads are quiet and the poor cat is verging on expiration and you on hysteria.

You may hear someone with a mainly *options* metaprogram use words and phrases like 'play it by ear', 'bend the rules', 'possibilities', 'Let's play with this', and 'try this other ways'.

A person who is more at the *procedures* end of the scale may be heard using expressions like 'follow the steps', 'obey the rules', 'step by step', and words like 'first', 'second', and 'finally'.

Internal/External

If you trust your judgement when it comes to making decisions or in knowing you have done a good job, you operate at the *internal* end of the scale for this metaprogram.

If you need feedback from other people to know how well you have done, you probably have more of an *external* preference.

The crux of this metaprogram is whether the location for motivating yourself, judging your actions, and making decisions lies within you or with other people.

Children have an external frame of reference as they absorb the conscious and unconscious teachings of their parents and teachers. However, maturity usually shifts the locus of reference to a more internal one as you gain greater understanding of yourself and therefore trust your judgements and decisions more.

A similar slide can occur when you learn something new. You may have more of an external reference, needing other people to tell you how well you are doing. Experience and knowledge can then shift the reference to internal.

You have a propensity for working at the internal end of the scale, in a given context, when you question the negative feedback you receive, even if several people have said more or less the same thing.

You do not need to be praised for doing a good job because you already know you did well. You will do well as an entrepreneur as you will not have to wait for someone else to tell you what to do or how well you are doing it.

Bosses, if you have an internal frame of reference, please remember to give feedback to your staff. They may have an external frame of reference and may be craving praise and wanting to be told how they are doing.

If you have an external bent you will need to receive feedback from other people to know how you are doing and to keep yourself motivated.

Unless you explain the need for the outcomes you want in a job, *internal* employees may prove difficult to manage, particularly if your management style is to micro-manage. They will want to do things their way and will operate from their own standards. *External* people, on the other hand, are easier to manage as long as you understand that they do need direction and praise.

To find out where on the scale a person is, you can ask 'How do you know you've done a good job, bought the right car, made the right decision. . . ?' An *internal* person might respond with 'I just know when I've done a good job', whereas an *external* person may respond with, 'My family really like the car'.

When speaking to a person who operates from an *internal* frame of reference you may gain greater leverage if you use phrases such as 'only you can be the judge', 'it's entirely up to you', 'see for yourself', and 'study the facts to help you decide'.

When talking to someone who is more *externally* referenced you may get a better response by using phrases such as 'the statistics/studies show . . .', 'they'll approve', 'the expert opinion is', and 'this has sold really well'.

Global/Detail

Some people find it easier to see the big picture when they start work on a project or when setting a goal. Others find it difficult to get a global perspective, but find it much easier to envisage the steps required to achieve the goals and prefer to work with smaller details.

Chunk size refers to the size of the task a person prefers to work with. A person with a *global* preference will break tasks into larger chunks than a *detail* person. A *detail* person will need to have a task chunked down into smaller, more manageable steps. The scale at which people work is referred to as the *chunk size*.

If you are one of the people who prefer to work at a global or conceptual level and have trouble dealing with details, you will want a *big picture* outline of what you are about to be taught when you learn something new. If your presenter launches straight into the details of the subject, you may have difficulty in understanding the new topic. You find it easier to see the forest but get confused by the mass of trees. If you prefer working with the big picture, you may find yourself switching off or getting impatient with the amount of information that a *detail* person may give you.

If, on the other hand, you prefer eating the elephant a bite at a time, you have a predisposition for handling details. You may find it difficult to share the vision of someone who thinks globally. *Detail* people handle information in sequential steps and may have trouble getting their priorities right because they are unable to make the more general connections to other areas within which they are working. These people are very good in jobs that require close attention to detail, especially over a period of time, for instance on an assembly line or conducting a test in a laboratory.

Detail people have a tendency to dive straight into working on a task without looking at the impact of the steps on the final, desired goal. As a result, they may not meet the actual goal or only see the goal after a great deal of time and energy has been spent following the steps getting to the wrong goal.

When training, give an overview of the course before going on to talk about the specifics otherwise you will lose the *big picture* people before you even get started.

When I (Romilla) worked in IT, weekly meetings at one multinational company were interesting to say the least. The manager was a *big picture* person and one of the programmers always gave him his progress in minute detail. The rest of the team had great difficulty in keeping a straight face when the manager's face went through its contortions of not understanding, boredom, and blatant irritation until he would snap at one of the project leaders, 'Explain what he means'. Fortunately the project leader was somewhere in the middle of the chunk size range and was able to translate the details for the manager. The poor programmer sweated buckets before the meetings and his stress levels would rise unbearably prior to the meeting.

Have you found yourself procrastinating over a particular task? You may find you are overwhelmed by the size of the job to be done. Use this process to break the task into manageable chunks:

1. **Stop!**

   If you aren't already paralysed into inaction, that is.

2. **Fetch some paper and a pen.**

3. **Sit down and make a list.**

   Think about, and write down, what is really important to you.

4. **Re-arrange the list in order of importance. You may want to transfer some of the points to another list of actions.**

5. **Get cracking!**

To learn where on the scale between *global* and *detail* someone is, ask them about a project they worked on. A *detail* person will give a step-by-step account, for example:

'Jim and I met for lunch on the second Tuesday last July. I remember having to ask Jim a lot of questions because he kept jumping all over the place and I had to keep him focused on each step. I was very nervous at first but felt much happier once we had spent time on capturing all the information in a project plan.'

A *big picture* person will present things randomly, summarising the outcome, as for example:

'Tom and I met for lunch last year sometime and decided to work on building the animal sanctuary. It's really important to focus on the biodiversity. I really think people need help managing their circumstances, don't you?'

A person who has a tendency to operate from a *global* perspective will find it easier to hear words like 'overview', 'the big picture', 'in a nutshell', 'generally', and 'essentially'.

A person at the *detail* end of the spectrum will listen better to someone using words such as 'plan', 'precisely', 'schedule', 'specifically', 'first', 'second . . .', 'next', and 'before'.

Fight, flight, freeze, and procrastination

Along with fight and flight, freezing is part of the stress mechanism. An impala caught by a cheetah will go into a state of hyper-arousal and freeze. The survival response behind this is to make the cheetah believe the impala is dead, thereby giving the impala an opportunity for escape if the cheetah stows it away for later consumption. The other reason for this survival response is that the impala will not feel the pain of being torn apart if the cheetah decides on an immediate feast.

Procrastination is the human equivalent of a freeze response. Are you in the habit of procrastinating? It may be that you take on too much and just don't know where to start.

Sameness/Sameness with Difference/Difference

If, when you learn or experience something new, you try and match the information to what you already know, you have a preference for *sameness*.

Or you could be someone who first notices the similarities in situations and becomes aware of the differences, in which case you have a *sameness with difference* preference.

If, on the other hand, you look at what is different to what you already know, you prefer sorting by *difference*.

As a *sameness* person, you have a head start when it comes to rapport because rapport is all about matching someone else's physiology and thinking – probably something you do automatically. You tend to delete a lot of incoming information if you cannot spot the similarities to previous situations. You may have difficulty in learning something new because you do not have hooks on which to hang the relevant information that is coming in. You are one of the people who does not like change, may even feel threatened by it, and find it difficult to adapt to changes in your work and home life. As a general rule, you only initiate major changes anywhere between 15 and 25 years. This means you probably move house or change jobs very infrequently.

As a *sameness with difference* person, you will first look for similarities in a situation and then you tend to spot the differences. You like the evolutionary approach to change, preferring a major change every five to seven years and you may resist sudden change.

If you operate a *difference* metaprogram, you thrive on change. You love a revolution in your life at least every 18 months and create change for the sake of change. As with *sameness* people, you too have a tendency to delete vast amounts of data, except in your case it is information in which you cannot spot the differences. Some people may find you difficult because of your tendency to always see the other side of the coin.

A close family member of one of the authors (Romilla) sorts by differences. Until she learned about NLP, communications between Romilla and her family member were difficult, to say the least. Now Romilla really values his input. When working on a new project, she does all the brainstorming with other friends and family members. Once she has worked out a fairly solid idea, she approaches her contrary relative who is able to identify the errors and problems the rest of the brainstormers have overlooked. This process saves a lot of time that would otherwise have been wasted in trial and error.

To uncover a person's preferred metaprogram in a given context, you can ask, 'What is the relationship between this job and your previous job?'

A person who sorts for *sameness* may respond with, 'There's no difference, I'm still writing programs.'

A person who runs a *sameness with difference* metaprogram may respond, 'I'm still writing programs for the accounting suite, but now I have the responsibility of supervising three junior programmers.'

The *difference* person may respond with, 'I've been promoted to supervise junior programmers and everything is different.'

A little party game is to ask someone the relationship between the rectangles shown in Figure 8-2. Each rectangle is the same size, but don't tell the person this before asking them.

A person who is operating a *sameness* metaprogram may say, 'They're all rectangles' or 'the rectangles are the same size'.

A person who runs a *sameness with difference* metaprogram may respond with, 'They're all rectangles but one is positioned vertically'.

A person who has a *differences* metaprogram is likely to say, 'They're laid out differently'.

If you do not have rectangles, bar mats, or coasters, you could use three one-pound coins and place two with their heads up and one with the tail up and ask about the relationship between the three coins.

Figure 8-2:
The
Sameness/
Sameness
with
Difference/
Difference
party game.

People with a preference for *sameness* will use words like 'same', 'similar', 'in common', 'as always', 'static', 'unaltered', 'as good as', and 'identical'.

People who operate from a *sameness with difference* base will use words and phrases like 'the same except', 'better', 'improve', 'gradual', 'increase', 'evolutionary', 'less', 'although', 'same but the difference is'. In order to gain greater rapport with these people, you should emphasise things that are the same, followed by what is different, for example, 'the work will be fairly similar to what you have done, however, you will be involved with implementing new solutions'.

In order to influence someone who operates at the *difference* end of the spectrum, use words and phrases like 'chalk and cheese', 'different', 'altered', 'changed', 'revolutionary', 'completely new', 'no comparison', and 'I don't know if you'll agree or not . . .'.

Combinations of Metaprograms

You have a combination of metaprograms that you prefer to adopt when you are within your comfort zone. You should try to remember that this preference may change depending on the different circumstances you find yourself in. For instance, a project manager may combine *difference, proactive, detail,* and *toward* when at work but may choose to be more of a *sameness, reactive, global* person when at home.

It is also important to realise that certain combinations of metaprograms may fit certain professions better than others and that there are many more metaprograms which may be of use to you.

Would you want the pilot of your 747 to have a high *options*, *global* and *difference* metaprogram combination? I think I might be a little nervous of being in the hands of someone who might decide to skip a couple of the flight checks because the procedure was boring and it might be fun to see what would happen if he could get that red light to flash.

Would you want your prescription filled by a chemist who would like to test the result of adding a couple extra drops of the pretty blue liquid to your angina medicine?

The above examples are meant to illustrate that jobs work best when the profile of the person fits the parameters of their job.

You might decide the best metaprogram fit for a quality controller is for her to have a preference for *detail*, *away from*, and *procedures*.

Developing Your Metaprograms

Metaprograms is one of the topics that excites the most interest in my (Romilla) workshops. This is probably because delegates realise the power of using the 'right' language. By this I mean words and phrases that mean the most to the person with whom you are communicating. This will allow you to build rapport and get your message heard better than someone who is not as skilled in the art of metaprograms.

With this thought in mind, we would invite you to develop your abilities by considering the following:

✔ Can you identify the metaprograms you run in different areas of your life? This can be particularly useful if you want to model a successful part of your life in order to improve another aspect of your life that isn't working as well as you would like. If you find you are better at planning your holidays than at progressing your career, is it because you are more *proactive, towards* and *procedures* when you come to plan your holiday? This may mean you go out and research holidays and plan what you want to do. Perhaps, after deciding on the big career goal, you may need to be more procedures driven in order to define and attain the steps that will get you there. You may also need to focus *toward* the goal and become more proactive in achieving it.

✔ If you are having problems with another person, is it because you are at opposite ends of a metaprogram scale? Can you identify the metaprograms being used by you and the other person? As we said when we discussed the *Global/Detail* metaprogram, this is one that can cause a lot of grief. If you talk about the big picture and the person with whom you are communicating is a *details* person, bite the bullet and chunk down!. Mismatched metaprograms can result in a great deal of conflict and miscommunication, so practise feeding back what you hear of someone else's language.

✔ If you are recruiting for a job, write down the traits for the ideal candidate once you have identified the roles and responsibilities inherent in the job. What questions would you ask to establish how well an applicant fits the role? Employing the 'wrong' person for a job can prove to be very costly. So if you are employing a tax accountant you may decide the person needs to be:

- *Proactive* in order to keep abreast of the changes in tax laws.

- *Procedures* and *detail* in order to implement the law to the letter.

- *External* so the tax accountant is receptive to the government's dictats.

- *Difference* in order to spot any discrepancies in the clients' taxes.

Part IV
Opening the Toolkit

The 5th Wave   By Rich Tennant

DOCTOR RUNTLOWE FOUND THE APPLICANTS COVER LETTER FOR CLINICAL HYPNOTIST TO BE MESMERIZING

In this part . . .

You've arrived at the heart of the core tools and techniques in NLP that enable you to cope with difficult situations. As you get more proficient with the tools, you are able to adapt your own thoughts and actions. From using anchoring techniques to travelling along your personal timeline, you discover the essentials that allow you to change and build your repertoire. Roll up, roll up for a more compelling future!

Chapter 9

Dropping Anchors

- -

In This Chapter

▶ Understanding the effect on you of certain sounds, sights, smells, and sensations

▶ Controlling the way you feel on the inside

▶ Overcoming stage nerves

▶ Changing the way you think about the past and the future

- -

'I just don't know what came over me!' Familiar words? Ever had that feeling that your reactions to a situation have been way in excess of what was called for? Your feelings may have overtaken or even overwhelmed you. Perhaps you'd even say that you weren't quite yourself.

Ordinary people like you and us have emotional responses all the time. Some are great – falling in love, joy, and pleasure. Others are not so great – falling out of love, sadness, and pain. It's what makes life and work interesting and fun, as well as confusing and unpredictable. Often in our work, we talk to managers who sigh and wish that their colleagues would leave their emotions at home. And at home, many people would prefer that their partners would leave their workplace stresses at work.

Maybe you've witnessed situations when someone has 'blown a fuse' unexpectedly. Often this happens at what, on the face of it, seems the slightest provocation. Most of us can identify with the discomfort or agitation of being in a bit of a state. In fact, NLP adopts the term *state* to look at, and become more aware of, how you are at any moment in time.

Taken to extremes, these feelings of being overwhelmed and of being out-of-control can scare people. They can affect your career and your social life. People will question if such a person can be trusted in responsible situations or if they have to represent the company.

You'll be pleased to know that with the stabilising influence of the NLP toolkit, help is at hand to control yourself, your state at any one time, and the effect you have on other people. And once you discover how, it's pure magic.

Starting Out with NLP Anchors

NLP tools that help you create positive states in yourself are known as anchoring techniques. NLP defines an anchor as an external stimulus that triggers a particular internal state or response. People set and respond to anchors all the time. You know to stop the car at a red traffic light. You find that certain foods get you licking your lips.

You may be curious as to why anchors are helpful. The answer is that when you learn how to anchor, you can take all your positive and challenging experiences and memories and play around with them to make yourself more resourceful in the future.

The idea of anchoring in NLP came from modelling the techniques of Milton Erickson, the hypnotherapist. Erickson often used cues as triggers to help a person change his or her internal state outside the therapeutic setting.

Humans learn behaviour in response to a stimulus: it's not just dolphins who learn amazing tricks. From conception, babies are programmed to respond to certain stimuli. We constantly move and change our state in response to our environment with incredible flexibility in our behaviour.

From Twitmeyer to Pavlov, or how it all started

What the Russian psychologist Pavlov found out with his famous dog experiments was an early example of anchoring. Set a stimulus – food – and get a consistent response – salivation. Pair the sound of a bell – the conditioned stimulus – with placing the food in the dog's mouth and soon the dog learns to respond to the bell.

Pavlov's less well-known colleague, Twitmeyer, was examining the human knee jerk reflex in 1902 even before Pavlov studied salivation in dogs. Twitmeyer took a hammer to the knee and he had a bell that sounded when the hammer fell. Like so many discoveries in science, just one accidental change in an experiment leads to the most exciting breakthroughs. One day he rang the bell without dropping the hammer. And

guess what? Yes, the subject's knee reacted to the sound of the bell alone.

Unfortunately for Twitmeyer, he was slightly ahead of his time and the medics of the day yawned at his Behaviourist contribution. (Or maybe with a name like that no-one could take him seriously.) Fast forward the story just a couple of years to 1904 and Pavlov's work on dogs grabbed people's attention and won him the Nobel prize in Physiology.

Since then studies of animal behaviour have become increasingly more scientific and sophisticated. Every day we can read new research on the brain and increase our knowledge about human intelligence and behaviour.

Setting an anchor and building yourself a resourceful state

Our memories are stored as associations with our senses. Smells are particularly powerful anchors to times and events. So, for example, you smell a particular perfume and it transports you back to your first date and splashing on the cologne or aftershave. Or if you've ever been drunk on whisky, perhaps the smell of it alone will be enough to make you feel nauseous. We create positive and negative anchors for ourselves all the time.

How do you set an anchor? NLP teachers suggest various techniques. Ian McDermott and Ian Shircore describe the following simple three-step NLP technique for taking control of your own state by establishing resourceful anchors:

1. **Get clear about the positive state you would ideally wish to be in.**

   Your confident state may be bold or witty, energetic, anticipatory, enthusiastic. Be clear and specific in your own words to describe it.

2. **Recall a specific occasion in the past when you have been in that state.**

   What you are looking for here is a comparable experience, even though the context can be very different.

3. **Relive it as vividly as you can.**

   Engage fully with the experience – the sights, sounds, smells, the physical feelings, and internal sensations.

Once you have followed these three steps and you are in the highest positive state, it's the moment to set an anchor for yourself. Hand movements work well as a physical (kinaesthetic) anchor. Simply notice what your hands are doing as you engage with the experience and hold a distinct movement – such as a clenched grip, or thumb and first finger in a circle. (A handshake won't work because it's too mundane and habitual.) Alternatively, as an auditory anchor, listen for a sound. For those with a visual preference, see a picture that symbolises the positive state.

When you need to get back into a positive state, you simply fire the anchor for yourself as a stimulus to change your state. For more information on using anchors to change states, head to the section 'Altering states with anchors', later in this chapter.

Anchors need to be:

- Distinctive – different to everyday movements, sounds, or pictures.

- Unique – special for you.

- Intense – set when you fully and vividly experience the peak of the state.

- Timely – catching the best moment to make the association.

- Reinforced – use it or you'll lose it. Anchoring is a skill to develop with practice.

It's easy to establish a *negative anchor* without planning it that way. Take the situation, for example, where a highly stressed manager drives home from work at night and arrives at the house having had mobile phone conversations all the way from the office about work problems. As he walks in the door, his negative feelings about work peak to a high intensity. What if at that moment, his wife comes and kisses him hello as he walks into the house? It could happen that he unintentionally connects his wife kissing him with work worries. This is how anchors are established. Then guess what? His wife kisses him, he begins to feel anxious and doesn't know why.

Common sense suggests that you would not deliberately set out to establish a negative anchor. So how could you avoid doing it? The key lies in recognising what triggers a negative response in you and realising you have a choice in how you respond. If you have got into the habit of responding negatively in certain situations, once you are aware of it, you are in a position to decide if that is an appropriate and helpful response, or whether you would like to make some changes.

Eliciting and calibrating states

Do you know when someone else is in a happy, positive state or not? What are the signals? When you meet someone and are building a relationship – socially or in business – it's useful to *calibrate* them.

NLP defines calibration as the process of learning how to read another person's responses. Good communicators have learnt to heighten their skills of observation. Instead of guessing how somebody else is thinking, they notice and recognise the subtle cues and facial expressions of people that they mix with.

For example, if you know that your boss goes quiet and clenches her facial muscles when she is faced with a tough deadline, you will be well advised to avoid a chatty social conversation when you spot those signs. Or, if you are negotiating a deal in business, it helps to take time to get to know the people you are negotiating with. Friendly, social questions asked at the coffee machine or in the lift can help you calibrate people's body language and develop your awareness of their responses.

Try this quick game with a friend to calibrate their states. As you do so, notice the changes in their physiology – what happens in their facial movements and colour change as well as their body language. Notice the difference.

1. **First notice their starting position – to check what your friend looks like in neutral.**

   To get them into a neutral state, you can ask a mundane silly question like: 'What colour are your socks today?' Or 'How many pens do you keep in your desk drawer?'

2. **Then ask them to think for a minute about someone they really like, whose company they enjoy – paying attention to any pictures, sounds, or feelings that come.**

   (Give them time to be with the experience.)

3. **Get them to stand up and shake that out.**

   NLP calls this *breaking state*.

4. **Ask them to think for a minute about someone they really dislike, whose company they do not enjoy – paying attention to any pictures, sounds, or feelings that come.**

5. **Compare the differences in your friend's reaction to a positive and a negative experience.**

With some people you'll find a dramatic change in the body language. For others it will be so subtle it's hard to tell.

There's an NLP presupposition that goes: We cannot *not* communicate. Like it or not, you're continually influencing other people. Just by a look or a word, you have the skill to elicit states in other people and in yourself. It's so easy – just by being who you are and doing what you do, without any conscious effort.

Setting your own repertoire of anchors

One great way to work with NLP concepts is to find optimal states for yourself. Simply the best way for you to be yourself. This is a bit like having a repertoire of tennis or golf shots. Ask yourself what might be the best way:

- ✔ To learn effectively
- ✔ To perform at your best
- ✔ To relate to other people

Notice times in the past when you've been particularly successful in these areas. What was going on for you at the time? Where were you, who were you with, what were you doing at the time that was helpful? What was important to you?

Build a range of visual, auditory, and kinaesthetic anchors that make you feel good about yourself and other people. You may want to enlist the help of a friend and work with each other on this.

Recognising your own anchors

What are the triggers, the stimuli that affect you most at home or work? Make a note in the chart below (Figure 9-1) so that you begin to become aware of the times you're feeling good and less good. Your aim is to concentrate more on your positive experiences and change or let go of the negatives.

	AT HOME		AT WORK	
	Good	Bad	Good	Bad
V-Sights				
A-Sounds				
K-Touch/feelings				
O-Smells				
G-Tastes				

Figure 9-1: A personal anchor chart.

Take some time to record some details of different experiences that make you feel good or bad. These can be seemingly insignificant everyday events and will be very individual.

You may feel good at home at the sight of a log fire or a vase of tulips on the table, the sound of your favourite CD, or the smell of a hot meal on the kitchen stove. Equally, the sight of your computer on a tidy desk, the buzz of the people, or the smell of a steaming hot drink may welcome you to work in the mornings.

Alternatively, if you flip when someone turns the TV up loud, or another e-mail or piece of paper plops into your in-tray, you may need to find some strategies to switch the negatives into positives. Only when you identify what you like and what you don't like can you start steering the minute details of your daily experience in the best direction for you.

We've organised this chart by the different VAKOG senses (head to Chapter 6, for more on these). Here are some anchors to notice:

Visual – pictures, colours, decoration

Auditory – music, voices, birdsong, sounds

Kinaesthetic – textures, feel of the physical elements, and emotional vibes

Olfactory – smells, chemicals, scents

Gustatory – tastes, food and drink

Come back to this framework every few weeks or so to help you get more of what gives you pleasure. If you have a dominant sense – with more visual anchors than auditory ones, check if you're missing out and filtering information unnecessarily.

Your anchors will change over time. As you concentrate more and more on the things that give you pleasure, you may begin to notice that those that upset at first seem less relevant over time. Here's an exercise that you may want to turn into a healthy daily habit.

As you go through every day, pick out five events or experiences that have given you pleasure. Keep a private notebook of what's going well for you. Often it's the small things that make a difference – a pleasant conversation, a kind gesture, the smell of a bakery, or the sun breaking through the clouds. When you're feeling under pressure, refer to it and ensure that you spend at least part of every day on important things that matter to you.

A taste of the past: anchors in common usage

Just for a moment look back to your very first day at school. Quietly listen for the sounds around you and what it feels like for you to be in that new environment. Sounds and smells are particularly evocative to bring back pictures of childhood memories . . . good and bad. Maybe there are some triggers today that immediately remind you of school. What makes you recall memories of your school days? Possibly the smell of certain foods or a polished floor, the sight of a school trophy, or the sound of a bell signalling the end of lessons.

For me (Romilla), the smell of cardamom transports me immediately into my idyllic and colourful Indian childhood . . . yet, for Kate, merely hearing the words 'school custard' brings sights, sounds, unpleasant tastes, and anxious feelings of the formal school dining room rushing back with a vengeance.

People who work with adults or children in training roles should be aware that there are those who've had unhappy learning experiences in school and then you'll come up against a natural sense of resistance. Luckily, with good teachers and trainers, most come to discover how rewarding, and how much fun, it can be to continue learning as an adult, even if that wasn't true in childhood.

Going through the Emotions: Sequencing States

Think back to yesterday. As you review the events of the day, ask yourself how you felt at different times. Were you in the same state all day? Unlikely. Just as with a temperature gauge, you may have blown hot or cold or experienced all the dimensions on the scale – cool and calm, warm and interested, hot and excited, plus any number of degrees of permutations along the way.

As humans, we are blessed with behavioural flexibility and the wonderful ability to change state. We need to shift. If we operated on a constant high, we'd soon get exhausted. Peak performers have to be able to switch off and regenerate, recharging the batteries. Otherwise they suffer burn out. During a presentation, for example, it's important to vary the pace and rhythm so that your audience stays interested. At times you'll want them to be relaxed and receptive to what you're saying, at other times highly alert to the details, at other times curious and interested.

Working in one-to-one coaching sessions and facing up to difficult problems, clients regularly demonstrate a full range of emotions from extreme anger, frustration, and worry to laughter in a very short space of time. At times when the going gets tough, the territory constantly sways to a point where someone exclaims: 'I don't know whether it's best to laugh or cry!'

Humour offers an incredibly resourceful and valuable way to change state. Cartoon characters often give us the ability to see the opposite perspective on our experience; to take a serious subject and put it into a new light. The skill of any leader – whether as parent or manager – lies in our ability to pace somebody through these different states and lead them to a positive outcome.

Altering states with anchors

Your states may be constantly shifting, and the value of anchors is that they enable you to alter your state to a more resourceful one when you need to. Say, for example, you have a difficult decision to make, a person to meet, or an event to attend – at weddings and funerals emotions run high and at these times you might want to manage your feelings closely. By being in the right state, you will make the best choices and act for the best result.

As an analogy, imagine that you're sailing a dinghy in a storm, and you want to reach a safe harbour. By developing the ability to fire anchors, you can secure a calm state for yourself or switch to an energetic, risk-taking mode. An anchor, by definition, is attached to a stable position: it keeps you safe and stops you floating away. Strength and stability are the keynotes here.

At any time when you notice that you are not in 'a good state', you have a choice. Either you stick with this uncomfortable state because, for some reason, you get some value out of it. Or you decide there is a 'better' state that you'd prefer to shift into. To change your state, you can fire off an anchor to create a more positive state for yourself. (See the earlier section 'Setting an anchor and building yourself a resourceful state' to remember how easily you can do this in just three steps.)

Constantly overriding negative anchors with positive ones can lead to problems. Negative anchors can be one way that the unconscious mind indicates to the person that there is an underlying issue that they need to address. Feeling tired may be an indication that your current work patterns are exhausting you. If you continue to override this with an energetic anchor you will get burn out.

Get with the Baroque beat

The Ancient Greeks knew it, early psychologists used it, and modern science confirms it: music affects both mind and body. Music alters our brain-waves which indicate the electrical activity in the brain. When we're relaxed, our brain-waves are slower and they speed up as we become more energised. Music with around 60 beats per minute seems to be the most comfortable across cultures because it corresponds with the beat of the human heart at rest.

Brain-waves, from alpha to delta

We have four types of brain-waves, measured in cycles per second:

1. Alpha brain-waves – clear, calm, and relaxed – 8–12 cycles per second

2. Beta brain-waves – alert and problem solving – 13–30 cycles per second

3. Theta brain-waves – creative and imaginative – 4–9 cycles per second

4. Delta brain-waves – deep sleep – less than 6 cycles per second

Baroque music is especially suitable for creating a state of relaxed awareness, known as the alpha state. To explore this kind of music, look out for the largo and adagio passages in pieces composed between about 1600 and 1750 – Bach, Mozart, Handel, and Vivaldi all offer good starting points.

Here are some different ways to think about the music you play. Perhaps you're stuck in a groove with your listening taste:

- **Vary the range of CDs you buy** – from Baroque to classical, jazz and blues, reggae, pop and rock, to opera.

- **Change the rhythm** – compare predictable rhythms with varied and unfamiliar ones to encourage your creativity. World music is good for this.

- **Instrumentation or lyrics?** Words can distract – solo instruments tend to encourage relaxation.

- **Intuition** – trust your own tastes. If you dislike a piece of music, don't struggle with it. Turn it off – it's unlikely to make you feel good.

- **Start the day differently** – when you feel good in the morning, you'll get off to a flying start. Try swapping the confrontational news channel on the radio for inspiring and uplifting music.

Here's an exercise to work through an issue with the help of music:

1. **Think of an issue or a decision that's bothering you – rate it on a worry scale of 1 to 10 and note the score on a piece of paper.**

2. **Select three pieces of music of different styles.**

   For example, try some Baroque, instrumentals, or soft vocals.

3. **Play the first piece of music while thinking about your issue; then rate your thoughts on a scale of 1 to 10. Make a note of how you now see and feel about the issue.**

4. **Play the second piece of music while thinking about your issue; then rate it on a scale of 1 to 10. Make a note of how you now see and feel about the issue.**

5. **Play the third piece of music while thinking about your issue; then rate it on a scale of 1 to 10. Make a note of how you now see and feel about the issue.**

Has your thinking shifted? Which music was most powerful for you to become more resourceful?

Walking in someone else's shoes

Another way to develop your NLP skills is to find a positive role model – someone who seems to behave how you'd like to. Then try their body language on for size. One way you can do this is to copy how they hold themselves – upright or soft, smiling or serious – and then try walking the way that they walk. You may hear this called the *moccasin walk* – imagine you're wearing that person's shoes and try walking around the room or down the street as if you're treading in their footsteps.

By changing your own physiology, you will change your internal state – how you think and react.

 If you're a small woman copying a large man or vice versa, this can give you new insights into how your physical shape makes a difference to the way you influence people. Gill, one of our petite female clients, was struggling to get attention at board meetings. By becoming more attuned to the physical mass of her male counterparts, she adapted her presenting style to be more expansive – moving purposefully across the stage as she spoke. She also now spreads her papers and takes up a larger portion of the boardroom meeting table. Both are moves to mark out her territory and authority. Similarly, large men working with children often find it better to talk to children from a seated position closer to the floor than by towering above them.

Getting Sophisticated with Anchors

This section shows you how further NLP anchoring techniques can help you face challenging and fearful situations. Perhaps you're battling with changing unhelpful behaviours such as smoking or eating the wrong foods. Perhaps you'd like to boost your confidence to perform a skill on the sports field or make a speech in public.

Realistically, NLP will not turn you into an opera singer or Olympic athlete overnight – NLP will not give you the competence to perform skills you do not possess – but anchoring techniques can help you access your innate resources to be the very best you can.

Changing negative anchors

Sometimes it's necessary to have a way of changing a negative anchor. As a simple example, you may want to change a destructive habit. A slimmer who reaches for the biscuit tin every time he has a cup of tea has created a negative anchor. Drink equals biscuit. Or an office worker who feels anxious each day when going into work because they once had an argument with their boss may be heading for a stress-related illness.

Desensitising yourself

One of the most common NLP approaches to releasing an anchor is by *desensitisation*. To do this you need to first get into a neutral or disassociated state – and then introduce the problem in small doses. So if the issue is the slimming one mentioned above, you'd need to get first into a strong state when you are able to say 'No, thank you' to fattening foods. Then practice being tempted while staying in the strong state. Essentially, it's about learning new habits.

Collapsing the anchor

Another strategy is to *collapse the anchor* by firing off two anchors simultaneously – the unwanted negative one plus a stronger positive one. What happens is that you are thrown into a state of confusion and a new, different state emerges. The pattern breaks, making way for a new one.

I (Romilla) have a client, Jane, who recently divorced and won custody of the couple's two young children. Jane felt uncontrollably angry every time her ex-husband called to make arrangements to visit the children. In turn, the children were becoming very anxious about weekend visits to their father and his new partner. Romilla enabled Jane to anchor a selection of different calm and positive states so that she could manage a strong and open dialogue with her ex-husband.

Lengthening the anchor chain

We talked earlier about how we move through different emotional states in one day. Anchors often work in chains with one trigger leading to another. Sometimes it is useful to create a chain of anchors, like the links in a bracelet.

Each link in the chain acts as a stimulus to the next link, building up a sequence of states. You can compare this to an opera singer getting ready for a major performance who paces herself through a sequence of states until she is mentally prepared, focused, and ready to go on stage.

You can also design a chain of anchors as the route to get into the state that you want at times when the shift from the current state to the desired positive state is too great a leap in one go.

For example, your current problem state might be 'Anger' and your desired state might be 'Relaxed'. This is quite a jump to achieve in one go. However if you first step from Anger to Worry, this has some overlap. Your second step could be from Worry to Curiosity. Again there are similarities between the two states. The final step can be from Curiosity to Relaxed. To move from step to step you need to fire off a new anchor, as explained earlier in the chapter, until you reach the desired state that you want to be in.

Confusion and curiosity are useful interim steps to achieve a change in state for yourself and others. They often defuse emotionally charged situations. I (Kate) once worked on a consultancy project where one of the senior managers would frequently interrupt highly charged conference calls with the statement: 'I'm confused here. Would someone please just go over that again for me?' Every time, it worked as a perfect strategy to defuse the situation and raise new ideas. By one person saying that he was confused, it made everybody else slow down and question their own understanding.

Stage anchors

For many people, public speaking represents speaking under severe pressure. A number of studies, borne out by our own experiences with clients, demonstrate that some people would actually rather die than stand up and speak in public! Apparently in the US, public speaking is the number one fear; in the UK, it's in second place to a fear of spiders.

We regularly work with clients who suffer performance anxiety which shows itself in hot sweats, loss of voice, stomach cramps, and upsets. When a dinner guest is invited to give an after-dinner speech, they often fail to enjoy the meal when faced with the prospect of entertaining the audience with their wit over the coffee, petit fours, and brandy.

If ever there was a reason to use anchoring to get back in control, this is it!

Using the Circle of Excellence

The NLP *circle of excellence* is a technique to help you summon up the confidence to perform a skill. So you can use it if you have a fear of public speaking, if you want to boost your confidence to play your best shot in sport, and in many other instances.

The circle of excellence is the classic NLP technique to practice with a partner if you are the after-dinner entertainment. It works best if you enlist a buddy or NLP practitioner who takes you sensitively through these steps while maintaining rapport with you, and not rushing.

First think of the situation where you are going to perform and imagine your own magic circle on the ground in front of you. Make it a generous circle of about three feet in diameter. These step-by step instructions take you in and out of your magic circle, telling you what to do at each stage, with the help of a partner.

CIRCLE   What to do

OUT   Identify your best state. Tell your partner what that state is.

Your partner says: 'Remember a time when you were xxxxxxxxxx' (use their words) . . . get back to it strongly . . . see what you saw then, hear what you heard.

IN   Step into the circle and re-live that experience. (Make it vivid, be there in it.)

Feel what your hands are doing and hold or anchor that state with a hand movement.

OUT   Step out of the circle and break state (see Chapter 9 for more on this), and repeat the exercise with a second experience of your best state.

In order to prepare for the future event, your partner says: 'Think of a time when this state will be useful.'

IN   With your hand in the anchored position, you move into the circle, and your partner asks you to see, hear, and feel how it can be now for you.

OUT   Relax . . . you've got it!

Spatial anchoring

Spatial anchoring is a way of influencing your audience through anchors. When you repeatedly do the same thing on stage in the same place, then people come to expect a certain behaviour from you according to where you move around stage. A lectern is a definite anchor – when you stand at the lectern, people expect you to speak.

When you are presenting, you can deliberately set up other expectations with the audience at different places on the stage. Perhaps you'll do the main delivery from the centre point of the stage, but you'll move to one side when you're telling stories and another when you deliver technical information. Very quickly, people learn to expect certain input from you according to where you position yourself.

A Final Point about Anchors

Anchors may or may not work for you when you first try them. As with all the tools in this book, you'll learn fastest by taking an NLP class and working with an experienced practitioner. Whichever way you choose to develop your skills – on your own or with others – then simply give it a go. Let us encourage you to persist even if it seems strange at first. Once you take control of your own state, you expand your choices and it's worth it.

Chapter 10

Sliding the Controls

· ·

In This Chapter

▶ Finding out how you can feel good and then even better

▶ Discovering how to fine tune input from your senses

▶ Learning how to let go of a limiting belief and create an empowering one

▶ Going from an unwanted state to a desired state

▶ Understanding how to take the sting out of a painful experience

· ·

*T*ry this: Think of a really pleasant experience that you have had. You don't have to share the experience with us so you can let rip and really get into it. As you think of the experience, do you get a picture, feel a feeling, hear any sounds? It's terrific if you can do all three and OK if you can only manage one or two out of the three; we'll work with you to experience all three. Can you begin to intensify the experience? Great! Now can you ramp it up some more?

Welcome back! So, as you relived the experience, how did you intensify it? Did you make the picture brighter, bigger, more colourful, or perhaps you brought it in closer to you. Maybe you turned up the volume of any sounds you heard and if you had a feeling, you spread that feeling further through your body. You have just discovered how to play with your *submodalities*.

Because submodalities are the basic building blocks of the way you experience your world, a very slight change in a submodality can have a significant effect on the changing of the experience. What this means is that you have control over the way you choose to experience your world. You can choose to change your mind to heighten a pleasurable time or to remove the negative emotions from an unpleasant one. You can also learn to take yourself from an undesired state, such as confused, to a better state, such as understanding. In short, *you* can *choose* the meaning you give to what happens to you in life. This chapter tells you how.

Submodalities: How We Record Our Experiences

You discovered in Chapter 6 – Seeing, Hearing, and Feeling Your Way to Better Communication that you experience your world through your five senses (six really but that's a story for another time). These five senses are called modalities in NLP. Submodalities are the means of fine tuning your modalities in order to change their qualities.

Examples of submodalities for your sense of sight may be the size of a picture, its brightness or colour, and whether it has a frame around it or not. Submodalities for hearing can be loudness, tempo, or the timbre of a voice, and for feeling could be a heaviness or butterflies in your stomach. You get the idea?

Contrastive analysis happens when you take two experiences and compare and contrast the submodalities of each. If, for example, we ask you to compare the submodalities of something you know is real – a dog – with something you know is fantasy – a unicorn – you will notice that each has differences in its submodalities.

Basic Info, or What You Need to Know Before You Begin

Submodalities are how you give meaning to your experiences – something is real or false, good or bad, and so on. You can use submodalities to change the intensity of the meaning. In the exercise at the start of the chapter, you gave your experience a meaning – it was pleasant. By changing the submodalities of the experience you were able to increase the experience and therefore the meaning of the experience – it became even more pleasant.

So now you know you can control your memories simply by changing the submodalities of the pictures, sounds, and feelings. Just as you are now aware that modalities can be broken down into submodalities, similarly you should be aware that the submodalities can have further distinctions. For example, a picture can be in _colour_ or _black and white_. It can be _framed_ or _panoramic_. Not clear about panoramic? Imagine standing on the top of a mountain and looking at the scenery in front of you as you turn your head, slowly, through 180 degrees. What you see is in panorama. Later in this chapter, you will discover how being associated into or dissociated from a picture can have an effect on your emotions. Sounds can be in your head or to the side. Feelings can have a texture.

You can change each of the modalities and to this end we have provided you with a list of these at the end of this chapter to help you with the changes. We recommend you fill out the form before you begin to make changes so that you can always revert back to the original structure of a modality if your change work raises any anxieties.

To associate or to dissociate

This section helps you experience how you can move in and out of your memories in order to offer you more choices over how you 'turn up' or 'turn down' your feelings. In our experience this is a very important submodality and one that needs a little extra clarification.

When you visualise yourself in a picture it is like watching yourself in a home movie. This is *dissociated*. Or you could actually be in the picture seeing out of your own eyes. This is *associated*. Being associated or dissociated into a picture can be an extremely important submodality when experiencing emotions as a result of the pictures you make.

Usually the emotions are heightened if you associate into the picture. Sometimes people find it difficult to either associate or dissociate. For instance, someone who has experienced a severe personal loss or been traumatised may find it hard to associate and may need to learn to do this.

To get the feel of being associated or dissociated, make a picture of yourself sitting in the front seat of a car. If you are dissociated, you will see a picture of yourself in the car, a little bit like watching yourself on television or looking at yourself in a photograph. If you want to associate into the picture, imagine opening the car door and sitting down. Now look out of your own eyes. The dashboard is in front of you. Can you see the texture and colour of the dashboard? Now look up at the windscreen. Is it splattered with the remnants of suicidal insects (or aliens, if you've seen *Men in Black*)?

Do you find it hard to dissociate? Picture yourself sitting in a car. Now imagine stepping out of the car and onto the pavement. Turn around and look back at the car and look at yourself sitting in the front seat. If you still cannot dissociate, pretend you are watching a movie and it's you there on the screen, in front of the car.

If you feel you aren't getting the hang of this, or any other exercise, feel free to leave it for the moment. You can always come back to it and give the exercise another go when you have more NLP embedded in your mind and muscle. Or you can find yourself an NLP practitioner or NLP practice group to work with in order to advance your skills (Appendix A is a Resource List to help you find these people).

Defining the details of your memories

If you are sitting down to read this book, you're probably unaware of the feel of the seat against your back and legs, although you are now because we mentioned it. Similarly, you are not always aware of the qualities of your memories until we ask you to remember a time when you were brushing your teeth, playing a game, reading a book, or cooking. Then you realise that there are a range of qualities to those memories. For instance, when reading the book – the picture you make of yourself, the book or the story, may have a frame around it. It may be in black and white. Perhaps you can hear the sound of distant traffic or of the pages turning. Maybe the book you were reading made you laugh and feel uplifted and happy. You can become aware of the qualities of the submodalities by paying attention to what you see, or hear, or feel when you think of an experience. The following sections present you with questions that can help you elicit the quality of the visual, auditory, and kinaesthetic submodalities.

Note: We have decided to focus on just the visual, auditory, and kinaesthetic submodalities in this chapter and put taste and smell aside just now. This is because we believe that culturally, unless you are a wine-, tea-, or coffee-taster, for example, these do not have the same emphasis that they do in some other cultures. Having said that . . . tastes and smells affect our emotional brain and you may find the smell of roasted chestnuts suddenly transporting you back to falling snows and Christmas carols.

Eliciting visual submodalities

You can define the quality of a picture in terms of where it is located in space as you look at it. For instance, it could be directly in front of you, to your left, to your right, or it could be slightly displaced to the top or bottom. If it is panoramic, it will look like you are standing in one spot and turning your head to look at the view in front of you. It will have other qualities of brightness, shape, and so on. You can discover how you make pictures in your head by thinking about the following qualities.

Visual Submodalities	*Questions to Discover Them*
Location	Where is it in space? Point to the picture. How close or how far away is it?
Colour/black-and-white	Is it in colour or is it black –and white?
Associated or dissociated	Is the picture associated or dissociated? Can you see yourself in the picture or are you looking out of your own eyes?

Visual Submodalities	*Questions to Discover Them*
Size	Is the picture big or small? What size would you say the picture measures?
2- or 3-dimensional	Is the picture in 2- or 3-dimensions?
Brightness	Is the picture bright or dull?
Still or moving	Is the picture still or is it a movie? If a movie, how fast is the movement of the movie?
Shape	Is the picture square, round, or rectangular?
Framed or Panoramic	Does the picture have a border around it, or is it panoramic?
Focused or fuzzy	Is the picture in sharp focus or is it blurred?

Eliciting auditory submodalities

Like the pictures you make in your head, the sounds you hear have certain qualities to them. You may not be aware of the attributes of the sounds you hear until you focus your mind on them by thinking of the questions below.

Auditory Submodalities	*Questions to Discover Them*
Location	Where do you hear the sound? Is the sound inside your head or outside? Point to where the sound is coming from.
Words or sounds	Can you hear words or sounds? If words, is it the voice of someone you know?
Volume	Is the sound loud or soft? Is the sound a whisper or clearly audible?
Tone	If you hear a voice, what tone does it have? Is it deep, rich, nasal, rasping?
Pitch	Is the sound high- or low-pitched?
Mono or stereo	Can you hear the sound on both sides or is it one-sided? Is the sound all around you?
Constant or intermittent	Is the sound continuous or intermittent?
Rhythm	Does the sound have a beat or a rhythm to it?
Tempo	Is the sound you hear slow or fast?
Tune	Does the sound have a tune?

Eliciting kinaesthetic submodalities

And guess what! Submodalities to do with feelings also have qualities that help to define them.

Kinaesthetic Submodalities	Questions to Discover Them
Location	Where is it in your body? Point to where you can feel the feeling.
Shape	Does the feeling have a shape?
Pressure	Does the feeling exert a pressure?
Size	Does the feeling have a size? Is it big or small?
Quality	Does the feeling make you tingle? Is it spread out or knotted in one place?
Intensity	Is the feeling strong or weak?
Still or moving	Can you feel the feeling in one place or is it moving around your body?
Temperature	Is the feeling warm or cold?
Constant or intermittent	Is the feeling constant or intermittent?
Texture	Does the feeling have a texture to it?

When you are playing at changing the submodalities of a memory, it is important you make a list at the start, before you start changing submodalities around. Because if you start to get uncomfortable with the process at any point, you can put the picture, sounds, or feelings back to how they were. At the end of this chapter you will find a worksheet designed for that very purpose. Make as many copies as you need.

Always remember to ask yourself if it is OK to go ahead with making any change. If you discover a resistance, a feeling that makes you uncomfortable, acknowledge the feeling and thank your unconscious mind for making you aware of possible internal conflict. For example, when I (Romilla) was working on resolving grief with a client he did not want to let go of the pain of loss. He believed that if he let go of the pain he would forget his father. In fact, by releasing the pain he was actually able to remember his father more vividly. You may simply overcome the issue by some quiet time to yourself or you may need to talk to someone, an NLP practitioner perhaps.

Getting a little practice

Imagine you have a remote control with three sliding buttons labelled V for visual, A for auditory, and K for kinaesthetic. You can change the qualities of any pictures you make in your mind, sounds you hear in your head, or any feelings you feel in your body just by sliding the V, A, and K controls. (For more information on VAK modalities, head to Chapter 6 'Seeing, Hearing, and Feeling Your Way to Better Communication'.)

Why would you want to adjust the qualities of your memories? Supposing, years ago, you were rehearsing for a school play and your highly stressed teacher screamed at you, 'You stupid boy you, you blew that again!' Now you are in a job where you need to make some strong presentations to colleagues and clients. Yet every time you get started you begin to sweat and stammer and the voice in your head goes, 'You stupid boy you, you blew that again!' You may need to adjust the qualities of your memories because they get in the way of what you want to achieve. Imagine you slide the brightness control and the picture of the teacher gets dimmer. Then you slide the size control and the teacher gets smaller and becomes insignificant. Finally you adjust the volume control and the scream drops to a whisper. Now you find you can make presentations the way you always knew you could.

To see how effective changing submodalities can be, try this exercise, using the worksheet at the end of the chapter:

1. **Think of someone you like.**

2. **Remember the last time you spent real, quality time with them.**

3. **Record the qualities of the picture you see, any sounds you hear, and any feelings you get.**

4. **Change the picture you made, *one visual submodality at a time*; notice how each change affects the memory of your time together.**

5. **Change the sounds you hear, *one auditory submodality at a time*; notice how each change affects the memory.**

6. **Change any feelings that you are feeling, *one kinaesthetic submodality at a time*; notice how each change impacts the whole experience of your time together.**

Understanding your critical submodalities

Some submodalities are very powerful in determining a person's response. An example of these may be the size or brightness of a mental picture. You may find that by making a picture bigger or brighter the experience is heightened. Or you may find that moving the picture to a different location or associating or dissociating into a picture can affect the sounds and feeling of an experience.

A *critical* submodality is one where changing it can change other submodalities of an experience. It also affects the submodalities of other representational systems. What this means is that by changing, say, the brightness of a picture, not only do other qualities of the picture change automatically, but attributes of sounds and feelings experienced in conjunction with the picture also change, without conscious intervention.

I (Romilla) was working with a client, Suzy, who was having trouble with a goal she wanted to achieve and had been struggling to reach for almost six months. I asked Suzy to explore the submodalities of the goal she wanted to reach. Suzy said it was over and up to the left (if you imagine a giant clock in front of you, it was at 11 o'clock and almost at roof height). I asked Suzy to move the location of the image so that it was in front of her and about three feet away. Suzy's reaction was phenomenal. She jumped in her chair so hard she almost fell off and then she turned bright pink and couldn't stop laughing. Changing the location of the picture had a real impact on Suzy and brought the goal to life for her as she could feel what it would be like to achieve the goal and made it much more immediate. Using some more goal-setting techniques, a delighted Suzy got to her goal in four months.

You experience your world through your five senses – visual (eyes), auditory (ears), kinaesthetic (feelings and touch), olfactory (smell), and gustatory (taste). You, more than likely, use one sense in preference to the others to collect data about your world, particularly at times of stress. This is called your *lead* or *primary representational system*. It influences how you learn and the way you represent your external world inside your head.

During a session with Charles, another of my (Romilla's) clients, I found Charles's primary representational system was auditory. He was more kinaesthetic than visual and felt emotions quite strongly. Charles was working to change a nagging voice that he was allowing to undermine his confidence when he was starting something new and which kept him awake at night with its chatter. On examining the qualities of the voice, he found that it was in fact his mother talking to him and that he heard her voice inside his head. Unfortunately she had had a rather negative way of putting things. Whenever Charles heard this voice he would feel sick and get a black, shiny rock in the region of his solar plexus. When I asked Charles to change the voice he muted it to a whisper and moved it to just below his left ear, outside his head. As soon as he had done this he blurted out in shock, 'The feelings have gone. I just have a warm glow in my middle.' However Charles was not prepared to change the voice further because he believed the voice actually served to watch out for potential problems. He just needed to change the quality so that it allowed him to get on with his life.

Making Real-life Changes

In playing with the exercises so far, we hope you're beginning to have a pretty good idea of which submodalities have the most impact on you – your critical submodalities, those that can change other submodalities – your driver submodalities. And we hope you have the conviction now that you are in control of your experiences and can change them so you can choose how you feel. In the light of this knowledge and belief we invite you to experience real change in your life by working through the exercises in the following sections.

Just think, you can sit and program your mind on the train, in a traffic jam, or even over a boring meal with your in-laws (or should they be out-laws, just joking). And remember, practice makes perfect so get practising, safe in the knowledge that you can't get arrested for playing with your submodalities, even in public.

Taking the sting out of an experience

Can you think of an unpleasant experience you have had? We don't mean something that is life-shattering, rather an incident which, when you think of it, makes you feel less than good. You can? Good. Now using the list at the end of this chapter examine and note the submodalities of the experience. With this knowledge, start changing the picture, sounds, and feelings that you get when you think of the unpleasant experience. What happened? You do feel better now, don't you? No? Then discover what happens when you change the submodalities of the unpleasant experience to those of the pleasant experience we asked you to recall at the start of the chapter.

Changing a limiting belief

How often have you heard yourself say such things as, 'I can't do that', 'I'm no good at maths', or 'I should learn to cook properly'? These are all examples of limiting beliefs. In Chapter 2 we explain that your beliefs are generalisations you make about yourself and your world. These can either disable you, holding you back, or empower you. Beliefs are really self-fulfilling prophecies which can start off just as a notion or a hint of an idea. Then your filters (metaprograms, values, beliefs, attitudes, memories, and decisions – see Chapter 5) begin aligning themselves like gates to only let in those 'facts' and experiences that will re-enforce your beliefs. For instance, let's say that you decided that you were a little more cuddly than you wanted to be and so you started on a diet. Perhaps you stuck to the diet for a few days but then temptation got the better of you. At this stage you got a hint of the notion that 'maybe I'm not good at following a diet'. Then you tried again and failed again until eventually you came to the limiting belief of 'I can't stick to a diet'.

1. **Think of a limiting belief you currently hold, one which you would like to change.**

2. **Think of a belief that you used to believe in but which, for you, is no longer true.**

   This can be a belief such as 'I am no longer a teenager'. It does not have to be a limiting belief that you may have overcome.

3. **Using the reference page at the end of this chapter, identify the submodalities of the belief which for you is no longer true.**

   For example when you think of a fictional character like the Tooth Fairy or Santa Claus, you may see her over to your right, in the distance, in colour, and very bright. You may get a warm, fluttery feeling in your chest and you hear the sound of a soft voice.

4. **Think of the limiting belief and put it into the submodalities of the belief you used to believe in.**

5. **When you think of your limiting belief, the submodalities, we would guess, are different.**

6. **Move the picture you get when you think of your limiting belief to the same position and distance you saw the Tooth Fairy at and give it the same colour and brightness. Then produce the same feelings in your body and listen for the same voice.**

Notice how your negative belief has changed, if it hasn't disappeared altogether!

Creating an empowering belief

Since beliefs are self-fulfilling prophecies it is useful to remember that you have control over choosing which ones you want to hold onto! In the previous exercise you learned how to let go of a limiting belief. Wouldn't it be really useful to learn how you can increase your choices in life by choosing to create a whole plethora of beliefs that will enable you to 'sing your song'?

1. **Think of a belief it would be really useful for you to have, we'll call it a desired belief.**

   It could be, for example, 'I deserve to be successful.'

2. **Think of a belief which *for you* is absolutely true.**

   For example – the sun will rise in the morning (yes, even behind those clouds).

3. **Using the reference pages at the end of this chapter, identify the submodalities of this absolutely true belief.**

   For example, when you think of the sun rising you may see it in front of you, about six feet away, in pale shimmering, orange colours and very bright. You may feel warm all over and hear bird songs.

4. **Put the desired belief into the exact same submodalities of the absolutely true belief.**

   Move the picture you get when you think of your desired belief to the same position and distance of the rising sun and give it the same colours and brightness. Then produce the same feelings of warmth and listen for the bird songs.

Getting rid of that backache

This process can be used for other unpleasant feelings, too.

1. **Calibrate your backache on a scale of 1 to 5.**

2. **Make a picture of the backache.**

3. **From the list at the end of the chapter, note the submodalities of the backache.**

4. **Change each attribute of the backache, one at a time.**

   If it has a colour, what happens when you give it a different colour, healing blue perhaps? What happens if you see that band of steel break up into strips of ribbon, fluttering in the wind? If there is a dull ache, can you change the feeling to a tingle? If it feels hot, can you change that feeling into one of a cool breeze blowing over the area? These changes should have already reduced the backache, if it hasn't already gone.

5. Now imagine you are sitting in front of a movie screen, remove the backache from your body and project a picture of the backache on to the screen.

6. Make the picture on the screen smaller and smaller until it is the size of a balloon.

7. Now watch the balloon float up, up, and away into the sky and as you see the balloon floating away your backache is getting less and less.

8. As the balloon reaches the clouds and you calibrate your backache, it is just a 1.

9. As the balloon disappears from sight, the backache fades to just the faintest memory.

Using the swish

This is a powerful technique for making lasting changes in habits and behaviours. The *swish*, as with a lot of NLP, is based on behavioural psychology. Assuming that learning to respond in a certain way results in you exhibiting a particular behaviour, then the swish teaches you a different way to respond in place of the unwanted behaviour. The idea behind using the swish is to use the learned pathways of the unwanted behaviour to create a new, desired pattern of behaviour. If you want to stop yourself biting your nails, think of what triggers the nail-biting and make a picture of the trigger. It may be you run your finger along a nail and find a jagged edge or it may be a response to getting nervous. The desired image is what you would rather have or see instead. In this case it may be a hand with perfect nails.

Identify the unwanted behaviour:

1. **Check with yourself that it is OK to go ahead with the change. Simply ask yourself: 'Is it OK?'**

2. **Identify the trigger that initiates the unwanted behaviour and make an associated picture. This is the cue picture.**

3. **Play with the image to discover the one or two critical submodalities.**

4. **Break state.**

   Break state means to change the state or frame of mind that you are in. You may stand up and give your body a good shake or move around the room when going from one phase of an exercise to another, allowing a natural break from the pictures and emotions of the first stage of the exercise.

5. **Think of the desired image. Create a dissociated image of you doing a preferred behaviour or looking a certain way.**

6. **Break state.**

7. **Recall the cue picture. Make sure you are associated into it and place a frame around it.**

8. **Create an image of the desired outcome.**

9. **Squash the desired image into a very small, dark dot and place it in the bottom left corner of the cue picture.**

10. **With a *swishhhh* sound, propel the small, dark dot into the big picture so that it explodes, covering the cue picture.**

11. **Break state.**

12. **Repeat the process several times.**

If you are more kinaesthetic than visual or auditory, you may find the swish more effective if you keep your hands far apart at the start of this exercise. Then as you *swishhhh* you bring your hands together quickly.

You have had a lot of experience now of playing with your submodalities and you know that you can change these to help you increase the choices in your life. You can use the process of putting *exhausted* into the submodalities of *relaxed* as you have done in the above exercises.

Submodalities Worksheet

Visual Submodalities	**Describe What You See**
Location	
Colour/black-and-white	
Associated or dissociated	
Size	
2- or 3-dimensional	
Brightness	
Still or moving	
Shape	
Framed or panoramic	
Focused or fuzzy	

Auditory Submodalities	**Describe What You Hear**
Location	
Words or sounds	
Volume	
Tone	
Pitch	
Mono or stereo	
Constant or intermittent	
Rhythm	
Tempo	
Tune	

Kinaesthetic Submodalities	**Describe What You Feel**
Location	
Shape	
Pressure	
Size	
Quality	
Intensity	
Still or moving	
Temperature	
Constant or intermittent	
Texture	

Chapter 11

Changing with Logical Levels

· ·

In This Chapter

▶ Finding out how easy change can be

▶ Playing with the core NLP tool for managing change

▶ Discovering your own sense of purpose

▶ Being more centred in your career, your life, and yourself

· ·

*O*ne of the key NLP presuppositions is 'The Map is not the Territory' (you can read more about this in Chapter 2): meaning that your map of reality is only part of the story, the territory surrounding your map is bigger. An added complication is that the territory of your experience changes as fast as the map. This landscape of reality that you are exploring continually changes. So, if you accept that the world in which you live and work is dynamic, how can you cope with this?

The NLP approach to change is that there is no single correct map of change at any one time. To survive and thrive, you need to acknowledge and embrace the fact that change is happening and put strategies in place to work with it rather than against it.

In this chapter we introduce you to a favourite model in NLP that has been developed largely thanks to the work of a man named Robert Dilts. This model is particularly helpful to apply in two ways:

✔ For understanding change for yourself as an individual

✔ For understanding change for organisations

What's Your Perspective?

Depending on the picture that you choose, change can be an opportunity and a positive energy force – whether you are looking at change with a personal or organisational hat on. What a shame that so much that's spoken about change assumes that it has to be difficult. Difficulties can be man-made. A question you may like to consider as you enjoy this chapter is: 'What would be different for you if you assumed the opposite – that it was going to be easy?'

Step inside as we invite you to meet one of the best guides from NLP, showing you a way of first understanding what you are experiencing during times of change.

✔ See how to break change into manageable steps.

✔ Work with it confidently rather than fighting, hiding in a corner with a paper bag over your head, or running away down the street like a headless chicken.

As you begin to consider the kind of changes that you experience, then logical levels can help you find a route forward in confusing times.

Understanding Logical Levels

NLP logical levels are a powerful way to think about change by breaking it down as a model into different categories of information (see Figure 11-1). (You'll also see them referred to in the NLP literature as a series of neurological levels.)

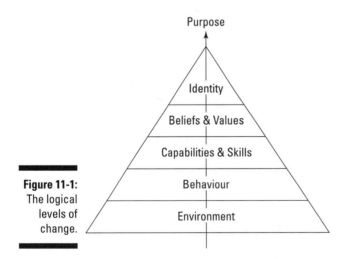

Figure 11-1:
The logical levels of change.

Although we've presented the levels to you in our diagram in a hierarchy, you may find it useful to look at them as a network of interrelationships or a series of concentric circles. All levels connect to each other. The device of the model simply creates some structure and understanding about how it all works.

In many cases it is easier to change at the lower levels on the diagram than the higher levels. So, for example, a company would find it easier to make changes to the building (environment), such as by painting the walls a different colour, than to change the culture or create a new identity for itself. Each level impacts those above and below it; the key value of the model is that it provides a structured approach to help understand what is happening.

The French have an expression to describe the feeling you have when you are comfortable in yourself and everything is running smoothly. They say: 'Elle va bien dans sa peau' (literally translated as 'She goes well in her own skin'). Similarly, NLPers use the word *congruence* to describe precisely how you are when you are truly being yourself. It means you're really comfortably on track, and consistent. The logical levels of behaviour, capability, beliefs, values, and skills are all lined up. Look out for this *alignment* in organisations as well as people. When either are going through periods of change then there's likely to be some misalignment. People may behave in unpredictable ways that are not a true reflection of what they really believe is right.

Asking the right questions

As you begin to think about some change you'd like to make, you can ask yourself some questions at the different levels.

- ✔ **Environment** refers to the factors which are external opportunities or constraints. Answers the questions **where?** and **when?** and **with whom?**

- ✔ **Behaviour** is made up of specific **actions** or reactions within the environment. Answers the question **what?**

- ✔ **Capabilities** are about the knowledge and skills, the 'how-tos' that guide and give direction to behaviour. Answers the question **how?**

- ✔ **Beliefs and values** provide the reinforcement (motivation and permission) to support or deny our capabilities. Answers the question **why?**

- ✔ **Identity** factors determine our sense of self. Answers the question **who?**

- ✔ **Purpose** goes beyond self-consciousness to relate to the bigger picture about mission to ask **what for or for whom?**

Why is 'Why?' the hardest question?

As a business writer, I (Kate) have spent many happy years of corporate life interviewing chief executives, interpreting their vision, and publishing their words of wisdom in an easily digestible format.

The who, what, when, where, why, and how questions form the essential journalist's weapons. Yet, it was only when coming across logical levels in NLP that it began to make sense just why some questions meet blank stares, even hostility, while others receive a warm welcome.

When you want to know something about a subject, work up the logical levels. Start with environment – the where, when, and with whom. These are easy factual questions to answer. Move through the what and the how. Leave the why question to last. It's so much harder to answer 'Why did you do that?', which rushes headlong into the realm of beliefs, than 'How did you do that?', a much gentler approach; or even 'How did that happen?', which disassociates the person from the question.

Taking logical levels step-by-step

You can use the logical levels to think about what's happening in the world around you, step-by-step. They'll help you to understand the structure and pattern as well as the content of different issues, events, relationships, or organisations, as we'll explain in the next few pages.

Let's just look at how you can apply this model when you're facing something like making a decision about change, or a dilemma that needs a solution. You can use the concept of logical levels to help you find the best way forward. Here's how the process works:

1. **First, you recognise that things are out of alignment.**

   You know this is the case when you're uncomfortable and you know that you want things to be different.

2. **Discover where the change really needs to take place.**

   You do this by asking yourself certain questions that can help you identify where the change needs to occur. Each logical level has certain types of questions. Head to the section 'Finding the Right Lever for Change' to help you work through the individual logical levels.

3. **Once you have identified the logical level, you bring that level back in alignment with the others.**

   At the lower levels of change, say at environment or behaviour, there may be some simple changes or habits you can adjust. Building your capability will take more time, while you may need to work with an individual coach (or business consultant in the organisational context) to help you examine your beliefs and values or develop a new identity for yourself.

John worked as the training manager of a hotel chain which was bought out by another hotel group, one of the fierce competitors. Once he'd got over the shock of the announcement, he had to decide whether to leave the organisation or to stay with it after the merger. On examining the similarities and differences of the two organisations, John ultimately made his decision to stay based on the fact that the core values were similar – both companies operated in different ways (their behaviours) yet shared a dedication to customer service and a strong respect for people.

For change to last, it's helpful to know where the change really needs to take place. Often we attempt to solve issues by changing the logical level – environment or behaviour – when we need to be addressing a separate logical level of values, beliefs, or identity. Similarly, when you have issues with someone's behaviour, remember not to challenge their identity, and to respect their beliefs.

To make change easy you need the right *resources* at the right time and in the right place. Resources are things that help you – they may be external things such as people and equipment, or internal things such as your own experiences or way of thinking. NLP assumes that people always have, or can get, the resources they need to accomplish whatever they want to do.

Wherever you are operating on the levels of change, it's important to make sure you get the resources in place at the logical level above. To make lasting change at the environment level, you'll need to do the right things (behaviour). To develop capability, you'll need to have useful beliefs in place.

Practical uses for logical levels

You can use logical levels to bring energy and focus to many different situations. Here are just a few examples:

- ✔ **Gathering and structuring information** – compiling a report, school essay, or any piece of writing.

- ✔ **Building relationships in a family** – exploring what all members of the family want for the family to work together. This is especially useful when dramatic change occurs in a family's structure such as happens in a divorce or remarriage.

- ✔ **Improving individual or corporate performance** – deciding where to make business changes that will help turn around a struggling company or one going through mergers and acquisitions.

- ✔ **Developing leadership and confidence** – stepping through the levels to get alignment and feel confident in leading a team or enterprise.

Open any toolbox of tricks – whether it's a box of coloured flipchart pens, a palette of paints, electric drill bits, or a mechanic's spanners, and some favourites always take centre stage. You keep coming back to these faithful friends and can depend on them for the feel-good factor. You'll discover that the logical levels model gives the *value-added* feature time and time again. It's there like a mate helping to decipher complex information, whether you need to make sense of a business project or unravel a difficult conversation. If you keep returning to any single well-loved tool in the NLP toolkit time and time again, this may well be the one for you.

Finding the Right Lever for Change

Carl Jung, one of the twentieth century's leading thinkers in psychology, once famously said, 'We cannot change anything until we accept it. Condemnation does not liberate, it oppresses.' And he was right because the first step to coping with change is to accept that it is happening. Then you are in a position to proactively work with it and give yourself choices rather than wait to be on the receiving end of whatever happens to you.

Three requirements need to be in place for change to happen. You must:

- Want to change
- Know how to change
- Get or create the opportunity to change

In the following sections, you delve further into the logical levels. As you explore, keep in mind one important question: 'How can you make change easy for yourself?'

In all of the questions we raise in the following sections, we have applied them to you as an individual. You can ask the same questions about your organisation, too.

Environment

The environment is about time, place, and people. It's the physical context where you hang out. It's about finding the right time and the right place. If you want to become fluent in a new language, then the easiest way to learn would be to go and live in the country for a while, fully immerse yourself in the culture, ideally by living with the locals. You would be in the best place to learn. Similarly, if you wanted to learn a new software package, then it would make sense to move onto a project to work with a person or team that applied it in their business. Again, the environment would be conducive to learning, which is itself a type of change. The timing would also be critical – you cannot learn if the time is not right for you – maybe if you're tied up with other needs.

Some *environmental* questions to ask yourself when you sense that you are not in the right place or this is not the right time for you to get what you want:

✔ Where do you work best?

✔ Where in the world do you want to explore?

✔ What kind of home environment is right for you – modern, minimalist, or traditional?

✔ What kind of people do you like to have around you? Who makes you feel good, energised, and comfortable? Who makes you feel drained? Or do you prefer to work alone?

✔ What time of day do you feel good – are you up with the lark in the mornings or a night owl?

Questions such as these will give you the right kind of data so you can decide what environmental issues you can work on.

Behaviour

Your behaviour is all about what you actually say and do, what you consciously get up to. In NLP terms, behaviour refers to what you think about as well as your actions. It also points out that all your behaviour is aimed at a purpose, it has a positive intention for you.

Change at the behavioural level is easy to make when you have a real sense of purpose, it fits with your sense of identity, and your beliefs and values.

Some *behavioural* questions to ask yourself when you think that you may need to change your behaviours in order to get the results you want: Do your behaviours support your goals?

✔ Do they fit with your sense of who you are?

✔ What do you do that makes life interesting and fun?

✔ What do you find yourself saying habitually? Can you detect any patterns?

- ✔ What do you notice about other people's words and sayings?
- ✔ How aware are you of people's behaviour – how they walk, the tone of their voice, and their smile?
- ✔ What colour changes do you observe in people as they talk?
- ✔ How does your breathing change and when?
- ✔ What body language do you adopt in different circumstances?
- ✔ What do you sound like?

Maximising effective behaviours

In order to create positive change, it's worth developing the behaviours and habits that serve you well. Often small changes have an incremental effect. If you are slimming to fit into a new outfit, then eating a healthy salad each day in place of your sandwiches would be a valuable habit to cultivate. In the same way, if you are trying to improve your meetings at work, then a good behaviour for a team would be to set clear beginning and end times.

When writing this book, and with deadlines pressing, we listened to the advice of successful writers. The one key message that we took away was the value of writing something every day – whether 200 words or 2,000 words. (We heard of one famous author who wrote precisely 600 words each day even if that meant stopping in mid-sentence.) An easy behavioural change for us to make was to get up early each morning and begin each day writing for a couple of hours. By focusing our energy at the start of the day, we felt a real sense of purpose and a clear identity as *Dummies* authors.

Practising the right behaviours until they become habitual will increase your capability. How many great sports people or musicians are born wielding a tennis racket or violin? Yes, they may have natural talent, but the key lies in their hours of dedicated practice and willingness to go that extra mile. One of our tennis coaches reminisced about teaching UK tennis star Tim Henman as a young lad. Tim was the one who was prepared to get out there and hit balls long after the others had had enough. The golfer Tiger Woods is renowned for being out on the golf course before anyone else. To stay at the top of the game requires constant hard practice.

Modifying unwanted behaviours

What about the unwanted behaviours, the things you do and wish you didn't do, silly habits such as smoking or poor eating habits? The reason they become hard to change is because they are linked to other higher, logical levels involving beliefs or identity.

'I'm a smoker' = a statement about identity.

'I need to have a cigarette when I get stressed' = a statement about belief.

'He's a big, strong lad' = a statement about identity.

'He can't live on salad and fruit' = a statement about belief.

To make change easier you can create a new identity for yourself such as 'I'm a healthy person' with beliefs such as 'I can develop the right habits to look to after myself'.

Capabilities

Capabilities are your talents and skills. They lie within people and organisations as highly valuable assets. These are the behaviours that you do so well that you can do them consistently without any seemingly conscious effort. Things like walking and talking are skills you learned without ever understanding how you did that. You are a naturally great learning machine.

Other things you've learned more consciously. Perhaps you can fly a kite, ride a bicycle, work a computer, or play a sport or musical instrument. These are skills you will have deliberately learned. Perhaps you're great at seeing the funny side of life, listening to friends, or getting the kids to school on time. All valuable skills that you take for granted and others could learn. You're likely to remember the time before you could do these things, while you probably can't recall a time before you could walk or talk. Organisations build core competencies into their business processes, defining essential skills that are needed to make the company function at its best.

NLP focuses plenty of attention at the capability level, working with the premise that all skills are learnable. It assumes that anything is possible if taken in bite-size pieces or chunks. The HR director of one of the UK's most prestigious retailers told us recently: 'We recruit primarily on attitude: once this is right, we can teach people the skills they need to do the job.'

Yet even attitudes can be learned and changed so long as you find the desire, know-how and opportunity to learn. The question to hold on to is: 'How can I do that?' Bear this in mind for yourself as you go through every day. The NLP approach is that by modelling others and yourself, you become open to making changes and developing your own capabilities. If you want to do something well, first find someone else who can do it and pay close attention to all of their logical levels.

Here are some *capability and skills* questions to ask yourself when you want to make an assessment of your capabilities and see where you can learn and improve:

- ✔ What skills have you learned that you're proud of – how did you do it?
- ✔ Have you become expert at something that serves you less well – how did that happen?
- ✔ Do you know someone who has got a really positive attitude that you could learn from – how could you learn from them?
- ✔ Ask other people to say what they think you are good at.
- ✔ What next? What would you like to learn?

As you build capability, the world opens up for you. You are in a position to take on greater challenges or to cope better with the ones you struggle to face.

Beliefs and values

Beliefs and values are the fundamental principles that shape your actions. You can read in Chapter 4 how beliefs and values direct your life and yet often you may not be aware of them. What *you* believe to be true is often going to be different to what *I* believe to be true. Here, we're not talking about beliefs in the sense of religion – rather your perception at a deep, often unconscious, level.

Lee is an amateur club golfer with a passionate desire to launch his career on the international circuit. He believes he has the same potential as top golfer Tiger Woods and that he too can create a living as a professional golfer. Such beliefs drive his capability – he is highly competent in his game. His beliefs also drive his behaviours – he can be found determinedly practising on the golf course every day of the year and he works at developing relationships with the media and sponsors. And his beliefs also determine the environment where he spends much of his time – when not on the golf course, he'll be working out in the gym.

Likewise values are the things that are important to you, what motivates you to get out of bed in the morning, or not – criteria such as health, wealth, or happiness. Beliefs and values and the way we rank them in order of importance are different for each person. This is why it's so difficult to motivate a whole team of people with the same approach. One size does not fit all when it comes to beliefs and values.

Values are also rules that keep us on the socially acceptable road. I may seek money, but my values of honesty keep me from stealing it from other people. Sometimes there will be a conflict between two important values – such as family life and work. In terms of making change, understanding beliefs and values offers huge leverage. When people value something or believe it enough, it's an energising force for change. They are concentrating on what's truly important to them, doing what they really want to be doing, and becoming closer to who they want to be. They are in a place that feels right and natural for them. Beliefs and values drive us and influence the lower levels of capability, behaviour, and environment. Thus all the levels begin to come into alignment.

Often we work with people who move from one job to another with increasing dissatisfaction. IT director, John, is a case in point. Every two years or so he'd get fed up, decide it was time for a change, and apply for another similar job with more money, a better benefits package, in a new location, hoping that things were going to be better somewhere else. He simply made changes at the environmental level – new company, new country, new people. 'It will be better if I work in New York.' As he began to evaluate his own values and beliefs he realised that some essential ingredients were missing. He'd invested time and energy into taking an MBA and valued professional learning and development as important. Yet he always ended up in 'hire and fire' organisations which were too busy to invest in their people or to work strategically: places that drained his energy. His beliefs and values did not match those of the organisations that he worked in. Once he understood this, he took his skills to a prestigious international business school that valued his learning and gave him the opportunity to develop further.

Here are some *beliefs and values* questions to ask yourself when you sense that there's a conflict at this logical level that is hindering you getting what you want:

- Why did you do that? Why did they do that?
- What factors are important to you in this situation?
- What is important to other people?
- What do you believe to be right and wrong?
- What has to be true for you to get what you want?
- When do you say 'must' and 'should' and 'must not' and 'should not'?
- What are your beliefs about this person or situation? Are they helpful? What beliefs might help me get better results?
- What would somebody else believe if they were in your shoes?

Armed with the answers to these questions, you may want to work on your beliefs and values to ensure that they support you through difficult times. As you question your beliefs about yourself you may choose to discard some of them that no longer serve you well.

In business change management programmes, you often hear talk of 'winning the hearts and minds' of people. This means you need to address people's beliefs and values. Once the right beliefs are firmly in place, NLP suggests that the lower levels – such as capability and behaviour – will fall into place automatically.

Identity

Identity describes your sense of who you are. You may express yourself through your beliefs, values, capabilities, behaviours, and environment, yet you are more than this. NLP assumes that a person's *identity* is separate from their *behaviour* and recommends that you remain aware of the difference. You are more than what you do. It separates the intention that lies behind your action from your action itself. This is why NLP avoids labelling people. 'Men behaving badly', for example, does not mean the men are intrinsically bad, it's just bad behaviour.

There's a saying that one of our corporate clients quotes: 'Easy on the person. Tough on the issue.' This is a positive management style consistent with the NLP premise that people make the best choices open to them, given their own situation at any time.

If you want to give feedback to encourage learning and better performance, always give very specific feedback about what someone has said or done in terms of the *behaviour* rather than commenting at the *identity* level. So, instead of saying: 'John. Sorry mate, but you were just awful.' Try instead: 'John, it was difficult to hear you at the meeting because you looked at the computer all the time and had your back to the audience.'

Here are some *identity* questions to ask yourself when you have a sense of conflict around your identity:

- ✔ How is what you are experiencing an expression of who you are?
- ✔ What kind of person are you?
- ✔ How do you describe yourself?
- ✔ What labels do you put on other people?
- ✔ How would others describe you?
- ✔ Would other people think of you as you wish?
- ✔ What pictures, sounds, or feelings are you aware of as you think about yourself?

A greater awareness of self is a valuable insight in any journey of personal change. Too often people try to change others when changing themselves would be a more effective starting point.

Purpose

This 'beyond identity' level connects you to the larger picture when you begin to question your own purpose, ethics, mission, or meaning in life. It takes individuals into the realms of spirituality and their connection with a bigger order of things in the universe. It leads organisations to define their *raison d'être*, vision, and mission.

Man's survival amidst incredible suffering depends on true self-sponsorship that goes beyond identity. Witness the resilience of the Dalai Lama driven from Tibet or the story of Viktor Frankl's endurance of the Holocaust in his book *Man's Search for Meaning*.

As we become older and approaching different life stages, it's natural to question what we're doing with our lives. Sometimes there will be a trigger to inspire action and light up our passion. A friend and logistics manager in industry, Alan, travelled to Kenya on holiday and saw at first-hand the educational needs of the country. Thus began a powerful one-man campaign that took over his life and led him to create an international charity taking educational materials into Africa thanks to his personal passion to make a difference. On speaking to him about it, he would often say. 'I don't know why me. It's mad, but I just know I have to do this.' His purpose was stronger than his identity.

Here are some *purpose* questions to ask yourself when you want to check whether you are steering your life in the right direction for yourself:

- ✔ For what reason are you here?
- ✔ What would you like your contribution to be to others?
- ✔ What are your personal strengths that you can add to the bigger world out there?
- ✔ How would you like to be remembered when you die?

In *The Elephant and the Flea,* management guru Charles Handy conveys the passion that comes from a sense of mission and underlying purpose. He talks of the entrepreneurs featured in *The New Alchemists,* another book by Handy and his wife, the portrait photographer Elizabeth Handy, as people who leap beyond the logical and stick with their dream:

> 'Passion is what drove them, a passionate belief in what they are doing, a passion that sustained them through the tough times, that seemed to justify their life. Passion is a much stronger word than mission or purpose, and I realise that as I speak that I am also talking to myself.'

When you are operating in a purposeful way, notice how you are unstoppable – you will be in the best place to gain true alignment at all the logical levels.

Figuring Out Other People's Levels: Language and Logical Levels

The intonation in someone's language, the way they speak, can tell you at what level they are operating. Take the simple phrase: 'I can't do it here' and listen to where the stress is placed.

> '*I* can't do it here' = statement about identity.
>
> 'I *can't* do it here' = statement about belief.
>
> 'I can't *do* it here' = statement about capability.
>
> 'I can't do *it* here' = statement about behaviour.
>
> 'I can't do it *here*' = statement about environment.

When you know the level that someone is operating at, you can help them to make change at that level. If they are working at the environmental level, the question to ask is: 'If not here, where can you do it?' If they are at the identity level, the question is: 'If not you, who can do it then?'

Logical Levels Exercise: Teambuilding at Work and Play

We've said that NLP is experiential. That means that to get the benefit of many NLP exercises you sometimes have to move physically as well as mentally. As NLP guru Robert Dilts puts it, 'Knowledge is just a rumour until you get it in the muscle.' You can lay out pieces of paper on the floor and walk through the different levels or use chairs, as in the following exercise.

This exercise helps you to brainstorm your team at its best. You could set this to some Baroque music to get the ideas flowing and speed it up as a musical chairs game – and you may want someone to capture ideas on a flipchart.

1. **Appoint one person to lead the exercise, ask the questions, and capture the answers.**

   This person is your question master.

2. **Place six chairs in a line; place a label on each chair to denote the logical level.**

3. **Seat one team member on each of the chairs.**

4. **Have the question master ask each person questions according to the chair they are on.**

   These are the questions to ask the team at each level:

   - **Environment chair** – 'Where, when, and with whom does this team work best?'

   - **Behaviour chair** – 'What does this team do well?'

   - **Capability chair** – 'How do we do what we do when we work well?'

   - **Beliefs and values chair** – 'Why is this team here? What's important to us?'

   - **Identity chair** – 'Who is this team?'

   - **Purpose chair** – 'How does this team contribute to the bigger picture? What is our mission to others?'

5. **After all the team members have answered their questions, let them move to a different chair; then repeat the questions.**

Keep people moving fairly promptly. They can always come around twice. Once you have captured your brainstorm, the next step will be to sift and work through the information you've gathered to spot patterns and new ideas to build on your strengths as a team.

Chapter 12

Driving Habits: Uncovering Your Secret Programs

In This Chapter

▶ Understanding the psychology behind your habits and behaviours

▶ Discovering how you can use strategies to communicate irresistibly

▶ Applying knowledge of strategies to overcome road rage

▶ Learning to spell well

When you woke up this morning did you brush your teeth first or did you shower first? When I (Romilla) was studying yoga with Swami Ambikananda, one of the tasks the class was set was to gain a greater understanding of the unconscious rituals that all of us have in our lives. Swami Ambikananda suggested we start our day by changing the sequence we had for getting dressed, eating breakfast, and preparing to go to work. Boy did that scramble the brain! It required real concentration to keep the rest of the day running smoothly. For me, at least, it felt like I had forgotten something crucial that day and my brain kept trying to remember what that was. It was a very uncomfortable experience.

Everyone has a strategy for everything and very few people are even aware that they do things on automatic pilot. The great thing now is that, once you realise you are running an ineffective strategy you will have the tools to change it and . . . you will also know how to find someone else's strategy that is working and model it.

As Tad James, creator of the Time Line Therapy™ technique, said, 'A strategy is any internal and external set (order, syntax) of experiences which consistently produces a specific outcome.'

You use strategies for all behaviours – feeling loved, loving your partner, parent, child, or pet, hating someone, getting irritable with your daughter, buying your favourite perfume, learning to drive, succeeding, failing, health, wealth, and happiness ad infinitum. In this chapter you will discover the mechanics of your behaviours, something that will put you in the driving seat of your life.

The Evolution of Strategies

The NLP strategy model has come about through a process of evolution. It started with Pavlov and his dogs and was enhanced by Miller, Galanter, and Pribram, who were cognitive psychologists, before being refined by NLP's founding fathers, Grinder and Bandler.

The S-R model

Behavioural psychologists based their work on Pavlov and his dogs. The dogs heard a bell which indicated food (Stimulus) and salivated (Response). Behaviourists believed that humans simply respond to a stimulus. For example, 'He beats his wife (Response) because he was beaten as a child (Stimulus)'. Or 'He always gives money to the homeless (Response) because he had a very poor childhood (Stimulus)'. The S-R model is illustrated in Figure 12-1.

Figure 12-1:
The
Stimulus-
Response
Model.

The TOTE model

Miller, Galanter, and Pribram built on the Stimulus-Response (S-R) model of behaviourism and presented the TOTE (Test, Operate, Test, Exit) model, which is illustrated in Figure 12-2. The TOTE model works on the principle that you have a goal in mind when you exhibit a particular behaviour. The purpose of your behaviour is to get as close to the desired outcome as possible. You have a test in order to assess whether you have reached your goal. If your goal is reached, you stop the behaviour. If it isn't reached, you modify the behaviour and repeat it, thereby incorporating a simple feedback and response loop. So if your outcome is to boil the kettle, the test is whether the kettle has boiled; if it hasn't then you carry on waiting for it to boil and test for the kettle having boiled and exit once it has.

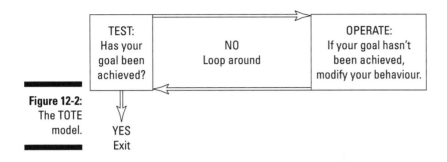

NLP strategy = TOTE + rep systems

You experience the world through your five senses – visual (eyes), auditory (ears), kinaesthetic (feelings and touch), olfactory (smell), and gustatory (taste). These are your *representational (rep) systems*, also called *modalities*. *Submodalities* combine to make up modalities. For example, if you make a picture in your mind's eye, you are using your visual representative system or modality. You can adjust the qualities or submodalities of the picture by making it bigger, brighter, or bringing it closer to you. You can discover much more about your submodalities and how they affect the way you experience your world in Chapter 10.

Bandler and Grinder included rep systems (modalities) and submodalities into the Test and Operate phases of the TOTE model, refining it further to give us the NLP strategy model. According to Bandler and Grinder, the goal you have when you initiate a strategy, and the means by which you assess whether or not it has been achieved, is dependent on combinations of *your* modalities. For example, you may make a picture of the goal and perhaps hear a voice telling you what to do. When you come to measure its success you may get a particular feeling and hear a sound as well as make a picture, so you judge success by whether or not you feel, hear, or see what you imagined you would through the submodalities.

The NLP strategy model in action

This section shows how the NLP strategy model works for someone enacting a basic road rage strategy. The TOTE model (see Figure 12-2) is enriched by adding modalities to give you the NLP strategy model which can be used to understand how someone operates a particular pattern of behaviour.

Figure 12-3 shows how the NLP strategy model works.

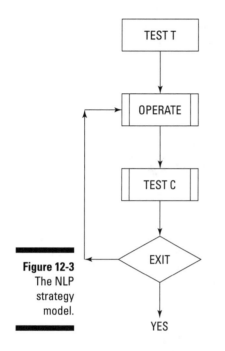

Figure 12-3
The NLP
strategy
model.

> ✓ **Test T(rigger)** – is the initial trigger that starts off a strategy. This test is where you assess whether the information coming in from your senses complies with data necessary to fire off the strategy. If you are prone to road rage, the trigger may be that you see someone undertaking and pushing in front of you in a traffic jam (visual confirmation), but because you are in a good mood (no kinaesthetic confirmation) you choose not to run the strategy. However, if you are in a bad mood (kinaesthetic confirmation), you fire your road rage strategy when you get the visual confirmation of someone undercutting you. The outcome is to make sure the driver in front knows exactly what you think of him and to thoroughly relish the feeling of giving in to the red mist of uncontrollable rage (kinaesthetic).

> ✓ **Operate** – is the process by which you gather the data that will help you carry out your strategy. So for your road rage strategy, you remember where the button for your horn is, where the light switch is, and which rude hand gesture you want to use. In this example you utilise the the visual modality as you visualise your arsenal to use for running your strategy. Although you do invoke the auditory digital modality as you recall all the juicy rude words you know. Then you launch yourself into your best road rage behaviour.

✔ **Test C(ompare)** – is where you compare the current data and situation to your outcome for running the strategy. Yes, you blew your horn (auditory); yes, you mouthed all your worst swear words (visual for the transgressor's benefit) and made the appropriate gestures (kinaesthetic for yourself and visual for the other driver). Yes, the red mist feels gooooood as it holds you in its deadly embrace (kinaesthetic). But . . . Oh no! You didn't flash your lights (visual).

✔ **Exit** – is where you exit your strategy. In this example, because you didn't remember to flash your lights, you would loop around to continue operating the strategy and exit once you had flashed your lights at the offending driver.

When I (Romilla) did my NLP Master Program, the exercise on modelling involved breaking a board. This was a fairly solid piece of wood which I was terrified of failing to break. My strategy for 'psyching' myself up was to see the board breaking (visual), feel energy in my solar plexus, pulsing up my chest and down my arm (kinaesthetic), and say repeatedly, 'You can do it' (auditory digital). The way this fits into the TOTE model is:

1. Test 1 – Stepping up to breaking the board is the trigger that starts this strategy.

2. Operate – Run my strategy for psyching myself up using the visual, kinaesthetic, and auditory digital representation systems (modalities).

3. Test 2 – Tested if I was psyched up.

4. Exit – Until I was ready, I looped around to operate the strategy, reinforcing my modalities. When I was ready I exited to the actual board break strategy.

The Eyes Have It: Recognising Another's Strategy

A strategy has very distinct stages. These stages can be Test Trigger, Operate, Test Compare, and Exit stages (explained earlier in this chapter). Consider this example: Ben has just started university and may well use the following strategy for phoning home:

✔ Feelings indicate that he is missing home. Test T (kinaesthetic).

✔ Makes a mental picture of his family. Operate (visual).

✔ Says the phone number to himself. Operate (auditory digital).

✔ Dials home. Operate (kinaesthetic).

For the purpose of this exercise, we will assume Ben got through, so satisfied his Test C, so exited the dial home strategy.

Once a strategy is embedded in your neurology, you have little or no conscious awareness of its steps. Yet if you know what to look for, you can figure out the other person's strategy. What you look for is eye movement. If, for example, we had asked Ben what he does when he phones home, his eyes would have gone down and to his right (feeling of missing home), then to the top and to his left (visual picture of his family). They would have stayed looking to the top and his left (as he remembered his phone number) before he pushed the buttons.

You can get a pretty good idea what someone is thinking about (images, emotions, and so on) by watching their eyes (see Figure 12-4). Generally, a person's eyes move in the following ways (you can find out more about the secrets that your eyes give away in Chapter 6):

When they're doing this	Their eyes do this
Remembering a picture	Move to the top left
Creating a picture	Move to the top right
Remembering a sound or conversation	Move horizontally to their left
Imagining what a sound will sound like	Move horizontally to their right
Accessing emotions	Drop down and to their right
Having a conversation with themselves	Drop down and to their left

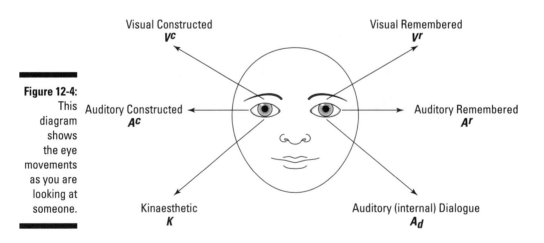

Figure 12-4: This diagram shows the eye movements as you are looking at someone.

How a person's eyes move can depend on whether that person is right- or left-handed. The diagram in Figure 12-4 illustrates a right-handed person. A left-handed person may look to the top and their right when they make a visual memory. So when you're trying to figure out someone else's strategy, it's always best to calibrate another person's responses by asking a few innocuous questions such as, 'Which route did you take to get here?' This will force them into visual recall and give you a clue as to which eye strategy they use.

Flexing Your Strategy Muscles

You develop strategies all through your life. Most of the basic ones like walking, eating, drinking, and choosing and making friends are created when you are young. Some you develop as you come across new circumstances in life. Sometimes what you develop for yourself may not be as effective as a strategy that another person uses, because they started from a more informed platform or had a teacher. If you can recognise the fact that your strategy may have grounds for improvement, that's a useful tool. For instance if your colleague is earning more than you are, for the same job, is it because she can present her success in a better light to the boss?

Acquiring new capabilities

Chapter 11 explains the NLP concept of logical levels, basically the idea that you have different levels at which you operate: identity, values and beliefs, capabilities and skills, behaviour, and environment. Your strategies relate to your capabilities and skills level. Sometimes you can improve your strategies by acquiring new skills. In the example of the higher earning colleague mentioned at the start of this section, you can learn how she has built and maintains rapport with the boss. Maybe she makes sure she keeps the boss apprised of progress on her project. Maybe you could try out talking to the boss of your progress.

Kay had always worked in an office where she felt safe and was confident of her abilities. When Kay decided to set up in business for herself, she discovered she had to learn a whole raft of new behaviours. Kay realised she had to learn to 'network' in order to spread the word of her new venture. Unfortunately, she would go to networking meetings and come away without really having achieved anything. She was quite vague about her objectives as she thought she was just going to meet new people who might prove useful in her business.

She realised she would have to learn new strategies in order to connect successfully with new people. She did this by observing Lindsay, a friend of hers, who was very successful at introducing herself and making a connection with someone new. She started to adopt Lindsay's strategies (outlines of which are listed below with how Kay used each step) and found she was making successful, new contacts.

- ✔ **Think of the outcome you want from a networking event.** Kay decided she wanted to exchange cards with at least six people who could be useful to her and she could be useful to them, either in a business or social context.

- ✔ **Go up to someone and introduce yourself:**

  'Hello, I'm Kay and you are . . . ?'

- ✔ **Ask questions to break the ice.** Kay's questions included:

  'This is my first time here. Have you been here before?'

  'How do you find these events?'

  'Have you travelled far?'

  'What line of business are you in?'

- ✔ **Stay focused on what the other person is saying as well as your outcome for the event.** Kay realised that she would get so caught up in the content of what the other person was saying she would forget to swap cards or would spend too much time with one person and forget to continue meeting people. She decided the way to stay focused on her goal was to hold the container with her cards in her left hand instead of putting it away in her handbag. This left her right hand free to shake hands, while keeping her mind on her goal.

Re-coding your programs

Strategies can be changed. In the road rage example earlier in this chapter, whose agenda were you fulfilling? Surely not yours? Particularly when you know how much physical damage anger and stress do to your body. How about developing another strategy that could go something like:

- ✔ **Test T:** Trigger: Someone undercutting you.

- ✔ **Operate:** Instead of accessing all your best rude words and gestures, think instead about the sun collapsing into a planetary nebula in about 5 billion years' time when all this angst will be completely pointless – and give yourself a quiet little smile and enjoy your life.

- ✔ **Test C:** Does your strategy for staying positive work? If so, move to last step, if not, return to previous step and try an alternative strategy.

✔ **Exit:** Choose to follow your own agenda and exit.

Chinese Qigong practitioners know that the 'internal smile' technique improves their immune system, gets the brain working more efficiently, and can reduce blood pressure, anxiety, and simple depression.

It's all in the 'How'

NLP is interested more in process – how you do something – than in the content of your experience. So the issue isn't that you get angry when you lose at badminton (content), rather 'HOW do you go about getting angry when you lose at badminton (process)?'

Because NLP is concerned with the 'how', it is possible to change a strategy that is not giving you the results you want. So instead of smashing your racket, you could see yourself writing a hefty cheque for another expensive racket – constructing a visual image. And because strategies can be modified, you can model the way you do something well to improve another area in your life you don't feel you do as well at.

Tim was extremely tidy and organised at the office. Unfortunately his home was a mess. Tim just could not work out how to keep a tidy house. I (Romilla) worked with Tim to help him identify the processes he used in the office to keep his work area tidy. He examined his strategy and discovered:

✔ **Test T:** Trigger: He would see papers and folders on his desk and decide he wanted to see clear desk space.

✔ **Operate:** Tim would do the following:

- Imagine his boss walking in and commenting on his untidiness. Interestingly, the tone of voice was very similar to the one Tim's mother used when he was a child.

- Get an uncomfortable feeling in his solar plexus.

- Picture where the files went.

- Get up and file away the papers and folders.

✔ **Test C:** He would look at his desk and see clear desk space and get a warm feeling in his solar plexus.

✔ **Exit:** If Tim didn't see enough desk space he would not get the warm feeling and he would proceed to tidy up further, before he would exit his strategy.

By understanding his 'tidy desk' strategy at work Tim was able to keep a tidy home. He organised his cupboards so he could tidy things away. When he couldn't see any floor space he would imagine his boss walking in and he would then run his strategy to keep his home tidy. A very successful transference of strategies.

Using NLP Strategies for Love and Success

Whatever you do, you do because you have either learned a strategy, usually unconsciously, or developed a strategy to carry out a particular function. For instance, if one eye is weaker than the other you may have learnt, also unconsciously, to hold reading material directly in front of the stronger eye by moving your head. It is very useful to learn to ask questions that will elicit a strategy, 'How do you know when to go to the gym?' and then watch the other person's eyes as they give their response. This will give you fairly obvious clues as to their strategies. If there is a doubt in your mind, fine tune the question!

Deep love strategy

Everyone has a particular strategy in order for them to feel truly loved. We call this the *deep love strategy*. When someone comes along who satisfies that deep love strategy, bingo! On go the rose-tinted glasses for Mr or Ms Right.

When you meet someone to whom you are attracted or whom you find interesting, initially you fire all modalities.

- ✔ Visual – You make the effort to look good. Perhaps you wear the colour you've discovered the object of your interest likes. You look deeply into those gorgeous blue/green/brown eyes.

- ✔ Auditory – You speak in dulcet tones and say the words you think he/she wants to hear.

- ✔ Kinaesthetic – You hold hands. You stroke the other person.

- ✔ Olfactory – Mmmm! Hope the perfume isn't too overwhelming. Oops! Forgot the mouthwash.

- ✔ Gustatory – Candle-lit dinners with herbs and spices to prove that someone is really special.

The person you desire is hooked and you walk into the sunset hand-in-hand. But then . . . after some time . . . there are rumblings of discontent. 'What went wrong?' you cry. Nothing really. Perhaps you and your partner just reverted to the modality you operate in most naturally. So where the wife may be craving physical contact with hugs and cuddles in order to feel loved, the husband may be proving his love by doing all he can for her, like keeping the house in good repair, washing the car and keeping it topped up with fuel.

Something GHOTI-y around here

Robert Dilts, one of the most innovative Gurus of NLP, says about his experience of learning to spell as a child: 'My consternation grew, however, as we began with basics – such as the names of the first ten numbers. Instead of "wun" the first number was spelled "one" (that looked like it should be pronounced "oh-nee"). There was no "W" and an extra silent "E". The second number, instead of being spelled "tu" like it sounded, was spelled "two" (as the comedian Gallagher points out, perhaps that was where the missing "W" from "one" had gone). After "three" ("tuh-ree"), "four" ("fow-er") and "five" ('fi-vee') I knew something was wrong, but being young, I figured it was probably just something wrong with me. In fact, when "six" and "seven"

came along I started to build back some hope – but then they struck with "eight" ("ee-yi-guh-hut") and I felt like the next number looked as if it should sound – "nine" (a "ninny").'

The vagaries of phonetics weren't lost on George Bernard Shaw either. He once demonstrated that FISH could be spelt GHOTI. 'GH' for example from laugh, 'O' as pronounced in women and 'TI' as in nation. Quite silly really as 'GH' never sounds like 'F' at the beginning of a word and 'TI' cannot be used at the end of a word because it needs to be followed by a vowel in order to make the 'SH' sound.

Reproduced with the permission of Robert Dilts.

To find a person's strategy for feeling loved, try saying words to the effect, 'You know I love you, don't you?' 'What would make you feel even more loved?' As you do, be sure to pay attention to the eyes and the body language. 'Uh, I'm not sure', with the eyes going to her bottom right (K), could give the clue that more cuddles might be in order. Test your hunch. If the eyes move to the horizontal left (A'), try asking what she might like to hear you say or what music she might like.

- ✔ Don't ask at moments of high stress, like a traffic jam – we can guarantee you won't like the response you get, but in that special, quiet time when there's just the two of you.

- ✔ Calibrate the response you get when you do something for the other person. Does bringing home a bunch of roses get you that special response?

In NLP, *calibration* is the process by which you read another person's response to your communication. A slap in the face is a pretty overt response and, hopefully, you won't repeat the words or behaviour that earned the slap. Most responses are much more subtle: a scowl, a puzzled look, flushed cheeks, a clenched jaw. A master communicator needs to be able to assess these, particularly when the signals are mixed; for example, a smile with a puzzled look may indicate the person doesn't get it but is too polite to say so.

There's nothing like positive feedback to achieve your own strategy, so let him or her know when he or she has hit the mark, especially if you know what your beloved's deep love strategy is. For example, I (Romilla) know a couple that have been very happily married for 27 years. The wife needs to have her face stroked just so with a particular look in her husband's eyes for her to feel the centre of her husband's universe and you can almost hear her purr.

Strategies for influencing people

By using your knowledge of strategies you can make yourself an irresistible communicator. Once you've discovered someone's strategies you can use them as a framework to feed information back to them, using the steps of their strategy. For example, suppose you want to utilise a teenager's strategy to help them do their homework.

In order to feed information back using the teen's own strategy, you first need to determine what that strategy is. So you ask a question, such as, 'How do you motivate yourself to play football?' and watch the teen's eye movements as he answers your question. Suppose your question elicited the verbal response with the accompanying eye movements shown in Figure 12-5.

Figure 12-5:
The Eyes
Reveal the
Strategy.

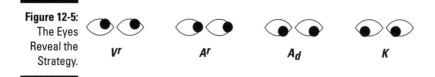

'I see myself in my kit, with the rest of the team (eyes move to his top, left – V^r) and I hear everyone talking excitedly (eyes move his left, horizontally – A^r), then I say to myself "we're going to win" (eyes move to his bottom left – A_d), and I feel really good (eyes move to his bottom right – K)'

Based on the teen's answer and his eye movements you can craft your response accordingly. You know that to motivate himself, he remembers a picture (V^r), then he remembers the excited chatter of the team (A^r). He then talks to himself (A_d) before, finally, feeling (K) good. Based on this information you may suggest the following:

✔ 'Can you recall the picture of when you finished your physics homework on time last week?'

You're asking your teenager to make a picture of the time when he had actually finished his homework, forcing him into the start of his strategy (V^r).

✔ 'When Mr Saunders really praised you. Do you remember what he said?'

You're asking your teenager to recall the words that were used in order to fire the next step of his motivation strategy (A^r).

✔ 'Can you remember the wonder with which you said to yourself, "For the first time, I really understand physics"?'

By asking your teenager to repeat his conversation with himself, you are directing him into the penultimate step of his motivation strategy (A_d).

✔ 'Do you remember how elated you felt and wouldn't it be terrific if you finished your homework now and you got that elated feeling back again?'

In this final step you are making the teenager motivate himself by hooking into feeling good (K) and suggesting he can re-create feeling good by getting his homework finished.

You can use this technique any time you need to be really persuasive. First, ask a question and watch the eyes as the person responds. And then phrase your suggestions in language that will get you the best response.

The NLP spelling strategy

Just as with other strategies, every literate person has a strategy for spelling. The good spellers have an effective strategy. The poor spellers have an ineffective strategy.

Spelling well is a very visual process. If you class yourself as a good speller, you will usually look up to your top left (visual remembered) when you visualise the word you want to spell. This means you have memorised pictures of words which you have built up into a library and you draw upon this store of words when you spell. Usually an ineffective spelling strategy is trying to spell phonetically.

So if you do spell phonetically and would like to be better, try the following:

1. **Think of a word you would like to learn to spell, then write it in big letters and keep it to hand.**

2. **Think of a word you know you can spell.**

The reason we ask you to spell a word you know is to create a good feeling in you. Sadly, when you learn to spell your teachers don't always teach you the strategy to spell well. Consequently you may get categorised as 'not the brightest student'. So when asked to spell, you may feel bad. Over a period of time, spelling may come to be synonymous with feeling bad. It may affect your identity – 'I am a bad speller' or even worse, 'I am a poor student'. Allow yourself to acknowledge any negative beliefs that may surface and be compassionate with yourself. You may not have got on with your English teacher and learning to spell may dredge up unwanted memories and that's OK. You are your own person now and you can give yourself permission to be the best at spelling as you can be. So play with the words and go for it.

3. **Move your eyes to visual recall (usually, your top left) and make a picture of the word you know you can spell.**

   Knowing you can spell the word gives you a positive feeling (satisfied, confident, happy, and so on).

4. **Really bring that positive feeling into your consciousness; focus on it and enhance it; then take a deep breath and enhance it some more.**

5. **Now have a quick glance at the word you want to learn to spell.**

6. **Keeping hold of the positive feeling, move your eyes to your top left and make a picture of the new word you want to learn to spell.**

   Make sure you make a clear, bright, big picture of the word and look at it, we mean *really look at it.*

7. **Next time you want to spell the word, move your eyes to visual recall and hey presto! As if by magic, it'll pop into your mind's eye and you can begin to believe that *you can spell*, can't you?**

When we were discussing the spelling strategy, I (Kate) discovered I use the visual recall section of my memory to remember things. Try this method to remember phone numbers or learning your multiplication tables.

To succeed or not to succeed

I (Romilla) was discussing success with Bernie, an acquaintance. He made me chuckle when he said, 'No one succeeds better than a toothless budgie.' Get it?! Succeeds – sucks seeds. The serious question is, 'Why are you successful in some areas of your life and perhaps not as successful in others?' You may discover that the answer could be that you are just running less effective strategies in the areas you are not as successful in. So change them! Here's how. Identify an area of your life in which you are successful and ask yourself, 'What strategy am I running now that I am succeeding?' This is playing the 'as if' game. Suppose you consider yourself a fairly successful tennis player and have always wanted to take up running. However, every time you've started running, you've given up because you just couldn't keep up the momentum. When examining the strategies you operate when playing tennis, you may realise that your breathing and mental focus are different when you are running around the tennis court to when you are running on the flat. By adopting the strategies you use when you play to when you run, you may find you achieve your desire of becoming a runner.

Chapter 13

Time Travel

In This Chapter

▶ Understanding what NLP means by time line

▶ Releasing the hold that negative emotions have on you

▶ Changing beliefs by going back on your time line

▶ Discovering how you organise time

▶ Learning to create your future along your time line

*T*ime has a strange, elastic quality. It goes really fast when you are engaged in something interesting and stretches when you allow yourself to get bored. Are you one of the time-rich people who has all the time in the world or are you time-poor, always short of time? Perhaps having time, like money, depends on where you focus your attention. Although day and night for the rich, poor, young, and old is 24 hours, the perception of time is different. Some people are stuck in the past, others have their gaze firmly staring into the future, and some people just live in the moment.

> *Time is a core system of cultural, social and personal life. In fact, nothing occurs except in some kind of time frame.*
>
> The Dance of Life (Edward T Hall, Anchor, 1984)

'American-European' time is a result of the Industrial Revolution when people would have to be in the factories at a specific time. It has a linear format, one event or transaction follows another. Time in Latin America, the Arab countries, and other countries in the Southern hemisphere has a multi-dimensional structure, allowing people to multi-task. Each has its strengths and weaknesses and the potential to cause conflict in cross-cultural exchanges.

Time also gives your memories meaning. You can change the meaning a memory has by changing its quality and its relationship to time. This allows you to release yourself of negative emotions and limiting decisions and gives you the means to create the future you would rather have, without the influence of disempowering past memories.

How Your Memories Are Organised

Think of something you do on a regular basis. This means that you can remember doing it in the past, imagine or experience doing it in the present, and can imagine doing it in the future. Do you notice that the pictures have different locations? By going into the past to examine a memory and again into the future, although with a pit stop in the present, you have just experienced a little 'land-based' time travel. (You can experience the airborne variety a little later; see the section 'Discovering Your Time Line'.)

Maybe you thought of reading a book, driving to a store, working at your desk, eating in a restaurant, or brushing your teeth. OK, so maybe you thought of something else and that's alright too. Did you notice the qualities of the three pictures, such as location, bright or dim, three-dimensional or flat, movie or still, colour or black and white? These qualities, or attributes, are called submodalities and you'll find loads of exciting applications to do with submodalities in Chapter 10 – 'Sliding the Controls'.

By asking you to think about these attributes we are getting you to realise that there is a structure to your memories. You know whether a memory is in the past or whether you are creating an image in your future by examining what the picture of the memory looks like.

If we were to ask you to define what you are made up of, if you're a woman you may say, 'sugar and spice and all things nice' and if you're a man you might say, ' hair, skin, and blood'. But . . . you, the whole person, are much more than your component parts. This is what is meant by the term *Gestalt*. The definition of a Gestalt is a structure, or pattern that cannot be derived purely from its constituent parts. So, in thinking about you, someone's mind makes the leap from your components to the whole you.

Your memories are arranged in a Gestalt. Associated memories form a Gestalt, although the formation of a Gestalt may start when you experience an event that first triggers an emotional response, a Significant Emotional Event, which is sometimes called SEE for short. The Significant Emotional Event is also referred to as the *root cause*. If you experience a similar event and have a similar emotional response, you link the two events. This continues and suddenly you have a chain.

One of psychology's founding fathers, William James, likened your memories to a string of pearls, where each related memory is linked along a string to the one before and to the one after. During any work with your time line, if you snip the string before the first occurrence, the Gestalt is broken (see Figure 13-1).

Figure 13-1:
A Memory
Gestalt.

Discovering Your Time Line

Memories are arranged in a pattern. Now, if you were asked to point to the direction the past memory came from, where would you point? Similarly, if you were to point to the picture of the thing you will do in the future, notice where you are pointing now. Could you also point to where your image for the present is? If you draw a line between the memory from the past, the one in the present, and the one in the future, you've created your very own *time line*.

People may identify their past as behind them and their future as in front of them. Some people may have a V-shaped line. Some may have their past to their left and their future to their right – this is interesting because, as you will discover in Chapter 6, the left is where most people move their eyes to when they want to remember something and the right is where they move their eyes to when they want to imagine something that isn't real, yet. Interestingly, some people arrange their time line geographically, with their past perhaps in Cornwall, Los Angeles, or Timbuktu and their present where they are currently residing. Their future may lie in the place they want to move to.

A woman who attended my (Romilla) workshop 'Future Perfect' (where people come to create the future they want to live) got very confused when it came to finding her time line. We discovered her past was in South Africa, her present in England, and she could not decide where her future lay. I asked her to trust her unconscious to point her finger to where her future could be. She pointed to her front and slightly to the right. By getting her to draw a line backwards to South Africa we were able to establish her time line.

If you find it easier, draw an imaginary line on the ground and, trusting your unconscious mind, walk along the line, from where you feel your past is to where you feel your future is.

Walking along a time line can be difficult if spatial restrictions get in the way, for example if you are in a small room. This exercise will show you how you can visualise your time line in your head by 'floating up' from where you are relaxing in order to get a clear view of the time line stretching out below you.

1. **Think of an event that you experienced recently.**

2. **Now take a deep breath and just relax as deeply as you can.**

3. **Imagine yourself floating up, up above your present and way above the clouds, into the stratosphere.**

4. **Picture your time line way below you, like a ribbon, and you can see yourself in the time line.**

5. **Now float back over your time line until you are directly over the recently experienced event.**

6. **You can hover there as long as you like until you decide to float back to the present and down into your own body.**

Hope you enjoyed that trial flight. Remember the process as you'll be doing a lot of it.

Changing Time Lines

When you got your time line, where was it in relation to you? For instance, did the line run through your body as in the first two *in-time* diagrams (see Figures 13-2 and 13-3)? Or was it out in front of you so that you could see the whole of your time line laid out in front of you as in the *through-time* diagram (see Figure 13-4)?

The shape of your time line can influence various personality traits. If you have a through-time line, you will have an American-European model of time, which means you may have the following tendencies:

✔ Very aware of the value of time

✔ Goal-oriented

✔ Conscious of turning up for appointments on time

✔ Good at planning activities

✔ Able to keep your emotions separate from events

✔ Living in the now is difficult

As a person with an in-time line you may have the following abilities and tendencies:

- ✔ Creative

- ✔ Good at multi-tasking

- ✔ Feel your emotions very strongly

- ✔ Like to keep your options open

- ✔ Good at living in the moment

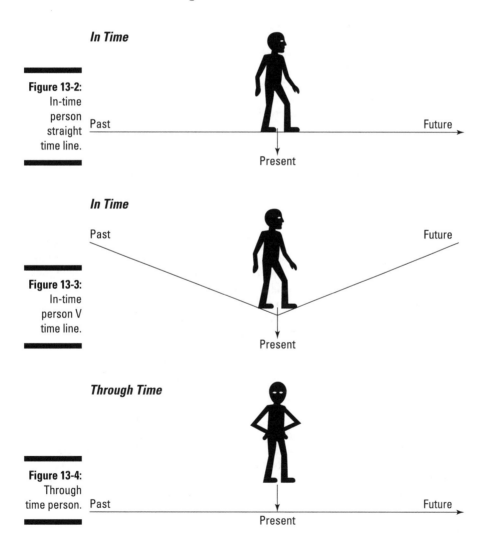

In Time

Past   Future

Present

Figure 13-2:
In-time person straight time line.

In Time

Past   Future

Present

Figure 13-3:
In-time person V time line.

Through Time

Past   Future

Present

Figure 13-4:
Through time person.

You can change the orientation of your time line so that you can experience a different mindset without changing any of the individual memories and events that your time line is made up of. If you are an in-time person, it may help you, when you have to keep to a time schedule, to turn your time line so that you are through-time with all of your time line in front of you. If you are a workaholic and would really like to chill with your partner in the evening, why not pretend that your time line is the other side of your front door and become an in-time person as you step through your door.

Switching time lines should only be practised when you are safe and sitting or lying down as it can cause some disorientation. If this does happen, slow down and revert your time line to its original orientation.

If you are a through-time person and your time line is laid out in front of you, you can change your time line by stepping on to it so that you have to turn your head or your body to face the past or the future. Another way you might decide to do this is to float above your time line so it is laid out below you and as you float back down to position yourself it is below your feet or running through your body.

If you are in-time, you can step off your time line so that it is laid out in front of you and you can see your past, present, and future as a continuum, without having to turn your body. If you prefer, you can float above your time line and when you float back down you can position yourself so that your time line is in front of you.

I (Romilla) always ask delegates on the 'Future Perfect' seminars to switch time line orientation and to keep the different orientation over lunch, *as long as they feel comfortable*. One of the delegates, a highly in-time person, experienced dizziness and nausea initially when she put her time line out in front of her (through-time) but was keen to persevere. After sitting down for a while she stabilised and went out. On her return from lunch, her relief at switching her time line back to an in-time line was visible for all to see.

Apart from switching the orientation of your time line, you may also find it quite useful to learn to change how you space your present and your future on it.

John was suffering from stress. He felt as though everything was pressing in on him and that he just couldn't cope with all his work. When John went back along his time line, using Time Line Therapy™ (co-created by Tad James), he remembered that he had failed to qualify for a scholarship when he was a young boy. His mother was very scathing and judgemental. John realised he had been trying to please her ever since and always tried to do too much. On examining the spacing of his time line, John discovered that he had his present up close to his nose and his future about six inches behind that. Once we had cleared up all the negative emotions behind his 'failure' (ugh! horrible term), John was able to move the present out to about a foot away and space his future further along up to about ten feet away. He had wanted to stretch his time line out and got into a panic because he felt he would 'never achieve anything in my life ever again'. Once he'd shortened his time line he felt comfortable because he knew he would be able to plan and meet his objectives.

Simon had the exact opposite problem to John. He said he could never meet his deadlines. On getting Simon to examine his time line, he discovered that his future was so far out in front of him that he couldn't generate enough of a sense of urgency about his goals. Simon compressed his time line and pretended that it was a conveyor belt. He placed goals at specific distances along the belt. In Chapter 3 – 'Taking Charge of Your Life' we suggest you make a 'to do' list for the next day. When Simon made his 'to do' list he would move the conveyor belt one notch closer. This had a real impact on Simon meeting his commitments.

Travelling Along Your Time Line to a Happier You

Your time line is made up of a sequence of memories which have a structure to them; pictures are in colour, sounds can be loud or soft, and feelings can make you feel light or weigh you down. For more information on this, read Chapter 6. Your memories are created by your mind – if we witnessed an event at the same time as you, each of us would remember the event differently. As you travel your time line, examining your memories and understanding the lessons that need to be learned can release the hold the memories have on the present and you can change their structure, making them smaller, softer, or lighter. So your past need no longer cast a shadow on your present – or more importantly on your future.

Releasing negative emotions and limiting decisions

Negative emotions are emotions such as anger, fear, shame, grief, sadness, guilt, regret, and anxiety, to list just a few. Not only can such emotions have a powerful, undesired, physical affect on your body, they can have a devastating affect on the way you conduct your life.

A limiting decision is a decision you made once upon a time when you decided you couldn't do something because you were too stupid, unfit, poor, or any number of other reasons; for example, 'I can never be slim' or 'I am bad at adding numbers'.

Negative emotions and limiting decisions reach far from your past to influence you in your present. If you can go into the past, by travelling back along your time line, and understand consciously what your unconscious mind was trying to protect you from, you will be able to release the emotions and decisions more easily.

Dealing with negative emotions can be, well, emotional. So before you attempt to use the techniques in this section to release negative emotions or understand your limiting decisions, keep these points in mind:

- ✔ In order to clear really heavy duty stuff such as very important emotional issues (such as the trauma of child abuse or divorce), we definitely recommend that you see a qualified NLP Master Practitioner or Time Line Therapist.

- ✔ This process is *not* for a trauma or phobia as you need a fully qualified therapist to ensure that your issues are dealt with professionally and sensitively and that you can handle resolving the trauma.

- ✔ It is better to work with someone else when working with time lines as they will be able to keep you grounded if you forget the exercise and succumb to the emotions you are experiencing. They can also ensure that you follow the steps in the exercise correctly.

The diagram shown in Figure 13-5 is very important to the following exercises as it clarifies the locations along your time line that you need to be aware of. It is particularly useful to people who are more visual, who make pictures in their heads.

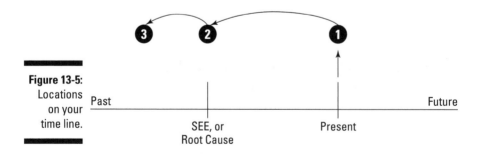

Figure 13-5:
Locations on your time line.

✔ Location number 1 in the figure represents the position you float up to which is directly above the present on your time line.

✔ Location number 2 is directly above the SEE (Significant Emotional Event) or root cause.

✔ Location number 3 is still way above your time line but 15 minutes before the root cause.

This exercise introduces you to a process which will help you remove negative emotions that you may be holding onto, for instance you may be prone to inappropriate feelings of anger. Once you have mastered this technique you can use it for eliminating negative decisions that you may have made in the past, for example 'I can never be truly successful'. Please remember to keep an open mind to the answers that your unconscious mind presents.

1. **Find yourself somewhere safe and quiet to relax and think of a mildly negative emotion you may have experienced in the past.**

2. **Check with yourself if it is OK to learn from the event and release the emotion. When you relax, ask your unconscious mind, 'Is it OK for me to let go of anger?'**

3. **Ask your unconscious mind, 'What is the root cause of this problem, which, when disconnected from it will cause the problem to disappear? Was it before, during, or after my birth?'**

When you ask your unconscious mind if the root cause was before, during, or after your birth, please keep an open mind about the answer it gives you. Your unconscious mind absorbs a lot of information and makes a lot of decisions without your conscious awareness. Romilla's clients have been surprised with the responses they got.

4. **When you get the root cause, float way above your time line so that you can see your past and your future stretching below you.**

   You are now at location 1 shown in Figure 13-5.

5. **Still above your time line, float back along your time line until you are above the SEE (location 2 in Figure 13-5), see what you saw, felt, and heard.**

6. **Ask your unconscious mind to learn what it needs to from the event in order for it to let go of the negative emotions easily and quickly.**

7. **Float to location 3 in Figure 13-5, which is above and 15 minutes *before* the SEE.**

8. **As you float above your time line at location 3, turn and face the present so that you can see the root cause in front of you and below you.**

9. **Give yourself permission to let go of all the negative emotions associated with the event and notice where the negative emotion is.**

   Have all the other negative emotions associated with the event disappeared too?

10. **If other negative emotions remain, use each 'out' breath to release all the emotions that are associated with the SEE.**

11. **Stay at location 3 until you feel, or know, that all the negative emotions have dissipated.**

12. **When you are ready, and by that we mean when you feel you have released the negative emotion, float back to location 1.**

    Go only as fast as your unconscious mind can learn from similar events and let go of all the associated emotions.

13. **Come back down into the room.**

14. **Just test – go into the future to when an event would have triggered the emotion you let go and notice that the emotion has gone.**

This exercise can also be used for getting rid of a limiting decision. For example, you may have decided to stay poor or unhealthy or made some other self-defeating decision. Follow the above process using the limiting decision in place of the negative emotion.

Finding forgiveness

With hindsight and maturity you can forgive someone in your past. This allows you to release all the energy you had invested in resentment, anger, or other emotions. You can then move on and have all that energy to be more creative or loving or anything wonderful you may want. One useful way to accomplish this is to understand the motives of a person who may have hurt you and realise that, because of their own issues, they were operating from a reality which provided them with a very limited choice.

As an example, imagine that you had a burning desire to become an actress and your parents gave you a hard time about it. Now acknowledge that they were actually showing parental concern for you. They were only doing their best for you with the resources they had at their disposal. Go back along your time line to a time when you can remember one such difficult time with your parents. You can then hover way above your time line while you learn any important lessons that you needed to be aware of. You can float down into the event and give your parents a hug and let them know you realise now that they were doing their best for you. If you find it easy, you can surround yourself in a bubble of light and just enjoy the feelings of love, compassion, and forgiveness.

Comforting the younger you

When you travel back along your time line and find an event that involves you when you were young, you can embrace the younger you, reassure him or her that all will be well, surround yourselves with light and let yourselves be healed. Now, imagine bringing all that joy and relief along your time line, right into the present.

Getting rid of anxiety

Anxiety is simply a negative emotion about a future event. You learnt that you can remove a negative emotion or limiting decision by going to *before* the event which has created the emotion or when you made the decision (see the section 'Releasing negative emotions and limiting decisions' earlier for details). Anxiety can be removed by going into the future *beyond* the successful conclusion of the event about which you are anxious.

Imagine what you would see, hear, and feel when the event which is causing you to feel anxious has been truly successful. Then, when you travel forward, above your time line to beyond the successful conclusion of the event, you will find that the anxiety no longer exists. Using Figure 13-6 as a reference, follow these steps:

1. **Find yourself somewhere safe and quiet to relax and think of an event about which you are feeling anxious; now check with your unconscious mind if it is OK for you to let go of the anxiety.**

2. **Now float way above your time line so that you can see your past and your future stretching below you.**

3. **Still above your time line, float forward along your time line until you are above the event about which you are feeling anxiety.**

4. **Ask your unconscious mind to learn what it needs to from the event in order for it to let go of the anxiety easily and quickly.**

5. **When you have the information needed, float further into the future, along your time line until you are 15 minutes after the *successful conclusion* of the event about which you were feeling anxious.**

6. **Turn and look toward now and notice that you are calm and no longer anxious.**

7. **When you are ready, float back to your present.**

8. **Just test – go into the future to the event about which you were anxious and confirm that the anxiety no longer exists.**

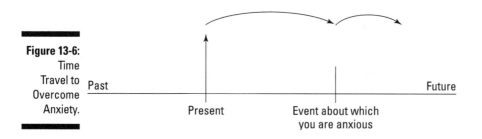

Figure 13-6:
Time
Travel to
Overcome
Anxiety.

Past

Present

Event about which
you are anxious

Future

Making a better future

Once you know how to travel your time line, think how wonderful it would be to take some goals that are so compelling that they are irresistible and put them into your future.

Always check your motives in setting and obtaining your goals in order to ensure they fit within all areas of your life, as described in Chapter 3 in the section on 'Creating Well-formed Outcomes'. By really examining your reasons, you will ensure there are no hidden negative emotions driving you, for instance if you are focusing on making a lot of money you may want to know that the desire stems from wanting to be comfortably secure and able to help those less fortunate than yourself and not because you are trying to escape from a poverty-stricken childhood. Checking your motives will also help you identify any lurking, unconscious fears, for example 'If I am rich people will only want to be friends because of my money, not because they like me'. Analysing these fully will help crystallise your exact reasons for your desire and you can take steps to overcome any unconscious issues.

1. **Find yourself somewhere safe and quiet to relax and design your goal.**

   Chapter 3 tells you what you need to know about creating goals.

2. **Float way above your time line so that you can see your past and your future stretching below you.**

3. **Still above your time line, float forward along your time line until you are above the time by which you want to have achieved your goal.**

4. **Turn and look back to *now* and allow all the events along your time line to align so that they support your goal, noting any actions you may have to take along the way.**

5. **When you are ready, float back to your present and back down into the room.**

ANECDOTE

Healing along the time line

My (Kate) friend, Tara, shared an inspiring experience with me. Tara had suffered severely with blocked sinuses since she was 18. This condition was so bad that she needed antibiotics at least three or four times a year in order to alleviate the debilitating symptoms. By the time Tara attended a workshop on Time Line Therapy she had undergone four unsuccessful operations to clear her sinuses and been told by her doctors that she would either have to live with her illness or stay on steroids. During the workshop, Tara discovered her symptoms became particularly severe when she needed attention from a particular person, when she became overwhelmed by people and events, or when she needed nurturing. Tara explored the possibility that her physical behaviour was psychosomatic. By investigating any limiting beliefs and benefits she was getting from her illness, Tara realised that she had built a Gestalt around illness. She remembered that, as a child, her brother had received a lot of attention from their mother because he was asthmatic and the only time Tara got the attention was when she had tonsillitis. Tara's father also suffered with chronic sinusitis and Tara found that her illness gave her something in common with her father. She also believed that she could not clear her disease by herself. Tara accepted that she could get attention from people without being ill, that she could ask for TLC (tender loving care) and that it was OK to admit to feelings of being overwhelmed. She went back along her time line to where she believed the first SEE happened. She realised that this was where she first became jealous of the attention her brother got. She was able to let go of the Gestalt associated with this event and has been free of sinusitis and antibiotics since March 2002.

Chapter 14

Smooth Running Below Decks

. . . .

In This Chapter

▶ Learning that your unconscious mind has parts that may be in conflict

▶ Discovering how to overcome self-sabotaging behaviour

▶ Experimenting with integrating parts of the unconscious mind

▶ Extrapolating personal conflict resolution to teams, organisations, and nations

. . . .

*C*an you remember participating in or watching a tug-of-war? Both sides expended an inordinate amount of energy but didn't really manage to move very far. Conflict, whether within your self or with someone else, is like a tug-of-war with two sides pulling in opposite directions and getting nowhere.

Conflict within yourself usually occurs between a conscious part of your mind and an unconscious part. 'I don't know what came over me', 'I just wasn't myself', 'Part of me wants . . . , another part wants . . .' – phrases like these give a clue to parts of your unconscious mind, which you may be unaware of. Take the example of a person who knows at a conscious level that smoking is bad for his health and yet continues to smoke because unconsciously he craves the companionship of his friends, most of whom smoke.

The *NLP Encyclopaedia* (which you can access at www.nlpu.com) defines conflict in this way: 'Psychologically, conflict is a mental struggle, sometimes unconscious, resulting when different representations of the world are held in opposition or exclusivity.' In other words, conflict occurs when two maps of the world collide. By reconciling these two different maps, you can eliminate the conflict and this chapter tells you how.

A Hierarchy of Conflict

Conflict can take place at different levels of a hierarchy which is made up of identity, values and beliefs, capabilities and skills, behaviour, and environment. When you are considering some of the conflicts you face, it can help to understand the level with which you need to engage. For example, if you, as a manager, believe that people are what make your company a success but you focus more on developing your technology than your people, you may need to modify your behaviour to bring it in line with the needs of your staff and ultimately with your beliefs.

This logical level hierarchy is also referred to as neuro-logical levels because they connect with your thinking processes and therefore the brain and its interaction with your body. (You can find out all about logical levels in Chapter 11.) These neuro-logical levels operate in a hierarchy – rather like the rungs on a ladder – with identity at the higher rung and environment down below. When you can identify the real logical level you're working at, then the conflict is easier to resolve.

Here are some examples of the conflicts you may face at the different *logical levels*:

- **Identity** – Often you have many roles to play in your life and work which pull you in different directions – parent or child. You may want to be a 'good parent' as well as a 'committed employee'. You may want be a 'nice, likeable guy' as well as a 'profitable manager'. Perhaps you're trying to be a 'supportive son or daughter' or 'volunteer in the local community' as well as an 'international jet setter'.

- **Values and beliefs** – Sometimes you have a mix of beliefs that don't seem to fit well together or match your values. You may want to be happy but there's a part of you that doesn't believe you deserve happiness. You may value both health and wealth but not believe it's possible to get them both at the same time. You may value family life and global success and be struggling to see how they fit because you have no role models of these two values sitting side by side as equals.

- **Capabilities and skills** – You may have a mix of wonderful skills and abilities and can't find a way to use them all in a way that satisfies you. So perhaps you would struggle to find a job that satisfies your desire to build or make things with your own hands at the same time as employing your skills at managing a team of other people. You may be a great musician and also a qualified medic and making a choice of where to put your energy.

✔ **Behaviour** – You can find yourself engaging in behaviour that doesn't seem to help you to achieve your goals. For example, have you ever had an important piece of work to do and spent hours tidying out your desk or a cupboard instead? Or maybe you've wanted to diet and found that a piece of buttered toast had somehow ended up in your mouth without you noticing how it got there.

✔ **Environment** – At times you may find yourself in a dilemma about the places where you hang out or the people you spend time with. Maybe you are mixing with the wrong sort of people – those who don't seem to have your best interests at heart, or those that your family disapproves of. Maybe part of you wants to move away from home and set up on your own; or perhaps part of you wants to live in the country of your birth while another part of you yearns to explore the world. You want to be in two places simultaneously and can't settle in either.

As soon as you hear yourself or others say phrases like: 'Well, part of me wants . . . and there's another part of me that wants . . .' you can be sure that there's an internal conflict going on that has defied logical reasoning.

You are in total harmony with yourself when each of your logical levels is aligned with the others. Personal conflict occurs when what you are trying to achieve, or what you believe, or perhaps what you are doing is out of kilter with other levels in the hierarchy. So if you want to satisfy a goal to earn a high salary, it may conflict with your identity of 'I am a good husband and father' because you don't get to spend time with your loved ones. Conflict resolution is achieved by brainstorming and asking questions of yourself and the people affected by your decisions about how you can come up with novel ways that may allow you to fulfil your goal and align your logical levels.

From Wholeness to Parts

Your memories are arranged in a Gestalt, which is an association of related memories. A Gestalt may start when you experience an event that first triggers an emotional response, a Significant Emotional Event (SEE). Starting from the premise that at some point your unconscious mind is a complete whole, parts are formed as a result of you experiencing a SEE. As a result of the SEE, a boundary forms around a part of your unconscious mind, separating it from the rest. This part functions like a 'mini you', with its own personality and values and beliefs. Just like the 'conscious' you, this part will exhibit behaviours which have purpose and intent. Unfortunately the behaviours can be in conflict with the actual intention of the part. Someone who believes they were never loved as a child may develop shoplifting tendencies because the unconscious part craves attention, although the attention this is likely to get is not what the person really wants.

Part's intentions

A major NLP presupposition is that *every behaviour has a positive intent*. For example, the positive intent behind someone smoking a cigarette may be to relax. (Head to Chapter 2 for more of the main NLP presuppositions.) Sometimes the behaviour that your unconscious part makes you exhibit doesn't satisfy its underlying need. An alcoholic may drink to numb the pain of being abandoned by his spouse. The unconscious part is actually crying out for love but the behaviour that is being manifested – drinking heavily – does not satisfy the underlying need. The answer lies in understanding what the real need is and satisfying it in a positive way. So if the alcoholic can come out of his stupor and recognise that what he needs is not alcohol but love, he may dry out, clean up, learn the lessons from his failed marriage, and pick himself up to find love.

Getting to the heart of the problem

Often a part of your unconscious mind can create problems for you. The reasons for these problems can be hard to understand logically. For example, you may suddenly develop a fear of an everyday activity like travelling or meeting people. You will be able to reach the real, hidden purpose behind the intention of the part by peeling back and exploring each reason or intention as it surfaces. Once you arrive at the true, underlying purpose of the part, you'll be able to assimilate this into the bigger whole of the unconscious mind. The following anecdote illustrates what happens when your unconscious mind drives the motivation of a part. Later in this chapter, in the section on 'Visual squash', you can discover how to integrate two parts that are in conflict.

Oliver is a very successful business school graduate who had his career mapped out. He knew what he wanted to achieve and the time scales in which he would meet his goals. He was thrilled when he was promoted to his dream job as Vice President of Planning and Strategy in a major global corporation. Just as he was about to embark on a tour of the European sites, disaster struck. Oliver started waking up in the night with heart palpitations, breathlessness and cold sweats. His doctor confirmed there was nothing physically wrong with Oliver.

In talking through possible reasons for his condition with his NLP coach, Oliver identified several issues connected with the promotion – he would be away from home for longer periods; he would be living in hotels; and would be spending less time playing sport, something Oliver was passionate about. Oliver and his coach explored each of the layers of objections that were presented and discarded them as superficial reasons for his health issues.

During a state of deep relaxation, Oliver recalled a memory of 'failing' at maths as a young boy. Oliver's teacher and parents had very high expectations for Oliver and he felt he had let them down when he did not meet the stringent exam standards. Oliver realised that, although the promotion gave him the opportunity to work at his dream job, it was very high profile and his unconscious mind was trying to protect him from the humiliation of yet another failure. It did this by creating the physical problems that would ultimately get in the way of Oliver succeeding at his dream job.

By working with his NLP coach, Oliver realised that his parents and teacher had pushed him beyond his level of capability and set him up for failure. Oliver recognised that he had succeeded at his career on the merits of his abilities and he could be an outstanding success. He learned that he could make mistakes and encounter failure and this too was alright as long as he was flexible enough to learn from the setbacks and use the lessons positively to move forward.

In achieving what you want in your career or a project close to your heart, you may hit a brick wall. Find your self a quiet space and some time to explore the ways that you may be creating barriers to your own success.

Help! I'm in Conflict With Myself

Self-sabotage is one of the symptoms you can experience when parts of you are in conflict, where every attempt you make to reach a goal is subverted by one of the parts. Two of the most common methods of self-sabotage you should keep an eye out for are detailed here.

Listening to your unconscious mind

As with any communication, if you understand that self-sabotage is just your unconscious mind's way of trying to communicate with you, you can assist it by examining its positive intention behind the behaviour that is stopping you achieving your goal. You can substitute the self-defeating behaviour with something that is more positive and which satisfies the intent of the unconscious mind. For instance, the smoker who wants to stop but continues smoking because unconsciously he craves the companionship of his friends who smoke, could satisfy his need for friendship by developing a new group of non-smoking friends or by undertaking a new activity which helps him develop a circle of friends with a healthier lifestyle.

Taking sides

Chances are you side with one part or the other, making a judgement that one is bad and suppressing it by sheer force of will. The result is similar to what happens when you squeeze a balloon. If the balloon isn't blown up to capacity, as you squeeze one end the air pushes the balloon out in another direction. If the balloon is filled to capacity, you just get a bang as you squeeze. Similarly, as you suppress a part of you, the suppressed part will show up as an aberrant behaviour, physical symptom (balloon distortion), or a breakdown (the bang).

Fiona suffered so badly from eczema that she kept her body well-covered. In therapy she realised the symptoms were a consequence of having been bullied at school, where all she had ever wanted to do was hide. Now her unconscious mind, in its own unique way, was presenting her with a means to hide.

Becoming Whole: Integrating Your Parts

More parts mean more potential for conflict, therefore the ideal to aspire to is complete wholeness. The *visual squash* and *reframing* are the more common of several techniques for integrating conflicting parts.

Not all parts of the unconscious mind are in conflict with each other. However, you become aware of the ones that are in conflict when you encounter problems like wanting to be healthy and still having a craving for cigarettes, or wanting to be slim but not being able to control binge eating. You can deal with these parts as and when they surface. If there are more than two parts, you can integrate them in pairs.

Visual squash

In principle, this process involves identifying the parts involved in a conflict and discovering their common intention before having the parts integrate.

As you work to integrate your parts, keep these tips in mind:

- ✔ When you are finding out what each part wants, you may get a negative answer. For example, if you want to do more exercise a negative answer might be 'I don't want to spend too much time on exercising'. You want to get to a positive outcome which could be, for example, 'I want to exercise to fit in with my lifestyle'.

- ✔ It is best if you work with a qualified NLP practitioner or with a partner who can record your answers and prompt you with them.

For this exercise to be successful you have to find out what the common intention is for each part before you try and integrate them. It is useful to talk to the parts and have them acknowledge that each part has a positive intention for the other and that their conflict is stopping both parts from achieving their common purpose.

1. **Identify two parts of yourself that may be in conflict.**

   For instance, a part of you wants you to be healthy while another part of you puts up an almighty fight when you want to exercise.

2. **Sit in a quiet place where you are not likely to be disturbed.**

3. **Ask the problem part to come out and stand on one hand.**

   In the example in step 1, this would be the part averse to exercise.

4. **Imagine the part as a person and see what the person looks like, sounds like, and what feelings that person has.**

5. **Ask the non-problem part to come out and stand on the other hand.**

   In the example in step 1, this would be the part that wants to be healthy.

6. **Imagine this part as a person and see what the person looks like, sounds like, and what feelings that person has.**

7. **Starting with the problem part, ask each part, 'What is your positive intention and purpose?' Keep repeating the question until both parts realise that they have the same intention.**

   The part averse to exercise may say things like, 'I get tired', 'it's important to conserve energy' or 'I want to make the world a better place'. In contrast, the part that wants to be healthy may say, 'I like the buzz I get', 'I have more energy', or 'I want to make the world a better place'.

8. **Ask each part what resources it has that the other part would find useful in attaining the common, positive purpose of each.** The part averse to exercise may say things like, 'I have the imagination to design better solutions' or 'I understand the problems people may experience'. Whereas the part that wants to be healthy may say, 'I have the energy to put into changing the world' or 'I have the discipline it takes to make the world a better place'.

9. **Bring both your hands together and fully integrate the parts and their resources, seeing a new you, hearing what that new you may say, and recognising new feelings that you may have.**

10. **Using techniques you learned in Chapter 13, go back to before your conception and travel back along your time line to now, with the new, integrated you, changing your history along your time line.**

Remember your memories are only a construct of your mind. If, in the past, you have chosen to make a decision, such as 'Exercise is tiring', your whole time line is based on this decision. If you then resolve this issue by integrating it with a decision you made to be healthy, you can now change your time line to accommodate the healthy new you.

Reframing – as if

The meaning of an interaction is dependent on the context in which it takes place. So by changing the context – reframing – of an experience, you can change its meaning. For instance if someone criticises you for being too subjective, you can thank them because you know that could mean you are good with people or great at coming up with ideas.

The 'as if' frame is excellent for resolving conflict because it allows you to pretend and therefore explore possibilities that you would otherwise not have thought of. Acting 'as if' you have the resources now, helps to shift any beliefs that may be holding you back.

When you are in conflict, either with yourself or another party, use the following 'as if' frames to help you resolve the problem.

✔ *Time switch* – step six months or a year into the future, look back to now and ask yourself what you did to overcome the problem.

Alan was in a well-paid job in which he was relatively happy. However, his boss had favourites in the department and Alan was getting sidelined. Alan had wanted to work for a large multinational for some time but did not believe his skills were good enough. Alan used the well-formed out-comes process (Chapter 3 – 'Taking Charge of Your Life' and Appendix C) to design his dream job. He then tried the time switch by stepping five years into the future and pretending he had his perfect job. He realised he needed to work for one of his company's competitors and two years later found he was actually in his dream job working for the multinational of his choice.

✔ *Person switch* – pretend you are someone you respect and ask yourself what you would do if you could swap bodies with the other person for a day.

Georgina really admired Amanda Tapping (Major Sam Carter in the tele-vision series *Stargate*). Georgina pretended to swap bodies with Amanda Tapping. She discovered that although her job supporting computer sys-tems paid the mortgage, it did not satisfy her soul. As Amanda Tapping, Georgina discovered that she really wanted to work in films, bringing stories from people's imagination to life. Georgina realises that life in the film world can be risky but has taken the first step by enrolling for a part-time course in scriptwriting.

✔ *Information switch* – suppose you had all the information you needed to get a solution, what would that knowledge be and how would the cir-cumstances change?

Georgina used the *information switch* to break down what she would have to do to live her dream of becoming a scriptwriter. Consequently she started evening classes in scriptwriting, worked weekends for a local college, working with projects for the students. She is now at the stage where she is planning on working part-time for production compa-nies so that she can spend more time following her dream.

✔ *Function switch* – ask your fairy godmother to wave her magic wand and change a component in the system within which you are experiencing a restriction, for example you are not progressing at work or your mar-riage is a little bumpy. What would change and how would this affect the outcome?

Colin worked as an animal nurse in a busy veterinary practice; he loved his job but felt as though something was missing in his life. He asked his fairy godmother for help. Colin's unconscious mind – in this case his fairy godmother – had him recognise that he wanted to do good where he was really needed by people and animals who couldn't afford to attend an expensive veterinary practice. Colin is now working at an animal sanctu-ary in India, still loves what he is doing, and feels completely fulfilled.

Bigger and Better Conflicts

If you've read through this chapter from the beginning, you should have a pretty good idea of *intrapersonal* conflicts (conflict within a person) and how to begin resolving these. What you may like to think about now is how you can extrapolate this model of intrapersonal conflict. You can apply the same principles to relationships and negotiations between two people, within a team, a family or social group, between different companies and organisations, and indeed between larger international entities. Here are some examples of these bigger conflicts:

- ✔ **Interpersonal conflict** – when two or more people have differing needs which cannot be satisfied at the same time.

- ✔ **Intragroup conflict** – between two or more people within the group, for example members of a team or department.

- ✔ **Intergroup conflict** – between two or more groups of people, as in gang warfare or companies battling for market leadership.

- ✔ **International conflict** – where two or more nations are in dispute over their needs.

- ✔ **Global conflict** – where human needs cannot be satisfied, although the people do not belong to a specific group, as in the case of the depletion of fresh water resources.

In all these situations, you can use the process outlined in the exercise below to negotiate a successful outcome.

This exercise is based on the NLP process for integrating conflicting parts, as you can read about in the sections on 'Visual squash' and 'Reframing – as if', elsewhere in this chapter.

1. **Imagine that you are in the role of negotiator to resolve a conflict between different parties.**

2. **Ask each party, 'What is your positive intention?' Keep asking both sides until you uncover some core and fundamental needs that each party can agree they both have. (Please refer to the section on 'Visual squash' elsewhere in this chapter.)**

3. **Ask each party to acknowledge the common ground they share and hold on to it.**

4. **Perhaps using the 'as if' frame, explore alternative solutions to the problem. (Please refer to the section on 'Reframing – as if' elsewhere in this chapter.)**

5. **Decide on the resources each party can bring to the table to help resolve the conflict.**

6. **Always keep the common aim in mind and aim for a win/win outcome.**

And, to paraphrase Einstein, it is more important to have imagination than knowledge because knowledge boxes you into the realm of the known whereas imagination allows you to discover and create new solutions. *So use your imagination for lateral thinking to come up with novel solutions.*

Part V
Words to Entrance

The 5th Wave   By Rich Tennant

SCREW-U

Screws 'n Screwdrivers
CUSTOMER SERVICE

Screw-U! How can
I... Hello? Dang!

Another, hang
up Dave? Just
a tip–next time try
answering with a smile
on your
face.

In this part . . .

This part explores the power of language – sharing with you the secrets of the world's best communicators. You discover that the language you use does not just describe your experience, but also has the power to create it. If you want to know how to use stories to good effect or send an audience into a trance (and not into a deep sleep!), you find out how to do that, too.

We've also added a chapter where we share the most powerful questions you can ask to help you to get straight to the heart of an issue.

Chapter 15

Heart of the Matter: The Meta Model

In This Chapter

▶ Reaching beyond the words people say

▶ Recognising how words can limit you

▶ Finding out about the NLP engine – the Meta Model

▶ Taking lessons from a great communicator

*H*ave you ever invited someone, even yourself, to: 'Say what you mean and mean what you say?' If only speech was so easy.

You use words all the time as important tools to convey your thoughts and ideas – to explain and share your experiences with others. Earlier in this book (in the Communication Wheel illustrated in Chapter 7) we explain that in any face-to-face communication, people take just part of the meaning from the words that come out of your mouth. Your body language – all those movements and gestures – and the tone of your voice transmit the rest.

Words offer just a model, a symbol of your experience; they can never fully describe the whole picture. Think of an iceberg – the tip above the surface is like the words you say. NLP says this is the *surface structure* of our language. Beneath the surface lies the rest of the iceberg – the home of the whole experience. NLP calls this the *deep structure*.

This chapter takes you from the surface structure and leads you into the deep structure so that you can get beyond the vague words of everyday speech to be more specific about what you mean. You'll meet the magic of the Meta Model, one of NLP's most important revelations that clarifies the meaning of what people say. No one gives a complete description of the entire thought process which lies behind their words; if they did, they'd never finish speaking. The Meta Model is a tool for you to get closer access to someone's experience that they code into speech.

It's been a hard day's work

Supper table talk in my (Kate) family often goes like this: 'So, has it been a hard day's work today?' In recounting the highlights of the day, our conversation invariably centres on what constitutes a hard day's work. Does a 12-hour-long stint in a warm, comfortable office surrounded by the latest computers and coffee-making devices qualify?

The question stemmed from watching a TV documentary of motorway maintenance men who work shifting traffic cones in the dead of night. We agreed that this really was hard work by comparison with the reality of a hard day for us as well as most of our friends and co-workers.

What's a hard day for you? In just one sentence, you can conjure up a wealth of different meanings. The qualities of the work experience if you're running a home or an office would be very different by comparison with the physical reality of, say, a firefighter tackling blazes or a builder constructing houses and exposed to the elements in all weathers.

A statement such as 'a hard day's work' will be interpreted in numerous different ways. To get to any one speaker's precise meaning requires access to more information– the facts that have been left out. As you read on in this chapter, you'll see how to gain easy access to relevant information to stop you jumping to the wrong assumptions about somebody else's experience.

Gathering Specific Information with the Meta Model

Richard Bandler and John Grinder, the founders of NLP, discovered that when people speak they naturally adopt three key processes with language, which they labelled as: *deletion*, *generalisation*, and *distortion*. These processes enable us all to explain our experiences in words to others without going into long-winded details and boring everyone to death.

These processes happen all the time in normal everyday encounters. We *delete* information by not giving the whole story. We make *generalisations* by extrapolating from one experience to another, and we *distort* reality by letting our imaginations run wild.

Figure 15-1 demonstrates the NLP model of how you experience the real world through your senses – visual (pictures), auditory (sounds), kinaesthetic (touch and feelings), olfactory (smell), and gustatory (taste). Your perception of reality is filtered or checked against what you already know through the processes of generalisation, distortion, and deletion. This is how you create your personal map or mental model of the real world.

By watching and analysing two different, highly experienced therapists – at work talking to their clients – Bandler and Grinder came up with the NLP Meta Model as a way to explain the link between language and experience.

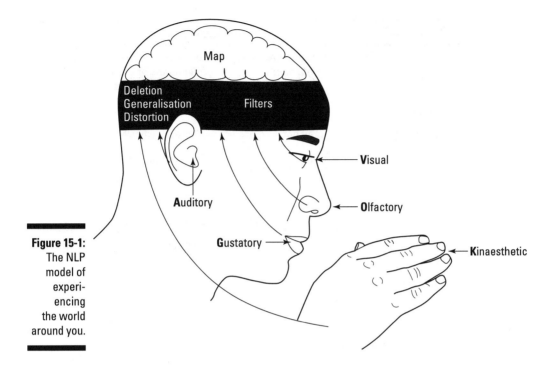

Figure 15-1:
The NLP
model of
experi-
encing
the world
around you.

Bandler and Grinder were interested in finding the rules that determine how humans use language so that others could learn similar skills. They were influenced by their own knowledge of linguistics and the field of *transformational grammar*, and idea that set out ideas on how people describe and record their experiences in language. They published the results in 1975 in *The Structure of Magic*. Although the early work came from the field of psychotherapy – because they wanted to enrich the skills of 'people-helpers' – the models shed light equally well for you and I in ordinary situations where we're simply talking with friends, family, and colleagues.

The Meta Model offers a series of questions that enable you to overcome the deletions, distortions, and generalisations that people make. You'll recognise some of the questions. They'll be questions you naturally ask when you want to clarify meaning. But perhaps you haven't thought about them consciously before. Asked in a gentle way and with rapport, these questions let you gather more information to define a clearer picture of what is really meant.

Table 15-1 summarises some of the different ways in which we can delete, generalise, and distort an experience through the language we adopt. Don't worry about the names of the NLP patterns just yet. It's more important that you begin to tune your ears into what people actually say. As you learn to spot the main Meta Model patterns that you prefer yourself, and that others favour too, you're in a great position to respond appropriately. We offer some suggestions of what to say when you respond to gather the missing information that helps you to be sure of understanding what the other person really means.

Table 15-1	Meta Model Patterns	
NLP Meta Model Patterns	*Examples of the patterns you might hear*	*Questions to help you gather information or expand the other person's viewpoint*
Deletion		
Simple deletion	I've been out	Where specifically have you been?
	Help!	What do you want help with?
Unspecified verbs	She annoyed me	How specifically did she annoy you?
Comparisons	She's better than me	Better at what than you?
Judgements	You are wrong	Who says so and what are the facts?
Nominalisations	Our *relationship* isn't working	How do we not relate to each other?
	Change is easy	Changing what is easy?
Generalisation		
Modal operators of possibility	I *can't* . . . it's not possible	What stops you?
Modal operators of necessity	We *have to* do this . . . we *should, ought to*	What would happen if we didn't?
Universal quantifiers	He *never* thinks about my feelings	Never, ever?
	We *always* do it this way	Every single time? What would happen if we did it differently?
Distortion		
Complex equivalence	With a name like that, he must be popular	How does having this name mean that he is popular?
Mind reading	You're going to love this	How do you know that? Who says?
Cause and effect	His voice makes me angry	How does his voice make you angry?
	I made her feel awful	How exactly did you do that?

Deletion – you're so vague

When you are listening, you naturally ignore many extra sounds, saving you the effort of processing every single word. When you speak, you economise on all the details you could share. This is called deletion because something has been removed. Figure 15-2 shows some everyday examples of deletion.

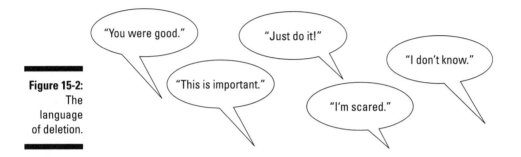

Figure 15-2:
The language of deletion.

Just consider that your central nervous system is being fed some two million pieces of information every second. If every bit of this information had to be processed, imagine the time and energy you would need; an impossible task with full information overload!

To help you operate at peak efficiency, deletion delivers a valuable critical screening mechanism. Selective attention is deletion. Deletions in our language encourage us to fill in the gaps – to imagine – to make it up. If I say to you 'I bought a new car', then you will begin to guess more information. If I don't tell you what new car I've bought, then you will have your own ideas about what make it is, the colour, and age.

The downside of deletion is that it can restrict and limit our thinking and understanding. For example – we can develop the habit of deleting certain information and signals from others. Compliments and criticism are the classic example. Some people are experts at deleting compliments they receive and only noticing the criticism. So, too, they ignore success and only notice failure. If this rings a bell for you, then it's time to break the habit.

To gather deleted information, ask these useful questions:

Who? What? When? Where? How?

What precisely?

What exactly?

Generalisation – beware the always, musts, and shoulds

Watch a young child getting on a two-wheeled bike for the first time. They pay tremendous attention to keeping their balance and steering it. Perhaps they'll need stabilisers for a time until they've mastered the skill. Yet, some weeks or months later, they're competent and don't have to re-learn each time they cycle away – they've generalised from one experience to the next.

Your ability to generalise from past experiences is another important skill that saves huge amounts of time and energy in learning about the world. These generalised experiences are represented by words. Think of the word 'chair'. You know what one is like: you've no doubt sat on many and seen it in different forms. As a child, you learned the word to represent a particular chair. Then you made a generalisation. So the next time you saw a chair, you could name it. Now whenever you see a chair, you understand its function.

The skill of generalisation can also limit our experience of options and differences in other contexts. When you've had a bad experience, then you may expect it to happen time and time again. A man who has experienced a string of unhappy romantic encounters may conclude 'All women are a pain' and decide that he's never going to meet a woman with whom he can live happily.

Romilla and I (Kate) were driving from a meeting on the motorway one afternoon when she ably demonstrated her natural ability to generalise and said: 'Gosh, have you noticed how *everyone's* driving my car?' Surprised, I asked how that could be the case. She pointed out to me that she had seen 15 new Mini Cooper cars in the last ten minutes. This was the car she had fallen in love with and she was deciding whether to buy it. All she could see everywhere were the possible colour combinations of this new car. I hadn't noticed one of them – I wasn't interested in a new car at all – just concentrating on getting through the traffic and out of London.

Think about the generalisations you hear about particular cultures or groups:

> British drink tea.
>
> Americans talk loudly.
>
> Scots are prudent with money.
>
> Italians are wild drivers.
>
> Unmarried mothers are a drain on society.
>
> Politicians can't be trusted.

Such rigid, black-and-white thinking that allows for no grey scale in between creates unhelpful generalisations about other people and situations. Stop and listen to what you say. And when you hear the verbal clues about generalisations in words like 'all', 'never', 'every', 'always' (Figure 15-3 shows several examples of everyday generalisations), then challenge yourself. Is *everyone* like that? Do *all* clients do that? Must we *always* do it this way?

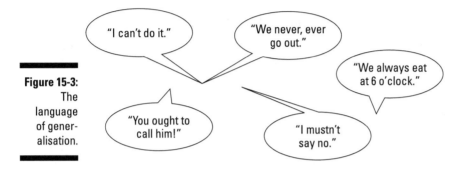

Figure 15-3: The language of generalisation.

"I can't do it."

"We never, ever go out."

"We always eat at 6 o'clock."

"You ought to call him!"

"I mustn't say no."

When you hear someone (or yourself!) generalising, ask these useful questions. They will make you stop and think about whether you are limiting your choices unnecessarily and encourage you to take a broader perspective.

What stops you?

Always? Never? Every?

So what happens if you do . . .?

Just imagine you could, what then?

To begin to explore your own thinking on what is possible and impossible, here's an easy exercise to play with in just ten minutes. Beware – it may change your life forever!

1. **Look at the following and jot down some of the statements you've made (to yourself as well as others) in the last week that start with these words:**

    'I always . . .'

    'I must . . .'

    'I should . . .'

    'I never . . .'

    'I ought to . . .'

    'I have to . . .'

2. Now stop.

3. Go back to your list and for each statement ask yourself three questions:

'What would happen if I didn't . . .?'

'When did I decide this?'

'Is this statement true and helpful for me now?'

4. Review your list in the light of the questions you asked.

5. Create a revised list for yourself that replaces the words 'I always', 'must', 'should never', 'ought to', and 'have to' with the words 'I choose to . . .'

By completing this exercise you are examining some of the types of generalisations that you make (which NLP calls modal operators and universal quantifiers). Then, in step 3, you ask Meta Model questions to explore choices for yourself. By revising the statements in step 5, you put yourself back in control of your own decisions and behaviour.

Distortion – that touch of fantasy

Disraeli was right when he said, 'Imagination governs the world'. Distortion, the process by which you change the meaning of the experience against your own map of reality, is one such example. Figure 15-4 shows some everyday examples of distortion.

The problem with distortion, though, is that most people don't realise that the distortion doesn't necessarily represent the truth. Instead, it just represents their own perception. For example, have you ever come out of a meeting with a group of people and all had a different understanding of what happened? Or been to the cinema or theatre with a group of friends and come away with a completely different viewpoint about the message it conveyed when you chat to your friends about it? Distortion happens when you take one aspect of an experience and change it according to what is happening for you.

Creativity relies on the ability to distort reality in a way that makes new and interesting connections. Science fiction and cartoon strips distort in order to entertain as does art, poetry, and literature. A visit to the cinema or theatre, or reading a novel leaves you free to make your own meaning and connections. Distortion supports your ability to explore your own inner world, your dreams, and lets your imagination run wild.

Abstract nouns and the wheelbarrow test

What we really like about the Meta Model is the way it helps you clarify vague statements. If you say to me 'Love is so painful', I would need more information from you to understand what was going on for you.

Abstract nouns – ones such as love, trust, honesty, relationship, change, fear, pain, obligation, responsibility, impression – are particularly hard to respond to. NLP calls these *nominalisations*. These are words where a verb (to *love*) has turned into a noun (*love*) which is hard to define in a way that everyone would agree on. In order to extract more meaning from your statement, I need to turn the noun back into a verb to help get

more information and then reply. My response to your statement above would be: 'How specifically is the way you love someone so painful?'

Imagine a wheelbarrow. If you think of a noun and can picture it inside the wheelbarrow, then it will be a concrete noun – a person, a flowerpot, an apple, a desk are all concrete examples. Nominalisations are the nouns that don't pass the wheelbarrow test. You can't put love, fear, a relationship, or pain in your wheelbarrow! Instead, when you rephrase these words as verbs, you put the action and responsibility back in them, which helps people explore more choices.

At the same time, it can be unhelpful to be mind-readers. Mind reading is a further example of distortion. You can never know what someone else is truly thinking, even though they give out interesting clues. When negative distortion is combined with generalisation it can become quite debilitating. An example of this is a child who comes home from school and says: 'Everyone stares at me every time I walk into the classroom and they all think I'm stupid.'

Beware making judgements about what other people think until you have actually gathered specific information and reviewed the facts.

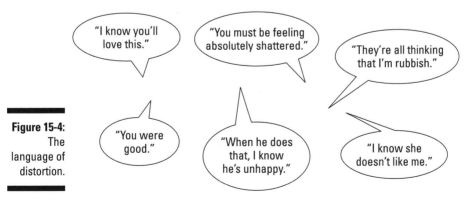

Figure 15-4:
The language of distortion.

Tennis anyone?

There will be times when people want something so badly, that they will believe it to be true even when the evidence is against them. As a tennis coach, John Woodward finds that the most frustrating people in the junior tennis leagues are the competitive parents.

'They so desperately want their children to win that they become blind to the facts of the game. They see what they want to see, even if it's not true, to the extent that as they watch their children play matches, they'll give faulty line calls in favour of their own budding tennis star.

Grandparents are even worse! I once saw a grandfather attack his grandson's tennis opponent with his umbrella because he was convinced that his grandson had won a shot that everybody else saw as out.'

Reproduced with the permission of John Woodward.

Here are some other useful questions to ask when you want to check for distorted meanings:

'Who says?'

'How do you know?'

'How exactly does x lead to y?'

Using the Meta Model

The Meta Model questions give you powerful verbal tools in business, in coaching, education, therapy, and in life. They let you use language to gain clarity and get closer to somebody's experience. You may want to adopt the Meta Model when you want to:

- ✔ **Get more information** to understand the objectives and scope of a new project.

- ✔ **Clarify the other person's meaning** to find out exactly what the other person has in mind. Are you both on the same wavelength or making assumptions that you really understand?

- ✔ **Spot your own and other people's limitations** to work through beliefs and habitual behaviour that can be unhelpful.

- ✔ **Open up more choices** to explore different ways of doing things for yourself and for others.

Two simple steps

When you use the Meta Model, challenge distortions first, then generalisations, and then deletions. If you begin with deletions, you may get more information than you can handle.

To use the Meta Model, follow these simple steps:

1. Listen to the words and spot the pattern (distortion, generalisation, or deletion).

   Refer to the section 'Gathering Specific Information with the Meta Model' earlier in this chapter for an explanation of the language clues that will help you recognise which pattern is being used.

2. Intervene with the right question.

   For distortion, ask:

   - 'How do you know?'
   - 'What's the evidence?'

   For generalisation, ask:

   'Is that always the case? Every time? Never?'

   'What if . . .?'

   For deletion, ask

   'Tell me more . . .'

   'What, when, where, who, how?'

A couple of caveats

There's a way of asking questions that is considerate and valuable. There's another way that sounds like interrogation by the Spanish Inquisition. So here are some points to remember, *please*. We don't want you falling out with your best friend.

- Rapport always comes first. Without rapport, nobody will listen to you. For information on rapport building, head to Chapter 7.

- People need to trust before they're ready to open up on difficult issues. Pace their timing. You can find information on pacing and leading people in Chapter 7, too.

✔ Make sure you are clear about what you are trying to achieve – your outcome – as you ask questions, otherwise you will get overloaded with irrelevant information and you are not being helpful.

✔ Soften your voice and be sensitive in your questioning. Feed the questions gently into conversations and meetings rather than firing them like a market researcher in the street.

✔ Try the Meta Model out on yourself before you rush off to sort out your family and friends uninvited. Go steady. Like Tom in the following example, they may wonder what's happening and not thank you for your new-found interest.

On Friday nights Andrew winds down after a busy week working in the City with a beer at his favourite pub in the picturesque village where he lives. After taking an NLP training course, he was enthusiastic to try out the Meta Model. His drinking partner, Tom, an architect, talked about the week he'd had, and especially about a major argument he had had with a colleague over an important project.

As Tom began his tale with 'I'll never work with him again,' Andrew questioned the generalisation with: 'What never? Are you sure? What would happen if you did?'

Tom looked puzzled and responded with: 'Our partnership isn't going to work; communication has just broken down.'

Delighted to spot not one but two nominalisations in one sentence, Andrew jumped in with: 'How would you like to be a partner with this guy? And how might you be able to communicate?'

To which, Tom looked aghast and said: 'Look, you're normally on my side. What's going on?'

In his keenness to try out NLP, he'd forgotten to match and pace his friend and ease in gently with some subtle use of the Meta Model. All Tom really wanted that night was to have a good moan to a friend who would listen and sympathise.

Chapter 16

Hypnotising Your Audience

In This Chapter

▶ Discovering your everyday trances

▶ Adopting the art of 'artfully vague' language to good effect

▶ Enlisting the help of your unconscious mind

Scenario one. You are driving along the road on an ordinary kind of day. It's a familiar stretch of road, one you've travelled on dozens of times. You know where you are going. You reach your destination, stop the car, and notice that you have no clear recollection of travelling the last few miles.

Scenario two. You are sitting in a group of people. Perhaps it's a meeting. Maybe it's a lesson of some kind. You wake with a start when someone turns to you and asks you a question: 'What are your thoughts on this?' Oh dear. Your attention has wandered. You really haven't a clue what the discussion is all about.

So what is happening here? You are in an everyday trance. It's as if your brain is operating like a computer in safe mode. You're daydreaming, an excellent example of the ability you have to delete the details of what is happening around you and sink into the relaxation pattern of the trance. Scenes like this happen the world over, every moment of the day.

In this chapter, we'll dip our toes into the world of trance and talk about how to turn it to your advantage and other people's benefit, too. Specifically, we'll look further at the language patterns you can choose to adopt to communicate even more effectively with other people by getting through to the unconscious part of their mind.

Milton H Erickson – the Master at Work

As a compelling teacher and therapist, Milton H Erickson (1901–80) inspired and enchanted those who came to learn from him or to be healed. His mastery of therapeutic skills brought positive results for many people and led him to be named as the most influential hypnotherapist of our time.

He had a profound effect on John Grinder and Richard Bandler, the founders of NLP. They modelled Erickson in 1974 and then published several books which demonstrated the language patterns they had noted. These form the basis of the Milton Model in NLP – that deliberately adopts language where the meaning is vague – as opposed to the Meta Model, explained in Chapter 15, which aims to elicit more specific information.

What Erickson excelled at was his ability to induce trance in his patients and effect real change that healed people. He *paced* people's reality, patiently describing what they must be experiencing before introducing suggestions and *leading* them to new thinking. His therapeutic style was much more 'permissive' than earlier hypnotherapists. And by this we mean that he adopted a flexible approach that worked with the client's map of the world – always respecting their reality and using it as the starting point for his work. He gently took clients into a trance by making general comments rather than saying: 'You will go into a trance now.' He believed that the client had the resources he or she needed and saw his role as the therapist to help the client to access them.

Language of Trance – The Milton Model

As humans, we have an amazing capacity to make sense of what people say – even when it's utter gobbledygook. There are times when it is valuable to be artfully vague – non-specific in the content of what you say to enable the other person to fill the gaps for themselves. When language construction is artfully vague, people can take what they need from your words in a way that is most appropriate for them.

The *Milton Model* is a set of language patterns that you can use to take somebody into a trance state, an altered state of consciousness, in which they are able to access unconscious resources, make changes, and solve their own problems. The Milton Model is named after Milton H Erickson, a man considered the most influential hypnotherapist of our time; you can read more about him and his technique in the sidebar 'Milton H Erickson – the Master at Work'.

The Milton Model uses all the same patterns that the Meta Model uses, except in reverse (head to Chapter 15 for details on the Meta Model). The Milton Model 'chunks up', deliberately adopting vague language that can be interpreted widely. While the Meta Model aims to gather more information, the Milton Model aims to rise above the detail. Table 16-1 outlines the differences between these two models.

Table 16-1	Meta vs Milton
Milton Model	*Meta Model*
Makes language more general	Makes language more specific
Moves from surface structure to deep structure	Moves from deep structure to surface structure
Looks for general understanding	Looks for precise examples
Aims to access unconscious resources	Aims to bring experience to conscious awareness
Keeps client internally focused	Keeps client externally focused

Language patterns and the Milton Model

In Table 16-2, we've highlighted some of the key language patterns of the Milton Model. Just as in the Meta Model, Bandler and Grinder's earlier explanation of language, the Milton Model identifies three key types of pattern. You'll see the same deletions, generalisations, and distortions that happen in normal speech (which are explained in full in Chapter 15). These are the ways in which we make sense of our everyday experiences and transform them into language.

You may notice from the comparison of the two models in Table 16-1 that the Milton Model makes statements that are deliberately very general in nature. The effect of this is to relax the person you're speaking to, while the Meta Model asks questions to gain specific details missing from general statements.

Table 16-2	NLP Milton Model Patterns
Patterns	*Examples of the vague language you might use to challenge deletions, generalisations, and distortions and to take a person into a receptive state*
Deletion	
Simple deletion	You are ready to listen
Unspecified verbs	As you make sense of this in your own time . . .
Unspecified referential index	There will be people who have been important to you

(continued)

Table 16-2 *(continued)*

Patterns	*Examples of the vague language you might use to challenge deletions, generalisations, and distortions and to take a person into a receptive state*
Comparisons	You are feeling more and more curious
Judgements	Remember that you have been through some tough times and survived them well
Nominalisations	You are gaining new insights, building new friendships
Generalisation	
Modal operators of possibility	You can become more successful . . . you are able to discover new ways
Modal operators of necessity	You must take this forward to where it has to go
Universal quantifiers	Every time you feel like this
	All the skills you need are easy for you to learn
Distortion	
Complex equivalence	This means that you are getting all the help you need
Mind reading	I know that you are becoming more interested
Cause and effect	On each breath, you can relax even more

Other aspects of the Milton Model

Erickson used a number of other linguistic devices to assist in communication with his clients. Here are a few.

Tag questions

A tag question is added to the end of a statement to invite agreement. Tag questions are a deliberate and very effective device that distracts the recipient's conscious mind with something they can agree with. The effect is the statement in front of the tag question goes directly to the unconscious mind and is acted upon:

This is easy, isn't it?

Your health is important, you know?

You can, can you not?

It's time to relax, don't you know?

 Even if you have never read or learned anything more about hypnosis, let us give you two of the most powerful words in the English language, which are also examples of tag questions. And they are: *That's right*. Don't take our word for it; just try them out.

Embedded commands

Embedded commands or questions are sentences that are constructed with the outcome Erickson wanted from the client stated in it, as with the italicised parts of the following sentences. The purpose of the embedded command is to send directions straight to the unconscious mind, with the conscious mind blocking it. Erickson's tone of voice would mark the commands out from the rest of the sentence. For example, by deepening his voice for the command element.

'I'm curious about whether *you will learn to relax and let yourself be comfortable* in a few moments.'

'What is interesting is *when did you last learn so easily?*'

Double binds

Double binds give people a choice, but limit it. You have covered the options and assumed the result you want will happen.

'When will you clean up your clutter, before you've had lunch or after?' (A typical one to use with messy teenagers or housemates!)

'Would you like to order it in blue or in green?' (How about this one in a sales situation?)

 As you adopt lessons from communicators like Erickson, do remember that what you say is important, yet the way you are with people will have the most effect.

 To help you understand the differences between the Milton Model and the Meta Model, do this little role-playing exercise. You'll need a willing friend. One of you will be the salesperson and the other the customer.

The tale is in the telling

Part of Erickson's therapy was to create stories – teaching tales – which helped people to make sense of their situations in new ways. Erickson was himself confined to a wheelchair, yet carried out an extensive therapeutic practice, travelled widely, taught and gave seminars right to the end of his life.

Vast libraries of transcripts of Erickson's tales and seminars are also available, which make fascinating reading. Yet, those fortunate enough to have met Erickson in person would point out that the written word conveys just part of the man's magical touch. If you think back to the communication equation we talked about in Chapter 7, 'Creating Rapport', you may remember that words play only a small part in any communication – something like 7 per cent of the effect. Erickson's smiles, gestures, the tone of his voice, his instinctive respect for and curiosity about his clients will be the missing ingredient in the written stories.

✔ **The salesperson** – Imagine you are a salesperson and your task is to sell an object or service to your partner. Your job is to persuade them to buy *without giving them any details of what you are really selling* – see how interested you can get your partner while you remain artfully vague in the style of the Milton Model.

✔ **The customer** – Imagine you are a customer and your job is to *get more specific information out of the salesperson* who is trying to sell to you. Challenge their vagueness, using tips from Chapter 15 in the Meta Model patterns to elicit detail from their generalised talk.

Afterwards, ask yourself which role felt most natural to you? Do you prefer to see and discuss the sweeping big picture or do you really feel more comfortable when you talk about detail?

The art of vagueness and why it's important

As you gain familiarity with the Milton Model, you can do what others before you have done: start to notice some of the language you hear as you listen to everyone you meet. You'll notice that most people have mastered the ability to communicate at a general level. In other words, most people have mastered the art of vagueness, which allows you to go inside so easily, does it not?

It's everywhere! Just consider these statements:

'We can work it out.'

'Things can only get better.'

'It doesn't have to be like this.'

'Someday, we'll all be free.'

'Everyone has got their problems.'

Sound familiar? Words like these are equally at home on the lips of politicians and pop stars, clairvoyants and copywriters. You hear them on the radio every morning and they pop out from the newspaper in your daily horoscope and the advertising pages for the latest 'must-have' products. They send you into a relaxed state. You cannot help but agree with highly generalised statements.

Good reasons to be vague

The power of vague language lies in the fact that you get people into a different state. It distracts people from the outside world. Then it's easier to connect with everybody in a group of people or get rapport with someone you do not know well. When you are vague:

- ✔ Your listeners find their own answers which will be more powerful and long lasting for them.

- ✔ You do not instil your own ideas or put inappropriate suggestions in the way.

- ✔ Your clients feel more in control because they are free to explore different possibilities that you could never have thought of.

In addition, being vague opens up your map, too. Remember that the language you adopt affects you too – not just other people. So often people impose their own limits by the way in which they talk about themselves – those naughty 'thought viruses' like 'I'm not good enough' or 'I'll never be able to do that' jump out and block our route to success. The Milton Model can help you to:

- ✔ Discover more empowering ways of acting

- ✔ Arouse your natural curiosity

- ✔ Think more clearly

- ✔ Find times when you were at your best and take you back into that resourceful state

NLP has adopted the idea of *chunking* from the world of IT; it simply means breaking things into bits. The NLP concept illustrated in Figure 16-1 is that for you to process information it needs to be in chunks of the right size – tiny details or the bigger picture – whatever is appropriate for the person you are speaking to. From what you can read in Chapter 15 on the Meta Model, this chapter, and in Chapter 17 on telling stories, you'll notice we're exploring the different ways in which giving people information at the right level of detail, or chunk size, aids communication.

The Milton Model is a style of communication that moves upwards and focuses ideas at a highly general level; the Meta Model has a downward direction concentrating on very specific details. When you use stories and metaphors, you are simply moving across sideways – chunking laterally – to match the same level of detail but using stories and metaphors to help people make new connections.

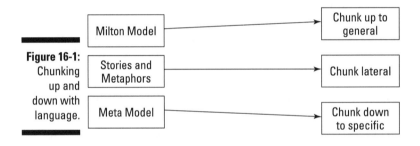

Figure 16-1: Chunking up and down with language.

You Are Going Deeper

Hypnosis has existed since the eighteenth century – its original founder is usually accepted as Franz Anton Mesmer. Hypnosis – or trance – is a natural state of focused attention, hence the word *mesmerised* when you are *entranced*. This is a state in which your main focus is on your internal thoughts and feelings rather than the external world around you.

Thanks to the more recent influence of Erickson, NLP views hypnosis and everyday trance as a safe and valuable route to your unconscious, or 'other than conscious', signifying simply those thoughts, feelings, and experiences which we do not currently have awareness about.

Erickson said that his patients were his patients because they were out of rapport with the unconscious mind, suggesting that mental health involves rapport between the two. His style of hypnosis enlists the help of the unconscious mind to facilitate change in patterns of thinking and behaviour. It works by a therapist talking to somebody in such a way that they 'go inwards'. In this altered or dream-like state, the mind is relaxed. Once the unconscious mind becomes more available, the therapist helps someone to make changes whether it's to give up smoking, let go of a phobia or fear, or make other positive changes to improve their health and well-being.

We've said several times throughout this book that the conscious mind can only cope with 7±2 chunks of information at one time. The real change work takes place at an unconscious level. The Milton Model allows change by pacing the person's reality, and by that we mean truly acknowledging and respecting the qualities of somebody else's experiences which are likely to be different to your own. The Model distracts the conscious mind and lets a person access their unconscious mind.

Some people go deep into this experience. Others are not as deep. Your brain will be less active; muscle movement, blinking rate, and swallowing reflexes all slow down.

Getting comfortable with the idea of hypnosis

Words are powerful – they conjure up all kinds of memories and sensations. They stir our imaginations into action. If we were to say one word to you, *hypnosis*, what does your mind's eye conjure up? If we asked you to let us hypnotise you, would you ponder the question for a second and answer 'Fine'. What sticks in your mind?

If you've ever experienced hypnosis, you'll remember it as a pleasant and relaxing state of being. If you haven't, you may be curious or even downright terrified. 'Don't start fiddling with my mind,' we hear you say!

Some stage hypnotists have given hypnosis a bad name by encouraging people to perform all kinds of embarrassing acts and making us fearful about the great control of a hypnotist over his subjects' minds. Therefore, it's little wonder that many people are sceptical when it comes to hypnosis.

If this is the case for you, perhaps you'd appreciate another way of looking at it. Simply think about hypnosis as a dream-like state in which the possibility of change becomes more available. The *Collins English Dictionary* defines hypnosis as: 'An artificially induced state of relaxation and concentration in which deeper parts of the mind become more accessible.'

When hard switches to easy

Registered hypnotherapist, Tom McGuire, of Seven Colours Limited, applies the Milton language patterns to diverse applications – from learning to release anxiety to breaking habits, controlling pain, and enhancing performance in sport or public speaking.

'At times we may wrestle with problems using all our conscious resources and yet find ourselves unable to reach a satisfactory solution,' Tom says. He cites the example of weight management: 'I acknowledge the fact that the client has tried really hard in the past to lose weight. I make a point of using the word "hard" and associating that with the methods they have used in the past. I then go on to explain that using the unconscious mind is an easy way to get the results, and they begin to activate images in their own mind about how they will feel and look.'

'The Milton approach is to assume that their unconscious mind already knows how to lose the weight. We enlist the help of the unconscious mind to achieve it. No need to force it to help. Because we do not go into detail about how it will be possible, the patient becomes curious. This curiosity provides the fuel to drive the unconscious.'

'Many clients have told me that they have found themselves putting food back onto the supermarket shelf when shopping, only realising after they have done it. Sometimes they tell me that they haven't felt hungry and so forgot about food altogether between meals. The thought of food sometimes drifts into their mind but then drifts out again. No fighting, just curiosity. To me, this flexible, indirect approach embodies the Milton Model and shows the utmost respect for the client.'

Reproduced with the permission of Tom McGuire.

Yet the truth is hypnosis works only if you allow it to. Only you have the power to control your thoughts, actions, and words. And here's why. The unconscious mind is a friend, not a foe. As we explain in Chapter 2, one of the NLP presuppositions is 'The unconscious mind is benevolent'. In other words, NLP presupposes that the unconscious is there looking after you. (Freud, by comparison, treated the unconscious as something to be feared, working against you, as the home of all your repressed drives that are outside of your control.)

Contrary to popular myth, under hypnosis people are in complete control of their situation. The hypnotherapist acts merely as a facilitator and the client will reject any suggestion that they do not consider appropriate.

Everyday trances

Throughout the day you move through a series of experiences which are trance-like. You naturally go in and out several times a minute. What a fantastic protection mechanism we humans have to cope with the overload of information!

There's an upside – your trance lets you meditate, plan, rest, and relax. Day-dreaming lets you open your mind to new ideas. It also enhances your natural creativity – this is when you make new connections between ideas and solve problems for yourself.

The downside comes when you replay anxieties, and are not reacting to the external world. It may be that you need a break or some outside help if this is happening to you. Therapy helps people break negative trances. Often hypnosis work is about bringing people out of a trance and back to reality.

What do you do to truly relax? To get yourself into that lovely, easy state where all is well with the world? Ask the same question of any number of friends, family, and colleagues and you'll get quite different suggestions. Relaxation is a light everyday trance that gives you some down time to balance out the highs.

Here's a simple way that you can induce a trance in yourself and others: just get with a group of people. Spend 20 minutes telling each other of all the things you do to relax. Talk them through gently and decide what appeals.

Groupthink

Have you ever noticed how group reactions to an event are bigger and more powerful than the sum of the individual parts? Perhaps you've been to a rock concert, religious gathering, the big match, or been caught in a serious airport delay. People have the ability to get into a group trance of mass hysteria – for better or for worse, like the whirling dervishes.

Groupthink is a term coined by Irving Janis to characterise situations where people are carried along by group illusions and perceptions. As a Yale social psychologist, he was fascinated with the question of how groups of experts, especially in the White House, could make such terrible decisions.

One of the most famous examples is found in the abortive invasion of Cuba at the Bay of Pigs by 1,200 anti-Castro exiles. Launched on April 17, 1961, by the Kennedy administration, it almost led to war. 'How could we have been so stupid?'

President Kennedy later remarked. In retrospect, the plan looked completely misguided. Yet at the time it had never seriously been questioned or challenged. Kennedy and his advisors had unwittingly developed shared illusions that stopped them thinking critically and engaging with reality.

When overcome by 'groupthink', chief executives or their advisors are not stupid, lazy, or evil was Janis's belief. Rather, he saw them as victims of 'a mode of thinking that people engage in when they are deeply involved in a cohesive in-group, when the members' strivings for unanimity override their motivation to realistically appraise alternative courses of action'.

When people operate in a groupthink mode, they automatically apply the 'let's preserve group harmony at all cost' test to every decision they face. Another everyday trance you may recognise.

Our challenge to you is to ask yourself: 'Am I spending time relaxing and allowing myself to daydream?' Build relaxation time into your diary each day and each week as a vital life-giving tonic. Become aware of your own trances and make a choice not to get drawn into the ones that are negative.

When I (Kate) asked a young friend, a teenager with a strong auditory prefer- ence and an 'away from' metaprogram (you can read more about metapro- grams in Chapter 8), what he most likes to do to relax, this was his response: 'Just find a good book and escape to somewhere pleasant and private. It's great when you're annoyed about something, because you're distracted by what you read, you get involved with the characters, and then you forget what you're angry about.' A mere two hours later that evening, I had come away from a late phone call feeling tense, having absorbed some strong nega- tive 'vibes' from an anxious client and I knew that I would not be able to sleep until I was fully relaxed. I took my young friend's advice, picked up a new novel, sank into the sofa and became so engrossed that I very quickly left all the angst behind me – and a good night's sleep followed. Sometimes the sim- plest solutions really are the best.

There's real truth in the advice that when you have a problem 'sleep on it' and a course of action will present itself in the morning. Once the conscious mind is allowed to rest, the unconscious mind is given the opportunity to process or retrieve information, and then the brain can really get to work in a positive way. When you are struggling with an issue, as you go to bed, ask your unconscious mind to help you find the answer and notice what comes to you in the morning when you wake.

When you're stuck, hypnosis simply accelerates the solution to get the help you need.

Chapter 17

Stories, Fables, and Metaphors: Telling Tales to Reach the Subconscious

In This Chapter

▶ Re-discovering your skills of storytelling

▶ Speaking so people remember your message

▶ Entertaining as you inform and influence

▶ Helping people solve their own problems

*T*here's a story about Nan-in, a Japanese master in the Meiji era, who received a university professor who came to inquire about Zen. Nan-in poured tea. He filled up his visitor's cup, and then kept on pouring. The professor watched until he could no longer restrain himself.

'It is overfull. No more will go in,' said the professor.

'Like this cup,' Nan-in said, 'you are full of your own opinions and speculations. How can I show you Zen unless you first empty your cup?'

What was happening for you as you read those words? What came into your head? Your response to this little story is unique to you. In the same way, if you were to ask a group of people for their reactions to a story you'll get totally different ones. Stories get to the parts that other words don't reach. They speak to you at an unconscious level.

Through stories you can get your message across in a way that is much more effective than any logical argument. They connect to people's experiences, to their memories and their emotions. In NLP terms, stories help build rapport. They enable you to convey information indirectly, to pace someone's current reality and then lead them on to a new one. To move away from problems to different outcomes. To open up new possibilities. So when you are sitting comfortably, let us begin . . .

Stories, Metaphors, and You

Your brain is a natural pattern-matching machine (in Chapter 4 you'll find more details on what goes on inside your mind) and all the time you are matching and sorting. When you hear something new you go: 'Aha. This is like *this*. This reminds me of *that*.' Brains naturally recognise patterns. Stories and metaphors transport you to a different place and put you into a trance – a deeply relaxed state in which you are very resourceful and your brain naturally recognises patterns.

NLP defines metaphors broadly in terms of stories or figures of speech that imply a comparison. The reason NLP suggests that stories and metaphors work as valuable communication tools is because they distract the conscious mind and overload it with processing. Meanwhile the unconscious mind steps in to come up with creative solutions and the resources you need. Thus you're able to make new meanings and solve the problems.

The Stories of Your Life

We live in a world of stories. And you too are an accomplished storyteller. Don't believe us? Consider this. When you recount the day's events to a friend or partner, you are telling a story. When you gossip on the telephone to your mates, or describe a business process to a client, you are telling a story. Events don't have to be make-believe to qualify as a story.

Storytelling basics

Good stories, whether they relate actual or imaginary events, have four key ingredients. Think about a child's fairy story handed down through generations such as *The Wizard of Oz*, *Little Red Riding Hood*, or *Cinderella* and see if you can recognise these elements:

- ✔ The characters – you need a hero, plus goodies and baddies along the way.
- ✔ The plot – the storyline of the journey that the hero takes.
- ✔ A conflict – the challenge that the hero takes up or difficulty they face.
- ✔ A resolution – the result or outcome that happens at the end of the tale (and hopefully it doesn't end in tears!).

Stories engage the left side of the brain to process the words and the sequence of the plots and the right side in terms of imagination, visualisation, and creativity.

The travelling storyteller

Throughout history, people have told stories, myths, and legends and used metaphors to communicate a message. The oral tradition preceded the written word and multi-media as a critical form of communication. Storytellers were typically travellers who would move from town to town, passing on important information by word-of-mouth. Without the luxury of email and PowerPoint, they used rhythm, rhyme, and visualisation to aid memory. The more fantastic and outrageous the story, the more you are likely to remember it.

Some stories are told solely to entertain, but you can use stories for a number of purposes:

✔ To focus concentration

✔ To illustrate a point

✔ To teach a lesson that people remember

✔ To sow new ideas

✔ To get people to recognise their own problems

✔ To make a complex idea simpler

✔ To change people's mood

✔ To challenge behaviour

✔ To have fun

Storytelling at work

Stories and metaphors work in business communication just as well as a social or religious context. We learn from others' experiences and take meaning from metaphors. Companies tell stories to:

✔ Communicate information

✔ Convey values of the organisation

✔ Educate people

✔ Give the listener the benefit of their wisdom

✔ Help teams to evaluate choices and make decisions

Stories engage people more fully. This is why customer examples, testimonials, and case studies work so well to reinforce a business message. They're so much more powerful than a pure product promotion.

In many companies, stories develop about the history of the birth of the company which keep people in touch with the fundamental values. During our early days working in Hewlett-Packard, everyone connected with the story of Bill Hewlett and Dave Packard's start-up in the Californian garage, the struggles for survival on the way to success in Palo Alto, and their continual dedication to the core principles that were written down and told to every one of the 100,000 employees as *The HP Way*. Corporate tales such as these engage people and align them to a common sense of purpose. They help to retain the same sense of teamwork and unity of a smaller business even as an organisation grows into a corporate giant. In Hewlett-Packard, employees respected the founders because they could identify with two fellow human beings who became renowned corporate leaders thanks to their skills, grit, and determination. They felt that Bill and Dave continued to value people as well as business performance in a way that was outstanding in the 'hire and fire' world of business culture.

We also remember ex-CEO Lew Platt speaking at an HP Women's Conference and telling the story of bringing up his children as a single parent after his wife had died. He talked about the worry of getting a phone call telling him his child was sick just as he was going into an important business negotiation. Lew knew how to connect to the heart of an audience by speaking from his own experience.

Storytelling is not a skill to confine to business leaders. At work, you can begin to develop your own stories as a tool for getting your message across to colleagues and clients as well as to your bosses. Business stories shouldn't be long-winded or amazingly elaborate. You might begin by noting some of your successes or interesting experiences and building them into a relevant anecdote to pull out of the bag at the appropriate moment.

Stories from your own experience can dramatically enliven an explanation of a dry subject like customer service, quality control, software programs, or safety procedures.

In a similar vein, if you want to influence a customer to buy your product or make the right decision, they are more likely to listen to you as you tell them how another customer solved a similar problem. This less 'in your face' approach can be more effective than putting forward a direct opinion on what you'd like them to do.

Follow your dream

Sahar Hashemi, co-founder of Coffee Republic, the UK chain of coffee shops, tells her own story of the ups and downs of building a £30 million enterprise from nothing. She talks passionately about giving up her highly-paid yet soul-destroying job as an international lawyer to follow a dream.

'When you do a job you hate, you lose optimism. When you start doing something you love, you tap into parts of yourself you never knew you had. I had a dream of who I was and what I did to be the same thing.'

Falling in love with an idea turned her into an entrepreneur. Her mission was to bring the skinny latte coffee and fat-free muffins she'd enjoyed in New York to the streets of London. And she stresses the importance of being clueless, which makes you think outside the box. Even though she set up the business with her brother, Bobby, an ex-merchant banker, they faced rejection from 19 banks before they found a bank willing to loan money on the back of their business plan.

Encouraging others who are keen to follow in her footsteps she suggests three essential tools: the first is sheer hard work; the second is a system to cope with failure – always expect nine 'nos' before you get a 'yes'; and the third is persistence – this kept her going when she had few customers for the first six months of trading.

So, too, if you want to positively manage your career progression, don't wait until your annual performance review for your boss to hear how you're doing. As some of our more successful clients have learnt, a few stories that demonstrate achievements fed into conversations as a weekly diet over lunch or coffee can be much more effective.

A gift to the next generation

The storytelling tradition forms part of our rich heritage to connect past, present, and future generations. We have Greek myths, Arthurian legends, Aesop's Fables through to modern writers. The stories you tell about your life (or hear about the lives of others in your family) perform the same function – they connect generations, as well.

What are the stories you love to hear and to tell about your life? Perhaps you've heard family stories about when you were born, your first day at school, the important events and people in your early life. Truth can be stranger and more entertaining than fiction. And the tales get told and retold, each time with fresh embellishment.

Family tales that get handed down the line by word of mouth get lost as families split and generations pass away. I (Kate) have a neighbour, Margaret, whose retirement hobby of tracing her family ancestors reaches further than drawing the family tree. Her more permanent legacy to her family is a fascinating bound collection of stories. Alongside the tree, she collected anecdotes from all living members of the family. She published them for the family and later generations to enjoy and understand more about their heritage. If you were to do the same, what stories would you like to record for posterity?

Here's a game of family anecdotes. Write out five cards with one of the following words on: farce, thriller, comedy, tragedy, TV soap. Take a card, think of a family anecdote and tell the story in the style that's written on the card.

Powerful Metaphors

Just as people tell stories all day, your ordinary conversations will be richly embroidered with metaphors. Consider these examples:

> 'Look, it's a jungle out there!'

> 'He was putty in their hands.'

> 'She's a pain in the neck.'

> 'He's a breath of fresh air.'

> 'We could have cut the atmosphere with a knife.'

Some would say that, while a picture is worth a thousand words, a metaphor is worth one thousand pictures.

Metaphors in NLP

The word metaphor is derived from the Greek, and literally means 'to carry across'. A metaphor makes a comparison, a parallel between two sometimes unrelated terms. It can be a powerful and innovative way of describing a situation; it can help the listener to reflect on himself or herself; or see a difficult situation in a new light, providing a novel way of resolving it.

In NLP, metaphors are used in a broader sense than that defined in English grammar – they are used to help people move across from one context to another. NLP calls this movement *chunking sideways*. As explained in Chapter 15, chunking is about moving up and down levels of detail (up to the big picture or down to specifics) in order to communicate with somebody at the most appropriate level.

As Nick Owen describes in his book *The Magic of Metaphor* (Crown House Publishing, 2001, reproduced with permission): 'Metaphors are not simply poetic or rhetorical embellishments, but powerful devices for shaping perception and experience.'

In my (Kate) Watercress training business, I help people to build their presentations. On a particular workshop, Janet, one of the delegates, was looking at creative ways to liven up a presentation to a group of teenage children. As a careers advisor, Janet's work takes her into schools where she needs to inspire groups with all the options of apprenticeship schemes. At first, she stood up and explained the choices open to the kids in the hope they'd listen because of her strong enthusiasm and in-depth knowledge. Later, as she thought about ways of refining her presentation with stories and metaphors, Janet hit on the idea of using the metaphor of a mobile phone – something that all the kids could identify with. She compared all the various career routes and choices with the sophisticated functions of the latest phone model. In this way, she bridged the gap from the advisor to the student and found a way to develop a more compelling talk. Thanks to the appealing metaphor, she discovered a fresh approach to enliven her story and inspire the kids.

To practice creating metaphors and have a little fun at the same time, try this exercise. You need three people: Person A has a subject (like writing a book, for example) that they'd like to communicate in a different way. Follow these steps:

1. **Person A says: '<Topic> is like . . .'**

   Using the book writing example, Person A would actually say, 'Writing a book is like . . .'

2. **Person B thinks of an object . . . any object at all to complete the sentence 'Writing a book is like . . .'**

   Person B, for example, might say, 'an apple'.

3. **Person C makes the connection.**

   For example, they might say: '. . . because you can get your teeth into it.'

This exercise makes a good suppertime game. And you can use it to find a metaphor to help you communicate a message in a more memorable way.

Using metaphors to find new solutions

One of Robert Dilts's tales in his book *Sleight of Mouth* is about the young man in a psychiatric ward suffering from the delusion that he is Jesus Christ. He spends his days unproductively, rambling around, annoying and ignored by the other patients. All attempts by the psychiatrists and their aides fail to convince the man of his delusion.

One day, a new psychiatrist arrives on the scene. After observing the patient quietly for some time, he approaches the young man. 'I understand that you have some experience as a carpenter', he says. 'Well . . . yes, I guess I do', replies the patient. The psychiatrist explains to the patient that they are building a new recreation room at the facility and need the help of someone who has the skills of a carpenter. 'We could sure use your assistance', says the psychiatrist, 'That is, if you are the type of person who likes to help others'.

And so the story ends well. The patient becomes drawn into a project, begins to interact with people again, and becomes able to leave the hospital and secure a stable job.

In this therapeutic story, the new psychiatrist connects with the client by working with his or her own metaphor. If the patient believes he is Jesus Christ, the psychiatrist accepts that and doesn't attempt to contradict. Instead the psychiatrist works with the patient's belief and adopts the same metaphor – Jesus the carpenter – to effect the cure.

Skilled therapists of all disciplines frequently work with the client's own metaphors to help shift problems. In the same way, you can work with other people's metaphors to aid communication in everyday conversation. This might be:

- ✔ To convey bad news like project delays or job changes

- ✔ To calm down an anxious teenager facing exams

- ✔ To explain a complicated subject to a group of people

- ✔ To encourage courage or confidence in a young child

Word plays on themes like weather and nature – rain and storms to sunshine and calm, or comparing a challenging situation to climbing a mountain or crossing a river – can defuse tension. Also, relating a message in terms of your friend's favourite sports – like golf, tennis, sailing, or football can help elicit shifts in thinking.

As an example, when your colleague at work tells you 'This project is a real nightmare', you can gently drop words around sleep and dreaming into the conversation to gain more information or lead them to a more positive state of thinking. So you might feed some of the following types of language into the discussion: 'What aspects of the project are keeping you awake at night?', 'Are there some scary bits?', 'Perhaps people need to sleep on this for a while', 'How would you like to get this put to bed?', and 'So in your wildest dreams, what would you see happening?'

Anthony is a therapist who works with clients with addictive behaviours. He told us: 'I had a client who told me about the pleasure she derived from her drinking until it got out of control. Initially she described the delight of her favourite tipple – the anticipation and smell of the first glass, how appealing it looked in the bottle, beautifully packaged and presented. But as she went on to describe the feelings of helplessness as the addiction overtook her, the alcohol was transformed into an ugly spirit that haunted and frightened her. Over a period of time, we were able to work with her story, develop the plot and re-work it to have a happier ending. She could then believe in a future where she could break free from the addiction that was overwhelming her life.'

Direct and indirect metaphors

NLP distinguishes between direct and indirect types of metaphors.

- ✔ A *direct* metaphor compares one situation with another where there's an obvious link in terms of the type of content. An example would be to compare learning a new software application with learning to drive. Both are about learning.

- ✔ An *indirect* metaphor makes comparisons which are not immediately obvious. So it might compare learning the software with cooking a meal or planning a holiday. Such indirect metaphors form the basis of the most creative advertising campaigns.

When I (Kate) set up a training venture with two partners, they held a brainstorming session to come up with a name that was memorable and different instead of the predictable 'ABC Associates'. They chose the name 'Watercress' as an indirect metaphor because of the subtle connotations of soft skills, a fresh approach, and building on hidden strengths.

Isomorphic metaphors

The hypnotherapist Milton Erickson had incredible successes with very sick people by telling them therapeutic stories while they listened in a very relaxed and receptive trance. The clients would then take their own meanings from the stories and apply these to their own situation to improve their own health.

Erickson's technique of these specially constructed stories that he'd tell to his clients is explained in NLP as an *isomorphic metaphor*. *Isomorphic* means *having equal dimensions or measurements*. Therapists will construct a story about a completely different subject that runs parallel to the structure of the client's problem and use it to lead the client to a desired resolution.

Here's a group exercise that you can have fun with. It builds in the use of metaphors to encourage new thinking.

Get together a group of three people and follow these steps.

1. **One person (A) thinks of an issue they are currently trying to resolve. A describes their issue to B and C.**

2. **The other two people (B and C) each think of a different object. (This can be ordinary or obscure, such as a loaf of bread or pink sunglasses.)**

3. **First B then C tells a story to the other two. This can be any type of story they like; the only rule is that the object must figure in the story in some way.**

Reproduced with the permission of Ian McDermott, International Teaching Seminars.

Building Your Own Stories

In storytelling, the most compelling stories are those that come from someone's heart. In this section we've gathered ideas for you to develop your own repertoire of stories and build your skills as an engaging storyteller. Even if you've not thought of yourself as a storyteller before now, you'll soon see how to capture your own story ideas and organise your thoughts for maximum effect.

As you begin to create your own favourite stories, think about:

- ✔ How you will *start* the story and how you will *finish*. Some great starts lose their way (and their readers) long before the finishing post.

- ✔ What happens in the *middle* to give the dramatic interest – what are the interesting landmarks, battles, dilemmas, or conflicts on the way?

- ✔ Who are the *characters* – who is the hero and what about the supporting cast? How will you make them memorable?

- ✔ Build the content around a strong framework.

Using the Personal Story Builder Journal

Everyday experiences can form the basis of your own compelling stories. Here's a way to capture and record storylines that you can adapt later.

1. Find a *situation* that has generated an emotion. Write down the emotion generated.

   For example, joy, laughter, fear, anger, surprise, confusion, disbelief.

2. Name the *characters*.

   Which people were involved?

3. Tell what happened by giving three key points of the *storyline*.

4. Tell what the *outcome* was; in other words, how did it end?

5. Describe something funny or *interesting* that was communicated.

6. Explain what you *learned* from this.

7. List your ideas for *developing* this story: Identify where, when, and to whom you will tell it.

Stories develop and change over time. Come back to the journal at regular intervals to extend your repertoire. Listen to speakers who inspire or entertain you and you may notice their storylines are quite simple. Feel free to record interesting stories you've heard others tell and put your spin on them to make them your own.

More ways to flex your storytelling muscles

Effective storytelling is a fabulous skill that it's worth learning – a well-told story captures the audience and remains with the people long after the other details of an event are forgotten. Here are some suggestions for you to hone your technique.

- ✔ Start with simple stories and then get more adventurous as your skills grow.

- ✔ Head for the children's library for all sorts of examples of folk and fairy tales that you can adapt well to any context. One of our clients describes *Alice in Wonderland* as the best business book ever written.

- ✔ Remember that when you tell a story the focus is on you. Practice and live with your story so that when you perform, you can command the audience's attention and gather everyone with you. Know the first lines and last lines by heart and simplify the structure to a few key points.

- ✔ Tell a humorous story with a deadpan serious face and you'll have so much more impact than when you smirk all the way through. The surprise element is powerful.

- ✔ Hold onto that essential ingredient of rapport to keep people listening. (Head to Chapter 7 for more details on creating rapport.)

- ✔ Arrange the time, the place, and the setting in which you tell the story. Make sure people are relaxed and comfortable. Campfire settings and flickering log fires make for perfect storytelling moments – as do seats under shady trees on a lazy summer's day.

✔ Think of your voice as a well-tuned musical instrument. Enjoy exploiting all your skills to play it to the full range of expression.

✔ Speaking from the heart rather than reading from a book or script is more powerful . . . and people will allow you to be less than word perfect.

✔ Stimulate your audience's senses so they can see vivid pictures, hear the sounds, get in touch with feelings, even smell and taste the delicious tale you've concocted for them. Delicious.

✔ Have a great beginning. For examples of memorable openers, head to the sidebar 'Hooking people in'.

And this reminds me of . . . : Adding loops to your story

Have you noticed how, in a novel, a writer will open up a number of 'loops' or storylines that run in parallel throughout the book?

In one of the greatest storybooks of the world, *The Thousand and One Nights*, a collection of a thousand tales tells how King Shahriyar had an unpleasant behavioural problem. He'd got into the habit of killing a succession of his young virgin brides after their first night of marriage.

Hooking people in

Once upon a time . . . notice how every great story intrigues the reader with its opening. Think about how you will begin your story to attract attention and retain interest. Here are some introductory lines for starters:

'Whether I shall turn out to be the hero of my own life, or whether that station will be held by anybody else, these pages must show.' Charles Dickens, *David Copperfield*

'It might have happened anywhere, at any time, and it could certainly have been a good deal worse.' Elizabeth Jane Howard, *The Sea Change*

'"Take my camel, dear", said my Aunt Dot as she climbed down from this animal on her return from High Mass.' Rose Macaulay, *The Towers of Trebizond*

'José Palacios, his oldest servant, found him floating naked with his eyes open in the purifying waters of his bath and thought he had drowned.' Gabriel Garcia Marquez, *The General in His Labyrinth*

'In the beginning, there was a river. The river became a road and the road branched out to the whole world. And because the road was once a river it was always hungry.' Ben Okri, *The Famished Road*

'I am doomed to remember a boy with a wrecked voice, not because of his voice or because he was the smallest person I ever knew or even because he was the instrument of my mother's death, but because he is the reason I believe in God.' John Irving, *A Prayer for Owen Meaney*

And finally, sit back, relax, and enjoy another story from the Sufi tradition

There was once a small boy who banged a drum all day and loved every moment of it. He would not be quiet, no matter what anyone else said or did. Various people who called themselves Sufis, and other well-wishers, were called in by neighbours and asked to do something about the child.

The first so-called Sufi told the boy that he would, if he continued to make so much noise, perforate his eardrums; this reasoning was too advanced for the child, who was neither a scientist nor a scholar. The second told him that drum-beating was a sacred activity and should be carried out only on special occasions. The third offered the neighbours plugs for their ears; the fourth gave the boy a book; the fifth gave the neighbours books that described a method of controlling anger through biofeedback; the sixth gave the boy meditation exercises to make him placid and explained that all reality was imagination. Like all placebos, each of these remedies worked for a short while, but none worked for very long.

Eventually, a real Sufi came along. He looked at the situation, handed the boy a hammer and chisel, and said, 'I wonder what is *inside* the drum?'

At the rate he was demolishing the female population, the source of potential brides began to run dry. Thanks to the cleverness of Shahrazad, the daughter of his senior statesman, and the King's potential next victim, the pattern was broken. It is said that Shahrazad had collected a thousand and one books of histories and poetry, fascinated as she was by the lives of kings and past generations.

On her marriage night, she entertained the King with a tale that hung in the air unfinished at dawn. The King's curiosity got the better of him awaiting the completion of the tale and he spared her life – again and again and again – as the thousand and one tales unfolded. And he broke the habit of killing his new brides!

You too can build story loops into your skillset. It's an advanced device to adopt in the stories you tell, whether in a presentation, training, or a social setting.

What you do is begin one story and before you complete it, you say: 'Ah that reminds me of, or have I told you the one about . . .'. The stories hang incomplete; people are left uncertain wondering what happened and how it's going to end. This device enables you to keep the audience's attention and concentration as the brain seeks to make order out of the confusion. You may do it naturally as you wander from subject to subject. Be sure to close the stories off eventually or you'll annoy your audience.

Chapter 18

Asking the Right Questions

. . . .

In This Chapter

▶ Revealing the assumptions that stop you being your best

▶ Heading straight to the heart of an issue

▶ Making tough decisions easier

. . . .

*W*hen you know the 'right' questions to ask, you'll get the results you want much faster. Throughout this book, in the true spirit of NLP, we've deliberately aimed to be non-judgemental; so you could quite legitimately say there are no 'right' or 'wrong' questions, only different ones.

Let's be more precise. When we talk about 'right' questions we are looking specifically for incisive ones – those that put your finger right on the nub of an issue, that have a positive effect in the shortest possible time. The 'wrong' questions are those that send you off-course, meandering down dead-ends, gathering interesting but irrelevant information.

Throughout this book, we explain and demonstrate that your language is powerful; it triggers an emotional response in *you* as well as others. This is one reason why you can make a difference as you begin to choose language with increasing awareness. In this chapter, we bring together some of the most useful questions you can ask in different situations to make things happen for yourself and for others. Knowing the right questions to ask might make a difference for you when you want to:

✔ Set your personal compass in the right direction

✔ Make the best decisions

✔ Help others to take more responsibility

✔ Select and motivate people

Before You Begin: Question-asking Tips and Strategies

Before rushing on to the critical question you'd probably like to get answered – 'What are the magic questions that do make a real difference?' – take a quick breather to consider *how* to ask questions when you are working with other people, which is just as important as the *what* to ask.

In this section we encourage you to challenge your personal style and assumptions and adapt your own behaviour to function at your best whether in the client or coaching seat.

Cleaning up your language

Have you ever wondered how many questions you ask that make assumptions based on what *you* want, and *your* map of reality, rather than what the other person wants? As human beings it's very hard not to project our ideas, our needs, our wants, and enthusiasms on to others – especially those closest to us. You influence other people all the time. You just can't help it. For that reason, most questions are not clean – they *assume* something, as in the famous 'When did you stop beating your wife?' question.

Even the one small word *beating* will have different meanings for each of us. Did you think of *beating* in the context of physical violence or did you think of it in the competitive sense of winning at a *sport* or game?

Therapists go into many years of training to work with their clients like a 'clean mirror' that can simply reflect the client's issues back to them to deliberate on. Some get to shine brighter than others! After all, you already know how much you can communicate just through one raised eyebrow or suppressed giggle. (This was why Freud had his clients lying on a couch while he, as the therapist, sat behind the client's head!)

If you want to be respectful of other people's views, then notice how well you can avoid prejudicing the result of a discussion. Are you telling somebody else what to do based on what you would do yourself?

Beware making the kinds of generalisations or limiting possibilities we talked about in Chapter 15 on the Meta Model. Listen for what you say and if you hear yourself issuing instructions that begin with words like: you must, you should, you ought to, you can't – then it's time to stop directing the action and imposing your stance on others.

Let's suppose you are coaching someone. Maybe it's a colleague, a friend, or a member of your family. In a coaching session, it's essential to begin with a clear aim in mind. So you might ask:

> 'What do we want to work on today?'

The question is simple, direct, and focuses attention on the fact that you're *working* on something.

Coaching is about exploring and challenging clients, leading them on to take responsibility and commit to action. Clean questions help you do that. It's important that suggestions are phrased in such a way that people think for themselves.

So a clean question that directs a client to think carefully for himself or herself might be:

> 'I wonder what that's about?'

Curiosity may have killed the cat, as the saying goes. We've never heard of it killing human beings. A different perspective is: curiosity is the pathway to understanding. You choose which saying suits you best.

It's the way you are that counts

Own up now . . . have you ever shouted at someone and said to him or her: 'Stop shouting at me!'? It's nonsense, isn't it, to expect someone else to do what you clearly are not demonstrating in your own behaviour. Yet people do it all the time. It's easy to see in someone else the negative qualities you want to change in yourself.

The art of influencing somebody else to change is to model that behaviour yourself. If you want somebody to be curious, then be curious yourself. If you want someone to be positive and helpful, then you too need to model that behaviour. If you think someone just needs to lighten up, inject some fun into the proceedings.

Instead of expecting other people to change, lead the way yourself. One of the best lessons we can pass on is: *'The way you are with other people will determine the way people are with you.'*

So as you ask questions, do so with awareness of how you are.

Press the pause button

Silence is golden. It's really helpful to pause for a moment when one person has finished speaking, and in turn let yourself think before you speak.

Pauses give other people critical space to process what you have said and consider their reply.

Simply giving people unhurried time to think within a structured framework of questioning is a huge benefit in business and in family situations, too. Listening to others is a generous act and an undeveloped, undervalued skill in most organisations. In her book, *Time to Think*, Nancy Kline sets out a framework which she describes as a *thinking environment* in which listening creates more productive meetings, solves business strategies, and builds stronger relationships.

To take time to think is to gain time to live (Nancy Kline).

Test your questions

If ever you have any doubts about whether your question is appropriate to help a person or situation move on to a better place, stop and ask yourself:

- ✔ 'Is my next question going to add value in this conversation? Is it taking us closer to where we want to go? Is it going to move us further apart?'
- ✔ 'What is the outcome or result I'm looking for here?'

Make positive statements the norm

When I say to you, don't think of a pink elephant, what happens? Yes, of course, you immediately think of a pink elephant, you just can't help it! Similarly, if I say to a child: 'Don't eat those sweets before tea, now!' What happens? The child is compelled to *eat the sweets* – you have inadvertently issued a command.

The brain doesn't distinguish the negatives – it ignores the 'don't' and thinks 'do'. Better to say to your child: 'Tea's coming, so save your appetite for just two minutes.'

Fishing for answers

There was once a therapist working with a client who told him he had a dream. All the client could remember was that it had been raining and he had been to a restaurant. Then he woke up feeling hot and anxious.

Therapist: Oh, so your dream was about fish, was it?

Client: I don't know.

Therapist: But you know that you were in a restaurant?

Client: That's right.

Therapist: And it's likely there was fish on the menu?

Client: Yes, most restaurants have fish on the menu.

Therapist: And it was raining, so that could represent water and fish swimming in water?

Client: Well, yes, you are right.

Therapist: Sounds like we're getting closer. Perhaps you were feeling like a fish that had been caught and then cooked even? What's that all about?

Of course, this is fiction. Reality is different. Yet, how easy it can be to listen to one point and lead somebody into your subjective interpretation of the facts.

Figuring Out What You Want

Knowing what you want can be the greatest challenge. It's a constantly moving feast. There may be times when you get what you *think* you wanted, yet you're disappointed because it turns out that it wasn't what you *really* wanted at all! So to figure out what you *really* want, you have to ask yourself two questions: 'What do I want?' and 'What will that do for me?'

What do I want?

If there's one great question that comes from NLP, the ultimate one is: 'What do I want?'

Sometimes you know very clearly what you don't want. This is a good starting point. When you know what you don't want, flip it over and ask yourself: 'What is the opposite?' And then check with yourself again: 'So, what is it that I do want?'

As you begin to articulate your answers, explore some details and allow yourself to dream a little. Imagine yourself in the future; fast forward your personal movie to a time when you have got what you want and maybe more besides. Employ all your senses and ask yourself what does that feel like, sound like, look like? Are there any smells or tastes associated with getting what you want? Check inside with yourself as to whether it seems right. Does it energise and excite you? And if you feel anxious or exhausted, that's a clue that something's wrong.

What will that do for me?

Once you've thought about what you want, and some words and ideas have come to you, then the next check question is: 'What will that do for me?' You may have a goal in place – it might be to bid for a new business project, or to take up a new sport, or to quit your work and go trekking in Nepal.

Ask yourself this question: 'What will that do for me?' And ask the same question three times – really drill down until you hit some core values that make sense for you. Otherwise you'll be choosing to do things that really take you meandering down the side lanes rather than staying on track for where you want to get to.

Keith was a successful, high-flying salesman who was evaluating his performance in his job. When he first worked with an NLP coach, his priority was to focus on developing specific skills he needed in place. His primary focus was to pave his succession route to become the next sales director in his company.

After a few sessions in which his coach asked him what he wanted and what that would do for him, he delved further into what he really wanted, taking into account all aspects of his life and work. He realised that if he achieved this career goal, he would have to give up much of the freedom and flexibility that his current role gave him. He realised that much of the new desirable role meant he'd be commuting into town in the rush hour, stuck most of the day at a desk in the corporate headquarters agreeing targets, budgets, and sorting out the legalities of the company pension schemes. ('I'd be like a puppy chained to a desk.')

In fact he thrived on being out with customers and winning deals. The promotion would not give him what he really wanted. With this realisation, he chose to reset his career direction and take his skills into another part of the corporation. From there he was able to use his initiative to open up new international sales territories.

Making Decisions

You make decisions all the time: whether to go to work or stay at home, what to have for lunch and supper, whether to accept an invitation to see a film, how much you should spend on a new computer or holiday, to lay on a Christmas party with your folks or not?

So let's imagine that one sunny day you're happily working at your job and there's a call from a head-hunter: there's a new job on offer, you're the person they'd like, and by the way, it means shifting your homebase to a town by the sea 200 miles away. You weren't even considering a change, but you're flattered, so you go and talk to them. The deal looks pretty attractive and, wow, wouldn't it feel good to be working near the sea in hot weather like this? But, there's a niggling little voice inside you saying: 'Is this the right thing to do? Are you sure?'

Should you go for it or should you stay doing what you know best? How can you decide this one?

Here are four key questions that you can ask yourself, or someone else, to guide you in making a decision – a life-changing one or something smaller.

- ✔ What will happen if you do?
- ✔ What will happen if you don't?
- ✔ What won't happen if you do?
- ✔ What won't happen if you don't?

The four questions you have here are based on Cartesian logic and you may find them referred to as *Cartesian Co-ordinates*. All you need to remember is that they offer some powerful linguistic patterns that enable you to examine a subject from different angles.

We often talk clients through these questions. The decisions can be major – shall I leave my wife, shall I move house, change career direction, have a baby? The questions focus your attention and challenge your thinking. When you reach the last question, you may stop and think, 'That's confusing.' Good. This means you're arriving at a breakthrough in your thinking.

If you make a change in one area of your life at the expense of another area, the chances are that that change is not going to last. So, for example, if you moved jobs but had to give up important interests or friendships where you currently live, then that change isn't going to make you happy in the long term, so you probably would not stick with it.

Don't take our word for it; try the questions out now on something you're deliberating. You'll see the questions encourage you to check out your decision based on the impact on the whole of your environment, in a healthy way – what we call an *ecology* check.

Challenging Limiting Beliefs

People's thinking may be stopping them from achieving a much sought after goal, but there are three simple questions you can ask that challenge such thinking. To help others (or yourself) overcome a limiting belief, you ask a series of three questions, explained in the following sections.

The way to ask the questions is to give people plenty of time to talk about an issue, then, as you sense they've 'got it off their chest', at that point begin asking the questions.

- ✔ **Question 1: 'What do you assume or believe about this that limits you in achieving your goal?'**

  Ask this question three times until you're sure you've reached the heart of the matter – what NLP describes as a limiting belief. As you delve deeper, you may say: 'That's right, and what else is there about this that limits you?'

  For example, the person may be thinking: 'I'm not good enough.' 'Nobody will let me.' 'I just don't know how.' When you hold a negative position like this, then you stop yourself from doing what you need to do to achieve what you want.

- ✔ **Question 2: 'What would be a more empowering belief, one that is the positive opposite of that?'**

  This question flips the limitation over to the positive side. For example, the positive opposite of the assumptions and beliefs above would be stated positively as: 'I am good enough.' 'Somebody will let me.' 'I do know how.'

  With this second question, your colleague or client may get confused or even cross because it is a challenging one to answer. Yet, it's a critical one to hold onto if you're going to get a switch in perspective and come up with a more empowering belief that helps someone shift forward. So stick with it.

- ✔ **Question 3: 'If you knew that (new freeing belief) . . . what ideas do you now have to help you move towards your goal?'**

  This question completes the process. At this point, your client comes up with his or her own ideas as to how to move forward: 'Oh well, if I knew that I was good enough, then I would do XYZ.'

The way this questioning works is to put somebody into an 'as if' way of thinking. If you act with the belief that something can happen, then you will find the behaviours to get there.

I (Kate) worked with a managing director who wanted to be successful in her business yet was struggling to make a decision on having a child. Her limiting belief was: 'It is not possible to be a good mother and a successful businesswoman at the same time.' By working through the three questions, she evaluated the new opposite assumption that: 'It is possible to be a good mother and a successful businesswoman at the same time.'

By working in this 'as if' framework, that is, operating as if it was possible to do both well, she opened up many ideas on how she could run the company differently in order to pursue motherhood at the same time as being successful in business. Not only did she go on to have two healthy well-adjusted children, she also put in place more flexible policies that benefited the men as well as the women in the company.

Finding the Right Person for the Job: A Question of Motivation

Getting the right people in the right job at the right time can be a tricky one. Asking the right questions can help you match the people to the qualities needed to succeed in the job.

To get somebody lined up in the right job, it's first important to ask yourself about the *personal qualities* of the person you need to do that job well, as well as the *technical skills* involved. How will they behave? This questioning begins before you recruit.

✔ What are some of the essential criteria for someone to perform this job well? Come up with about five key words. (These might be things like: teamworking, self-starter, clear processes, creativity, customer service, learning, variety, stability, flexibility, well-organised, intellectual challenge, good product, attractive environment, travel.)

✔ Do they need to be motivated to achieve results or to sort out problems?

✔ Do they need to be primarily self-motivated or get consensus from customers or a team?

✔ Does the style of working mean they must follow processes or will they have lots of choices about how they do things?

By using the following questions at the interview, you can gain specific information on how people are likely to behave in a given context, as well as their technical skills to do the job you have in mind. They are based on the NLP metaprograms that you can read about in Chapter 8.

The same questions apply as you check in with members of your team to see how things are going and what adjustments you can make to keep people motivated.

What do you want in your work?

This question enables you to match the criteria or hot buttons that you are looking for with those that are important for one individual. If you hear that someone wants lots of freedom and flexibility, they would do well in a creative environment, but not if you want them to tightly project manage an implementation of a new system. If they thrive on change, they'll be good for a short-term contract, but unlikely to stay more than a year or two at most unless you can give them new roles.

Why is that important?

Taking each of the criteria in turn, ask: 'Why is that important?' This question enables you to identify the direction in which your colleague is motivated either *away from* a problem or *towards* a solution. A person with an *away from* preference might say: 'Salary is important so I won't have to worry about not being able to pay my mortgage.' A person with a *towards* preference might say: 'Salary is important so I can buy my own home easily.'

The clues to understanding people are in the language style they adopt. For example:

- ✔ If someone is motivated *towards,* you might hear these kinds of words – attain, gain, achieve, get, include.

- ✔ If someone is motivated *away from*, you might hear these kinds of words – avoid, exclude, recognise problems.

How do you know you have done a good job?

This question enables you to identify the *source* of your colleague's motivation.

If they are *internally focused*, that is they know within themselves, you might motivate them by using these kinds of phrases: 'Only you can decide', 'You might want to consider', 'What do you think?'

If they are *externally focused*, that is they need to be convinced by other people and by gaining facts and figures, you might motivate them by using these kinds of phrases: 'Others will notice', 'The feedback you'll get', 'So and so says so.'

If you were employing somebody in customer service, it would be important that they value external approval, rather than being internally focused. However, if you want to give someone a project to get on with on their own, someone with a strong external focus is likely to struggle without regular approval from others.

Why did you choose your current work?

This is a great question to ask if you want to know if someone is motivated by having choices or by being told what to do. If somebody has an *options style*, you'll hear words like: opportunity, criteria, choice, unlimited possibilities, and variety. On the other hand, if somebody has strong *procedures style*, they are likely to give you a step-by-step response, the story of how they got into their job. You're likely to hear them talking about processes and using phrases like: the right way, tried and true.

Both styles can work in the same team quite happily together. To motivate your options people, build in as many choices as you can offer. Get them to brainstorm new ways to do things. To motivate your procedures people, get them to focus on the necessary systems and processes to bring more structure and controls to the team.

Checking In with Yourself

In order to keep on track to where you want to get, either on a daily basis or longer term, it can be helpful to question yourself. So allow us to leave you with a final checklist of questions to ask yourself each day.

Daily checkpoint

What do I want?

What will that do for me?

What's stopping me?

What's important to me here?

What's working well?

What can be better?

What resources will support me?

If you accept the NLP presupposition that there's no such thing as failure, just feedback, then you won't be afraid of asking questions in case you get answers you'd prefer not to hear. Tune into the feedback you get for yourself as well as others as you ask the right questions.

Part VI
The Part of Tens

The 5th Wave   By Rich Tennant

"It's called that because we feel that people are entirely free and therefore responsible for what they make of themselves and for themselves. Now, do you still want the double anchovy with the fried mozzarella strips?"

In this part . . .

You see why the famous *For Dummies* Part of Tens is so well loved for putting more information quickly and simply at your fingertips. This part gives you a taste of the broad impact of NLP on everyday life, from parents and teachers to sales success and personal development. There's something for everyone: ten applications of NLP, other books to read, online resources to use, and films to watch. And you see just how much more you can find out now that you've become curious.

Chapter 19

Ten Applications of NLP

In This Chapter

▶ Getting a quick road map to NLP in practice

▶ Understanding what you can do now to enjoy the benefits of NLP

. . . .

*I*n our experience as coaches, consultants, and trainers we find daily applications at work. At home with family and friends, it's equally important. How can you use NLP? In this chapter, we present ten suggestions which we hope will get you thinking about how you could apply the contents of the book. You choose what will make a difference for you.

Developing Yourself

When you read this book, we hope you'll take away one lesson. NLP offers a means for learning, for growing, and for developing yourself and you can choose to take it. You can use NLP to coach and help others too (as explained in other sections in this chapter), but it pays to be strong and healthy yourself so that you are an authentic role model.

The NLP toolkit is the collection of models and exercises, as well as the inquisitive mindset, which lets you:

✔ Choose your most resourceful emotional state and use anchors, a mental technique to access and hold that good state when you're feeling challenged. You will learn best when you feel safe to have a go at something new. To explore how to set and fire anchors, look at Chapter 9.

✔ Guide your thinking in different ways using the NLP presuppositions, the assumptions on which NLP is based. More on these in Chapter 2.

✔ Find out what makes you function at your best – gathering information about how you reflect your experience through your senses, what NLP calls representational systems. You can get to grips with these in Chapter 6.

✔ Take responsibility for your own learning rather than waiting for someone else to do it for you.

✔ Increase clarity on what you really want in all aspects of your life. The well-formed outcomes we introduce in Chapter 3 are fundamental to looking at what you want.

✔ Learn to make change at the most appropriate logical level of experience to improve your ability and self-confidence – whether this is about environment, behaviour, capability, beliefs, identity, or purpose. All is revealed in Chapter 11.

✔ Pace yourself as well as other people, to ensure that you don't get burnout by pushing yourself too hard, and learn to build rapport more easily. We devote the whole of Chapter 7 to creating rapport.

Managing Your Personal and Professional Relationships

'Help. This relationship isn't working!' If you think you have a bad relationship with someone, that can be a horrible, stuck experience. The door is closed in your face. One statement you'll hear a lot in NLP is this: *If what you are doing isn't working, then do something different.* Fortunately, NLP offers a couple of ways for you to get unstuck and open the door with more possibilities.

✔ **The Meta Model:** A key one is the Meta Model described in Chapter 15. It provides a way for you to delve below the surface of vague everyday language like 'I'm not happy with this' with useful questions that gather specific information and challenge assumptions that get in the way of happy and rewarding relationships. By knowing how to communicate more precisely you can get to the heart of what you and other people really mean to say.

✔ **The NLP meta-mirror:** A second one you can go back to is the NLP meta-mirror in Chapter 7, where we encourage you to stand in different perceptual positions. The meta-mirror is a favourite technique for exploring challenging situations by looking at how you relate to other people. By taking different viewpoints into account, you'll come away with fresh ideas to move relationships forward – or say a polite goodbye.

Negotiating a Win-Win Solution

Suppose you are going to enter into an important negotiation in your life. Perhaps you've spotted the home of your dreams. How can NLP help you to get the best deal when you're confronted by estate agents pushing you to buy the new house at the highest rate while selling your current one as low as possible? By giving you principles and strategies you can use to everybody's advantage. These same principles apply if you're negotiating for a job, buying a car, hiring contract staff at work, or allocating chores with your flatmates.

✔ Go for the positive outcome – begin with your desired result in mind. Talk in positive language. Always focus on what you want rather than what you don't want. For the full story on outcomes, see Chapter 3.

✔ Engage your senses – make your outcome more specific by noticing what it will look like, sound like, and feel like when you have achieved a successful negotiation. You can get a sense of this in Chapter 6.

✔ Note down your criteria or hot buttons – focus on five key elements that are important to you in making the move. Put them in order of priority and keep returning to them to check you are getting what you want.

✔ Note down the seller's criteria or hot buttons – what's important to them? Imagine what it's like to be in their shoes and remind yourself of what they want every time you have contact.

✔ Positive by-products – keep in mind what positive elements you get from the house you already have that you don't want to lose. This might be the number of bathrooms, the sunny south-facing garden, or the good local transport.

✔ Know your bottom line. Be prepared to walk away with no deal rather than getting carried away in the moment just to complete a deal that is disappointing for you.

✔ Manage your state. Staying calm and relaxed when the negotiation gets to you will help you make the best move. You can read about anchors in Chapter 9.

✔ *Chunking*, the ability to be able to shift someone's view to the big picture or whiz down to specifics confidently, is a key skill in any negotiation. If you are disagreeing on details, then chunk upwards from the specifics of your contract to gain common agreement on key points, then you can chunk downwards to smaller issues once you have achieved that common ground. Chapter 15 will help you get specific when necessary, while Chapter 16 can teach you how to put people into a relaxed trance so they hear your message more clearly.

✔ Keep rapport with everyone in the chain. Even when you disagree with the content of what they are saying, match and mirror their body language and tone of voice. It helps when you all listen! We cover the all-important NLP skill of rapport building in Chapter 7.

Meeting Those Sales Targets

NLP principles apply to creating strong sales relationships. They teach you how to build rapport, how to get clarity on what someone wants, understand their values and criteria, and how to be flexible along the way until you close a deal or decide to walk away because you know the fit isn't right.

Taking the NLP approach will lead to a winning situation that's highly considerate and respectful. Integrity is the key word that comes to mind here. Good salespeople are able to take the customer's perspective and match the benefit of their product to the customer's need. Nobody wants to be blatantly sold to, but they do want to be listened to and to find solutions to their issues, they want products and services that will help them run a business or enjoy life more; they want the 'feel-good' factor. NLP deals with influence and how people make decisions. Successful sales match the customer needs at many levels.

There's a saying: 'People buy on emotion and justify with fact.' Whether you are selling a product or an idea, you connect primarily with people on an emotional level. People buy *you* first, before they buy what you are selling.

Creating Powerful Presentations

The ability to communicate well is fundamental to your success. In fact, you may find it's the single most important skill that affects your future. Those who can present well have the leading edge in so many areas of life whether your passion is to be a politician, sportsperson, teacher, TV presenter, cheerleader, or business leader of the year. Have you got the self-confidence to go out and stand up for what you believe in? Do you really want to sit through a celebration dinner scared because you have to give the vote of thanks at the end? If you can present well, you can get ahead. Or simply relax and have a good time.

And what stops you? In one word – YOU.

Sadly, so many people we meet are terrified of presenting. And if they are not terrified, then many certainly prefer to hang around backstage than get out there and sock it to an audience.

NLP can make a difference for you in three ways:

✔ It shows you how to make your purpose in presenting crystal clear.

✔ It shows you how to touch everyone in an audience through your use of language.

✔ It shows you how to feel confident about standing up in front of any group.

Imagine that you've been invited to do a talk at the annual meeting of your favourite local gardening club. (And for gardening, substitute here your own hobby from hamster-training to glider-flying.)

Using NLP, your first task is to engage your brain to decide on the outcome of your presentation. What is the result, or action, you want to happen, once people have been so inspired by your speech? Map this out clearly for yourself, bearing in mind what the audience would like to learn from you.

Secondly, as you begin to build the content of your talk, think VAK – Visual, Auditory, and Kinaesthetic (head to Chapter 6 for tips on engaging with people's dominant senses). How are you going to connect with people who like pictures, those who hear the words, and those who just go with their gut feelings? As you develop your script, remember there are those who just need the headlines, and also those who like the nitty-gritty details.

The third thing to remember is that NLP gives you the tools to prepare mentally for any presentation. Get clear about how you want to be at that presentation – laughing and jovial, full of deep and meaningful gravitas, or perhaps somewhere in between? Find a time when you were like that in the past, so you can hold, or anchor, the previous experience to regain that feeling for yourself. You can learn how to set stage anchors by referring to Chapter 9.

And the most important tip – the Holy Grail – don't get hung up on tips and techniques. We all present differently and it's refreshing when you are just yourself. When you speak from the heart about something you care passionately about people will connect with you.

Managing Your Time and Precious Resources

We all have the same amount of time. It's how we use it that makes a difference. How is it that some people spend their lives racing against the clock while others gently amble along?

Understanding how you relate to time makes a difference to your daily experience. NLP distinguishes between those of us who operate *in time* – that's if you live in and for the moment – and those of us who operate *through time*. Planning time is much easier if you're *through time*. Being in the moment is easier if you are *in time*. Time travelling tips are waiting for you in Chapter 13.

As a coach, I (Kate) encourage my clients to use time wisely, to really understand the impact of spending time on what they don't want to be doing and freeing up their energy for what really motivates them. It's a precious resource and if you lose it or waste it, you can't go back to reclaim it.

Taking on too much to please others has the opposite effect if you let people down.

Being Coached to Success

Is there something you'd like to do, that you've maybe thought about for a long time, but have yet to start or to achieve? Yes? If so, then NLP coaching can help you make that leap from the idea, the desire to make some change, to really making it happen.

When you work with a coach who embraces the principles of NLP with skill, they will believe in your unlimited potential – and help you to achieve goals that seemed impossible. And that can be serious fun. No joking.

Coaching focuses your attention on getting the results you want – the outcomes – and stops you dithering along the way, dissipating energy on all the things that you don't want. It helps you to jump over or remove the barriers that stop you. Coaching closes that gap from where you are now to where you want to get to; from your *present state* to your *desired state*.

Action is what turns the dream into reality. One of the key reasons that coaching gets you results is that you make a commitment to action. Another is that you break down your goals into bite-sized, realistic chunks. When you work with a coach you make a commitment to somebody else. It's like somebody standing there with the stopwatch and clipboard and checking in with you at regular intervals to make sure that you're on track.

The principles of NLP apply to achieving success in sports and business. So you'll often find sports coaches using the anchoring techniques of NLP to help you get into a confident state before a big match.

Coaching is often about helping people to restore the balance and harmony once more. I (Kate) believe that coaching is about much more than simply excelling on the golf course or in the boardroom battles. I take a holistic view – considering all aspects of a person's life to enable them to create their own future. I coach highly successful executives who want to be outstanding in their work. By examining the whole picture of their lives as well as their work patterns, people unleash their own energy and direction to get what they want.

If you excel in one aspect of your life to the detriment of others, say your work, then life at work is great but your home life is miserable. You then have an unbalanced and potentially unhealthy existence. Clients who succeed at the extreme heights in business can damage their health or important relationships along the way. And those who have a very comfortable home life can neglect their professional potential. If these scenarios describe you, then finding an NLP coach can help you restore the balance and harmony to your life.

Using NLP to Support Your Health

'Stressed' spelled backwards is 'desserts'. Little wonder that dieting is so stressful when you keep seeing those puddings in front of your eyes – puddings can be very attractive when you're stressed.

Seriously though, NLP has much to offer you if you want to stay healthy because it recognises the inextricable connection between mind and body. It views a person like a system which needs to stay balanced for you to be healthy.

Have you ever had a time when you had too much to do, not enough time to do it, and not much say about when and how it was done? Perhaps you've felt like a hamster on a treadmill going nowhere? Most people go through times when things are tough – peaks and troughs are normal. The danger zone hits when people don't recognise what is happening and their lives are spiralling out of control. When people get out of control in one aspect of their lives the body will step in with a braking mechanism. Tension headaches, neck and back pains, as well as outbursts of anger and anxiety can all be warning flags from your body that you're not in control of your own life.

NLP helps people stay centred and focused on who they are and what their core values are, and to stay in tune with their health.

A delegate, Cassy, on my (Romilla) 'Beyond Di-Stress' workshop had worn herself to a frazzle, trying to meet her commitments at work, where she had been recently promoted, and trying to meet the demands of her family. During the workshop Cassy realised she was pandering to the demands of her boss and her family because she had a deep need for love which stemmed from the fact that she had been adopted. Despite loving adoptive parents and a very stable and happy childhood, Cassy had always felt she was one of life's rejects because her biological mother had given her away. Another delegate heard Cassy's story and said, 'But you're really one of the chosen.' Cassy was a joy to behold as she processed this new slant on her identity. After the workshop Cassy was able to say 'no' to a lot of people in her life, one of the unforeseen benefits of which was that her children became more responsible for their own lives.

Connecting to Your Audience: Advice for Trainers and Educators

NLP recognises that individuals all learn in very different ways and the only person who really knows what that is, is the pupil. Good teachers take responsibility for teaching so that pupils learn – they truly connect and inspire. What NLP does is to move the emphasis from teaching to learning and gets people to begin to notice how they learn in the best way.

The learning process involves many rich dimensions beyond just being taught facts or given the right answers. For learning to connect and last, people need to be put into a good positive and receptive state to learn. Putting the trainer and the group into a receptive state will be far more important than covering all the curriculum.

If you are learning a new skill, become curious about how to make that work for you. Think of your best learning experience; a time when you felt good about learning. What are three things about that? I (Kate) know that I learn best when having fun, being with people, and feeling OK to experiment and make mistakes. But this will not be the same for other people when I train.

NLP will show you how to discover people's preferences for taking in information – so as a teacher, it will be important to recognise that some people respond to pictures, some to words, and others to touch or feelings. Using highly general language at the beginning of a session will enable you to connect with different levels of expertise in a group. So your introduction can go something like . . .

We will cover many aspects of the subject today. Some of you will already have a lot of knowledge in this area and will have your own ideas, opinions, and experiences to contribute.

For some of you, the concepts will just reinforce what you already know and give you time to sit back and consider the implications of what you do already.

For others, there will be new perspectives and, during the course of the day, we will have the opportunity to explore some new ways to add value and power to what you are currently using.

You will make up your own minds on how these ideas will be applied.

Also keep in mind the stages of learning. When you learn a new skill, such as driving a car, you move through different levels of competence. When you start out you are blissfully ignorant – *unconsciously incompetent*. You don't know what you don't know. Then you move to *conscious incompetence* and you've woken up to what you don't know. As you build your capability you are *consciously competent* until you become *unconsciously competent* when, as an expert driver, you forget what it was like to be a learner. This is why it's often hard to learn from someone who is an expert – they can be so far removed from what it is like to be a beginner, that they say 'Just do it' and cannot break down the skill into easy stages.

Getting That Job

Shifting jobs can be like changing the wallpaper or buying yet another blue shirt. You can change jobs and realise that it was just the change that was attractive rather than the job itself.

NLP thinking can help you get the right job rather than a different job. Career planning needs to be done proactively or you'll end up like Alice in Wonderland, and not too bothered about where you get to, just so long as it's somewhere. And making informed decisions ensures that you don't chuck out a perfectly good job to end up somewhere that you'll be very unhappy.

Make your job search a well-formed outcome using the checklist in Appendix C. Do your homework about the person with the power to appoint you to your dream job and decide how their map of the world operates. There's a checklist in Chapter 7 to help you think about the person you need to influence.

Be creative about making yourself stand out from the crowd. If you were a product, what would your features and benefits be? In front of a mirror, practise being the person they want to employ. How would you dress and talk? What would you be saying about yourself and your capabilities? Remember, you need to believe in yourself for others to feel confident in you – and buy you.

Chapter 20

Ten Books to Add to Your Library

In This Chapter

▶ Book recommendations for NLP practitioners and newcomer alike

▶ Broadening the horizons of your NLP knowledge through the printed word

*W*e are voracious readers. This is a trait that has enabled us both to expand our knowledge of personal development and NLP. We would like to offer ten NLP-related books that have had a major impact on our development as a shortcut to your growth and which we hope will enrich your life and the lives of those you touch.

Changing Belief Systems with NLP

Robert Dilts, the author of *Changing Belief Systems with NLP* (Meta Publications, 1990), is one of the most creative trainers and authors in the world of NLP and one of the people who really walks his talk. In this book, he describes how your beliefs can prevent you from getting to a desired state of existence. The book helps you explore your beliefs and gives you exercises to change them in order to get alignment at all levels of your personality for permanent change.

The User's Manual for the Brain

In *The User's Manual for the Brain* (Crown House Publishing, 2001), authors Bob G Bodenhamer and L Michael Hall, two of the most prolific writers in the field of NLP, have produced a book for someone who wants to get to the NLP practitioner level without going on a course. Unlike some other NLP books for beginners, this book is very easy to follow and will give you a really good foundation prior to attending a practitioner course. Master practitioners of NLP will find this a brilliant book with which to revise their existing knowledge.

Core Transformation

Core Transformation (Real People Press, 1996) offers techniques in Neuro-linguistic Programming, discovered and developed by Connirae Andreas, designed to bring greater wholeness to the reader in order to facilitate personal change. The technique for *Core Transformation* is based on the premise that there are conflicting parts in every person's unconscious, yearning to reach a core state and thereby wholeness. This book is a breakthrough in the field of personal development because it enables you to use limitations as a springboard to reaching core states like inner peace and love.

From Frogs into Princes

From Frogs to Princes (Real People Press, 1979) is one of the seminal books in the field of NLP. The book is actually the transcript of a live training session conducted by the founding fathers of NLP, John Grinder and Richard Bandler and beautifully edited by Steve Andreas. Although there have been further developments in NLP since this book was first published, this is a 'must read' for starting you on the path of learning about NLP.

Influencing with Integrity

In *Influencing with Integrity* (Crown House Publishing, 1984), Genie Z Laborde, the author, has made use of lots of line drawings and cartoons to make this book easy on the eyes. She has simplified a complex subject to give the reader a set of state-of-the-art skills to use in all areas of communication. The straightforward approach with its focus on business applications makes this a very useful book for people in the corporate world.

Manage Yourself, Manage Your Life

If you want to learn the theory of NLP, *Manage Yourself, Manage Your Life* (Judy Piatkus Publishers, 1999) by Ian McDermott and Ian Shircore isn't for you. However, if you want to experience NLP while you 'plan to make change happen on your terms', this is just the one you should read and practise. Actually experiencing NLP with this book, prior to going on an NLP practitioner course, will provide an invaluable basis for your learning.

Presenting Magically

If you are a trainer or presenter this elegantly written book by David Shepard and Tad James is a must for you. The techniques in *Presenting Magically* (Crown House Publishing, 2001) use NLP and accelerated learning and will show you how to captivate your audience from the start. Practise the exercises in the book to model 'natural-born' presenters and raise your presentation skills to mastery level.

The Magic of Metaphor

In *The Magic of Metaphor* (Crown House Publishing, 2001), Nick Owen has put together a collection of stories designed to transform the reader with nuggets that will motivate you and provide you with strategies for excellence. The stories uplift you and promote positive feelings and confidence while challenging the very foundations of your ideas, attitudes, and beliefs. This book will prove extremely useful to people in professions as diverse as counselling, psychology, professional-speaking, management, and teaching.

Words that Change Minds

With *Words that Change Minds* (Kendall/Hunt Publishing Company, 2nd edition, 1997), Shelle Rose Charvet has turned what could be a dry subject into an unputdownable book. You do not have to know NLP to understand about NLP metaprograms because Shelle has used her enthusiasm and easy charm to illustrate the practical applications of learning the connection between behaviour and language. The book is packed full of everyday anecdotes which allow a lay person to understand aspects of communication such as how to aim a job or product advert to reach the optimum audience, connect with that recalcitrant person in your life, and which questions will help you match the perfect person to the job.

Awaken the Giant Within

Anthony Robbins wrote this very application-focused book. *Awaken the Giant Within* (Simon and Schuster Trade Paperbacks, 1992) is packed full of ideas for finding out what things you want from life and how to go about achieving these. There are loads of techniques for taking control of areas of your life that may be causing you hiccups like health, relationships, wealth, and managing your emotions.

Chapter 21

Ten Online NLP Resources

. . . .

In This Chapter

▶ Surfing the web for free knowledge

▶ Finding more useful information to broaden your horizons

. . . .

*T*he Internet has opened up a whole new way of distributing and accessing information on so many subjects, and NLP is no exception. This chapter lists ten Web sites that you should really try to take a look at.

Advanced Neuro-dynamics

This is a very interesting site, found at `www.nlp.com`. It has some meaty articles on the NLP Communication Model and Strategies as well an explanation of Time Line Therapy™, among other topics. A good site if you want a taster or to get clarity on the listed NLP topics.

Anchor Point

Anchor Point is at `www.nlpanchorpoint.com`. This site is crammed full of very informative articles on NLP. Anchor Point Publications publishes an excellent NLP magazine. Visit this site for a variety of books, audio and video tapes, and products on NLP and related topics.

Association for Neuro-linguistic Programming

Association for Neuro-linguistic Programming (UK) is at www.anlp.org. This site is a fount of information for the lay person and NLP practitioner, with information asking 'What is NLP?', a list of NLP practitioners if you need help to resolve issues, and some frequently asked questions.

Shelle Rose Charvet

You will find details of Shelle Rose Charvet on www.successstrategies.com/html/english/index.htm. This is a good site for beginners and practitioners of NLP alike, with humorous articles illustrating principles of NLP. There are some very useful products for use in the business and personal world available from this Web site.

Crown House Publishing

Crown House Publishing – www.crownhouse.co.uk – has a wonderful selection of books on some fascinating subjects stretching from 'Mind Body Spirit' to business, education, and psychotherapy. They carry titles that you may not find elsewhere and are lovely to deal with on the phone, nothing is too much trouble and they give some good advice too!

Design Human Engineering.com

Richard Bandler, co-founder of NLP, can be found at www.designhuman engineering.com and at www.richardbandler.com. Visit this site if you want to know what Richard Bandler has developed, and for opportunities to train with him. This site provides links to other sites and gives lots of information on articles and what to buy by way of books, tapes, and CDs, and what seminars and training programs are available to extend your knowledge.

Encyclopaedia of Systemic NLP and NLP New Coding

If there is only one NLP resource you could access, this is the one. nlpuniversitypress.com is an encyclopaedia of NLP, created primarily by Robert Dilts and Judith DeLozier. Details of the NLP University set up by Robert, Judith, and other leaders in the field can be found at www.nlpu.com. The encyclopaedia is a fabulous resource, given freely in the spirit that shows NLP at its best. This site will enrich the knowledge of both a newcomer and an NLP practitioner.

Michael Gelb

For some more ideas on creativity visit www.michaelgelb.com. Michael Gelb encourages people to use all of their senses to realise their potential for optimum individual and corporate growth. A good site for anyone interested in learning about improving their creativity.

The International Society of Neuro-semantics

Find Bob G Bodenhamer and L Michael Hall, two of the most prolific writers on NLP, at www.neurosemantics.com. Their site is packed full of information by way of articles introducing you to 'self-mastery and success' and has a good review of books for increasing your knowledge of NLP and NLP-based applications. An excellent site for beginners and practitioners.

Quantum Leap, Inc

www.quantum-leap.com is the website for John Grinder, one of the founders of NLP. The site access is free to use and has information on books by John and Carmen Bostic St Clair, the current presidents of Quantum Leap, as well as links to other NLP sites. Probably a site for an NLP practitioner, rather than the newcomer.

Chapter 22

Ten Movies That Include NLP Processes

In This Chapter
▶ Finding the NLP processes hidden in the movies
▶ Exploring your NLP skills through the media of movie

*W*e have selected ten films for you to watch. These are films that we found, in most cases, uplifting and in some cases thought provoking, but most of all we were able to identify aspects of NLP in all these films. We have identified some of the NLP features in each film to illustrate the sorts of things you can look out for as you hone your skills.

As Good As It Gets

Jack Nicholson's portrayal of a curmudgeonly, obsessive-compulsive recluse is hilarious. The way his neighbour's dog trains him in rapport building will delight animal lovers. Starring: Jack Nicholson, Helen Hunt. Director: James L Brooks. Studio: Columbia/Tristar Studios (1997).

Bend It Like Beckham

A delightful movie about girl power, friendship, and fulfilling dreams and aspirations in spite of obstacles. Starring: Parminder K Nagra, Keira Knightley. Director: Gurinder Chadha. Studio: Twentieth Century Fox Home Video (2002).

The Color Purple

The message of this movie must be 'To thine own self be true' or 'what doesn't kill you, makes you stronger'. A moving portrayal of the strength of the human spirit. Keep the tissues to hand! Starring: Danny Glover, Whoopi Goldberg. Director: Steven Spielberg. Studio: Warner Home Video (1985).

Field of Dreams

This is a movie classic about the fulfilment that comes from manifesting one's dreams. Starring: Kevin Costner, Ray Liotta. Director: Phil Alden Robinson. Studio: Universal Studios (1989).

Frida

A powerful movie about a woman, born ahead of her time, nonetheless, living life on her terms. Starring: Salma Hayek, Alfred Molina. Director: Julie Taymor. Studio: Miramax Home Entertainment (2002).

Gattaca

An inspiring sci-fi movie where determination overcomes genetic 'flaws' and proves that having it handed on a silver platter does not ensure success. This film illustrates how focusing on your goal can help you overcome even the most insurmountable obstacle. Starring: Ethan Hawke, Uma Thurman. Director: Andrew Niccol. Studio: Columbia/Tristar Studios (1997).

The Matrix

A thrilling sci-fi exploration of reality and what you can come to see and achieve when you begin to believe in yourself. Starring: Keanu Reeves, Laurence Fishburne. Director: Larry Wachowski, Andy Wachowski. Studio: Warner Studios (1999).

The Shawshank Redemption

Nominated for seven Academy Awards including Best Picture, Actor, and Screenplay, this is an uplifting movie about friendship and survival in a brutal environment. Starring: Tim Robbins, Morgan Freeman. Director: Frank Darabont. Studio: Castle Rock (1994).

Stand and Deliver

Nothing to do with Adam and the Ants, but instead a terrific movie based on a true story, of a high school teacher motivating his class of East Los Angeles barrio kids to believe in themselves and overcome stereotyping. Starring: Edward James Olmos. Director: Ramón Menéndez. Studio: Warner Studios (1988).

The Three Faces of Eve

A very entertaining movie which brought mental illness into the public awareness by exploring the complexity of the human mind. Starring: Joanne Woodward, David Wayne. Director: Nunnally Johnson. Studio: Twentieth Century Fox (1957).

NLP at the Movies

Now that we've given you a taster of the NLPisms that you can look for in a movie, why don't you try your hand at sharpening your NLP skills by spotting some of the items from the list below:

✔ Which NLP presuppositions are demonstrated in this movie?

✔ What do you notice about rapport in this movie?

✔ What maps of the world are depicted – how do they match up to your reality?

✔ Listening to the words people say, what do you notice about their use of language and the metaprograms they run? What about the soundtrack?

✔ What message is there in this movie about dreams, goals, and outcomes?

✔ Are the characters victims of circumstance and if they are, what is the process by which they take control of their lives?

✔ What are the beliefs and values demonstrated in the movie?

✔ How do the characters pace and lead each other?

✔ Which characters, if any, display flexibility in their behaviour?

✔ Looking at the movie, what is the visual impact? How do you experience the kinaesthetic dimensions of feelings and touch, plus a sense of taste or smell?

Part VII
Appendixes

In this part . . .

We've pulled together a resource list to get you started with some addresses for further NLP contacts and training, plus two of the most useful everyday templates from the book. Use these templates to help you build relationships with people and set well-formed outcomes in everything that you do.

Appendix A

Resource List

· ·

*I*n this appendix, we've drawn together a selection of the wealth of resources available on NLP to help you along when you've read everything you wish to in this book. This is not an exhaustive list and you will find many more worthy people and organisations as your interest deepens.

Contact the Authors

Romilla Ready
Ready Solutions Ltd
Tel: 0845 6444759 (UK local rate)
    +44 (0)118 9547744
Fax: +44 (0)118 9547722
E-mail: Enquiries@readysolutionsgroup.com
Web site: www.readysolutionsgroup.com

Kate Burton
Watercress
Tel: +44 (0)118 9734590
E-mail: learn@watercress.uk.com
Web site: www.watercress.uk.com

United Kingdom

The Association of NLP (ANLP)
PO Box 5
Haverfordwest
Wales SO63 4YA
Tel: +44 (0)870 8704970
Web site: www.anlp.org

International NLP Trainers Association
Coombe House
Mill Road
Fareham
Hampshire PO16 0TN
Tel: +44 (0)1489 571171
Fax: +44 (0)1489 885704
E-mail: inlpta@aol.com
Web site: www.inlpta.com

David Straker
Syque (Consulting and Publishing) Ltd
Tel: +44 (0)7966 754976
Web site: www.syque.com

Frank Daniels Associates
103 Hands Road
Heanor
Derbyshire DE75 7BH
Tel: +44 (0)1773 532195

International Teaching Seminars (ITS)
ITS House
Webster Court
Websters Way
Rayleigh
Essex SS6 8JQ
Tel: +44 (0)1268 777125
Fax: +44 (0)1268 777976
Web site: www.itsnlp.com/contact.htm

John Seymour Associates
Park House
10 Park St
Bristol
Avon BS1 5HX
Tel: +44 (0)845 6580654

Performance Partnership
11 Acton Hill Mews
310 Uxbridge Road
Acton
London W3 9QN
Tel: +44 (0)20 8992 9523

Realisation at Stenhouse
36 Plasturton Gardens
Pontcanna
Cardiff CF1 9HF
Tel: +44 (0)1222 377732

PPD Learning Ltd.
PO Box 127
Ashtead
Surrey KT21 1WT
Tel: +44 (0)1372 277123
Fax: +44 (0)1372 277123
E-mail: enquiries@PPDLearning.co.uk
Web site: www.ppdlearning.co.uk

CMT
CountyMark House
50 Regent Street
London W1R 6LP
Tel: +44 (0)20 7470 7262
Fax: +44 (0)20 7470 7243
E-mail: hecmt@aol.com
Web site: cmt-london.co.uk

Customised Management Consultancy Group
Oak Tree Lodge
Bluebell Drive
Burghfield Common
Reading RG7 3EF
Tel: +44 (0)118 9831659
Fax: +44 (0)118 9831659
E-mail: amh@cmcgconsultancy.com
Web site: www.cmcgconsultancy.com

Accelerated Success
Ground 2
50 Hopehill Road
Glasgow G20 7JP
Tel: +44 (0)141 5608714
E-mail: rintu.basu@accelerate
Web site: www.acceleratedsuccess.biz

Chris Rasey
Tel: +44 (0)1488 685488
E-mail: Aquilla@aol.com

Bob Janes
E-mail: bob.janes@bobjames.com
Web site: www.bobjanes.com/modules/sections

USA and Canada

Canadian Association of NLP (CANLP)
Web site: www.canlp.com/welcome.htm

Success Strategies
1264 Lemonville Road
Burlington, Ontario
Canada L7R 3X5
Tel: +1 (905) 6396468
Fax: +1 (905) 6394220
Web site: www.successtrategies.com

NLP Comprehensive
PO Box 927
Evergreen CO 80437
Tel: +1 (303) 9872224, (800) 2331657
Fax: +1 (303) 9872228
E-mail: learn@nlpco.com
Web site: www.nlpcomprehensive.com

Michael Neill
Tel: +1 (818) 3404464
E-mail: michael@successmadefun.com
Web site: www.successmadefun.com
For Michael's Coaching Tip of the Week every Monday morning, please send
a blank e-mail with the word "subscribe" in the subject line to:
subscribe@successmadefun.com

Robbins Research International
9191 Towne Centre Drive
San Diego CA 92122

Advanced Neuro Dynamics
Web site: www.nlp.com

Denmark

Jernbanevej 1
5771 Stenstrup
Fyn
Tel: +45 70 26 01 01
Web site: www.futurepace.dk

NLP Center Danmark
Marianne Kjær
Groskenstræde 7
3000 Helsingør
Tel: +45 49 20 25 17
Web site: www.nlpcenter.dk

Appendix B
Rapport Building

. . . .

*T*his form is a copy of the form you will find in Chapter 7. You may have important people with whom you may want to build stronger relationships – either at home or at work. By asking you to keep a written record we intend for you to take time out to think about these individuals. This in turn will give you the opportunity to focus on what you want from the interaction in order to achieve a win/win outcome. Feel free to photocopy and complete this form as and when you please.

Fill out this form for anyone you'd like to have better rapport with:

Name: _____

Company/group: _____

What is your relationship to this person?_____

Specifically, how would you like your relationship with this person to change?
_____
_____

What impact would this have on you?_____
_____
_____

What impact would it have on the other person?_____
_____
_____

Is it worth investing time and energy?_____
_____
_____

What pressures does this person face?_____
_____
_____

What is most important to them right now? _____
_____
_____

Who do you know who you could talk to who has successfully built rapport
with this person? And what can you learn from them? _____
_____
_____

What other help can you get to build rapport? _____
_____
_____

What ideas do you have now in moving this relationship forward?_____
_____
_____

What is the first step? _____
_____
_____

The Well-formed Outcome Checklist

⬤ ⬤

*T*he checklist below is a summary of the process of creating well-formed outcomes that is described in full in Chapter 3.

Feel free to photocopy this list and complete the questions whenever you want to set very clear goals for yourself.

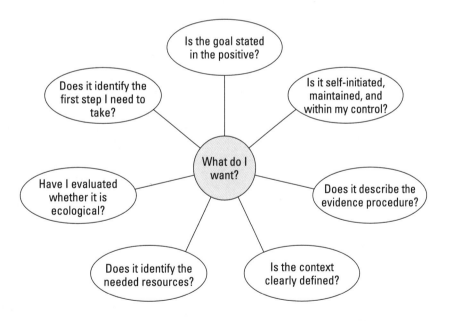

Index

• A •

abstract nouns, 233
abuse
  alcohol abuse, conflicts and, 214
  negative emotions, 204
Accelerated Success, contact
  information, 303
accidents, life-changing experiences, 161
achievement, values and, 66–67
Advanced Neuro-Dynamics Web site,
  291, 304
adventure, values and, 66
alcohol abuse, conflicts, 214
alpha brain waves, 146
analysis, conscious mind control, 51
Anchor Point Web site, 291
anchors
  altering states with, 145
  anchor chains, lengthening, 148–149
  auditory, 143
  being yourself, 142
  breaking state, 141
  calibration, 140–141
  circle of excellence, 150
  collapsing, 148
  in common usage, 144
  desensitisation, 148
  disassociated states, 148
  distinctive, 140
  eliciting, 140–141
  emotional states, altering, 145–147
  gustatory, 143
  intense, 140
  kinaesthetic, 143
  negative, changing, 148–149
  negative, discussed, 140
  olfactory, 143
  patterns, breaking, 148
  personal anchor charts, 142
  physical anchors, hand movements as,
    139–140
  recognition, 142–143
  reinforced, 140
  resourceful states, building, 139–140
  spatial anchoring, 151
  stage anchors, 149–151
  timely, 140
  unique, 140
  usefulness of, 138
  visual, 143
and word, when to use, rapport, 112–114
Andreas, Connirae (*Core
  Transformation*), 288
anger
  away from values, 64
  internal state, 71
  negative emotions, 205
animal loving people, extrovert
  tendencies, 77
ANLP (Association of NLP), contact
  information, 301
anxiety disorders
  negative anchors, changing, 148
  phobias, 57–59
  PTSD (Post Traumatic Stress Disorder),
    56–57
  public speaking, 149–151
  releasing, through time lines, 207
As Good As It Gets, obsessive-compulsive
  disorder, 295
asking questions
  belief sets, challenging, 270–271
  clear and concise questions, 236,
    264–265
  decision making, 269–270

asking questions *(continued)*
  effective listening, 267
  influencing people, 265
  job interviews, 271–273
  pauses during, 266
  positive statements, 266
  rapport-building techniques, 235
  within self, 273–274
  strategies, 264–267
  tag questions, 240–241
  triggers, 263
  voice sensitivity, 236
  what to ask, 267–268
association
  memories, 32
  pictures, 155
  submodalities, 155
Association for Neuro-Linguistic
    Programming Web site, 292
Association of NLP (ANLP), contact
    information, 301
assumptions
  clarification, 234
  presuppositions, 29
attitudes
  belief systems and, 79
  concentration, 16
  negative beliefs, changing, 162
  positive, achieving, 15–16
  positive, life style change, 16
  positive, SMART model, 38
  positive, unconscious mind control, 52
auditory senses
  anchors, 143
  deep love strategy, 192
  discussed, 23
  sound, 87
  submodalities, 157
  word association, 91
authors, contact information, 301
Awaken the Giant Within (Anthony
    Robbins), 289
awareness
  belief systems, 55
  thought processes, 86

away from tendencies, values
  discussed, 64–65
  metaprograms, 122–124

• *B* •

bad behaviours
  eliminating, using swish technique, 154,
    156
  misconceptions about, 26–27
Bandler, Richard
  communication management, 72
  From Frogs to Princes, 288
behavioural flexibility
  discussed, 13
  perspectives, 13
  repetitive behaviours, 16
  success formula, 42
behaviours
  bad behaviours, eliminating, using
    swish technique, 154, 156
  bad behaviours, misconception about,
    26–27
  conflicts, 213
  effective behaviours, maximizing, 174
  external, communication, 70
  inconsiderate, 25
  logical levels of change, 173–175
  metaprograms and, 120
  negative, health values and, 38
  obnoxious, 25
  out-of-character, 58
  positive intent, 25–26, 214
  racists, 26
  self-defeating, 216
being yourself, anchoring
    techniques, 142
beliefs
  attitudes and, 79
  awareness, 55
  belief systems, 62
  challenging, question-asking
    techniques, 270–271
  changing, 61–62

choosing carefully, 78–79
conflicts, 212
convenient, 16
empowering, 163
generalisations and, 75
health values and, 60
logical levels of change, 176–178
negative beliefs, changing, 162
perception, 20, 33
positive beliefs, empowerment, 163
power of, 60–62
religious, 60
self-beliefs, 45
visual senses and, 33
Bend It Like Beckham, NLP process
   examples, 295
beta brain waves, 146
blame, 34
Bodenhamer, Bob G (*The User's Manual
   for the Brain*), 287
body language
   eye accessing cues, 94–97
   rapport-building techniques, 106, 109
brain functions
   brain waves, 146
   left versus right brain functions, 51
   PTSD (Post Traumatic Stress Disorder),
      56–57
breaking rapport, 111–112
breaking state, anchoring techniques,
   141
breathing rates, rapport-building
   techniques, 109
brightness, visual submodalities, 157
Burton, Kate, contact information, 301
but word, when to use, rapport, 112–114

• C •

calibration, anchors, 140–141
Canadian Association of NLP (CANLP),
   contact information, 304

capabilities
   acquiring new, 189–191
   conflicts, 212
   logical levels of change, 175–176
career and work ethics, values, 63
cause and effect, distortion patterns,
   228, 240
change, positive attitude towards, 16
Changing Belief Systems with NLP (Robert
   Dilts), 287
charts, personal anchor, 142
Charvet, Shelle Rose (*Words that Change
   Minds*), 122, 289, 292
chats, rapport in, 111
checklists, outcome thinking, 309
childhood experiences
   imprint period, creation of values, 65
   time lines, 207
choices
   as healthy way of life, 28
   I have no choice misconception, 28
   outcome thinking and, 13
chunking, defined, 244
cigarette smoking
   conflicts, 214
   self-initiated goals, 38
circle of excellence, anchoring
   techniques, 150
clarification, assumptions, 234
Clinical Hypnotherapy (Milton H
   Erickson), 11
CMT, contact information, 303
coaching success, 282–283
collapsing anchors, 148
The Color Purple, NLP process
   examples, 296
colour
   colour associations, dissociation, 155
   sensory awareness, 12
   visual submodalities, 156
commitments, goals, 44
communication
   chunking, 244
   communication model, 14–15

communication *(continued)*
  communication wheel, rapport-building
    techniques, 106–107
  effective, 81
  elicit responses, 69
  external behaviour, 70
  facial expressions as, 24
  generosity and kindness techniques, 81
  honourable intentions, 22
  internal response, 70
  Internet, rapport in, 110
  lack of, problems associated with, 24
  neurological system, 10
  NLP communication model, 70–72
  observation, heightening skills through,
    140–141
  presentations, 280–281
  processes, Seven Plus or Minus Two
    theory, 72–75
  response and, 22
  think before you speak, 81
  translation, 92–94
  verbal, 24
  virtual communication, rapport in,
    110–111
comparisons, deletion patterns, 228, 240
compassion, in place of fear, 33
competence, educators and trainers,
    284–285
complex equivalence, distortion
    pattern, 228
concentration, attitudes, 16
conceptual words, digital processing, 92
conference calls, rapport in, 110
confidence
  extrovert tendencies, 76
  logical levels of change, 171
  rapport-building techniques, 107
confirmation, visual senses, 186
conflicts
  alcohol abuse, 214
  behaviour, 213
  beliefs, 212

capabilities, 212
cigarette smoking, 214
discussed, 211
environmental, 213
function switch resolution
    technique, 220
global, 221
hierarchy of, 212–213
identification, 212
information switch resolution
    technique, 220
intergroup, 221
international, 221
interpersonal, 220
intragroup, 220
intrapersonal, 220
lateral thinking resolution
    technique, 221
logical levels of change, 212
parts intentions, 214
person switch resolution technique, 219
reframing resolution technique,
    219–220
root of problems, identification,
    214–215
within self, 216, 220–221
self-sabotage, 216
skills, 212
time switch resolution technique, 219
of values, 66–67, 212
visual squash resolution technique,
    217–218
confusion, curiosity and, 16
congruence, logical levels of change, 169
Conjoint Family Therapy (Virginia
    Satir), 11
conscious mind versus unconscious
    mind, 50–51
contextual values, 78
contrastive analysis, 154
convenient beliefs, 16
conversation starters, rapport-building
    techniques, 106

Core Transformation (Connirae Andreas), 288
creativity
distortion and, 232
story telling, 250
unconscious mind control, 51
critical submodalities, 160–161
Crown House Publishing Web site, 292
cultural backgrounds
generalisations, 230
perception and, 19
curiosity and confusion, 16
Customised Management Consultancy Group, contact information, 303

● *D* ●

The Dance of Life (Edward T Hall), 197
day dreaming, 68
decisions
decision-making, question-asking, 269–270
decision-making strategies, metaprograms and, 120
limiting, 80
deep love strategy, 192–194
deep structure of language, 225
deletion
Meta Model patterns, 228–229
Milton Model patterns, 239–240
nominalisations, 233
Seven Plus or Minus Two theory, 73
DeLozier, Judith (*Encyclopedia of NLP and NLP New Coding*), 120
delta brain waves, 146
desensitisation, anchoring techniques, 148
Design Human Engineering Web site, 292
detail preferences, metaprograms, 128–129
determination, performance, 29

difference preferences, metaprograms, 130–132
digital processing, conceptual words, 92
Dilts, Robert
Changing Belief Systems, 287
Encyclopedia of NLP and NLP New Coding, 120, 211
meta-mirror development, 115–116
direct metaphors, 257–258
disagreements, rapport-building techniques, 107
disassociation
desensitisation, 148
disassociated states, anchoring techniques, 148
memories, 32
phobias, 59
submodalities, 154–155
discipline, mind control, 11
distinctive anchors, 140
distortion
from bad memories, 80
cause and effect pattern, 228
complex equivalence, 228
creativity and, 232
Meta Model patterns, 228, 232–234
Milton Model patterns, 240
mind reading, 228
misinterpretation, 74
science fiction, 232
diversity, rapport in, 110
divorce, negative emotions, 204
double binds, Milton Model, 241
dream diaries, goal setting, 44–45

● *E* ●

ecology checks, goals, 40–41
educators, competence, 284–285
effective behaviours, 174
effective communication, 81

elicit responses
  anchors, 140–141
  communication, 69
e-mail, rapport in, 110
embedded commands, Milton Model, 241
emergency service personnel, Post
    Traumatic Stress Disorder, 56
emotional states, altering, 145–147
emotions
  negative, abuse, 204
  negative, anger, 205
  negative, divorce, 204
  negative, phobias, 204
  negative, releasing through time lines,
    203–206
  negative, trauma, 204
  response and, 22
  touch senses and, 87
  unconscious mind control, 51
empowerment, positive beliefs, 163
Encyclopedia of NLP an NLP New Coding
    (Robert Dilts and Judith DeLozier),
    120, 211
Encyclopedia of Systemic NLP and NLP
    New Coding Web site, 293
ends values, 64–65
energy levels, rapport-building
    techniques, 109
environment
  conflicts, 213
  logical levels of change, 172–173
Erickson, Milton H
  Clinical Hypnotherapy, 11
  Milton Model, 238–242
evidence procedure, SMART model, 39
excellence
  discussed, 35
  NLP approaches to, 15
  outcomes, knowing what you want,
    36–37
  SMART model, 37–41
  successful performance, 29
  well-formed outcomes, achieving, 37

expectations, setting clear, 39
experiences, subjective, 10
external behaviours, communication, 70
external preferences, metaprograms,
    126–127
extrovert tendencies
  animal loving people, 77
  metaprograms, 76–77
eye accessing cues, 94–97, 194
eye-to-eye contact, rapport-building
    techniques, 107

• *F* •

facial expressions
  as communication, 24
  eye accessing cues, 96
  rapport, breaking, 111
failure
  learning from, 21–22
  worrying about, 21
family environments
  family values, 63
  story telling in, 253–254
  wheel of life demonstration, 43
faxes, rapport in, 110
fear, compassion in place of, 33
feedback
  normal, 21
  positive, 23
  rapport-building techniques, 106
  unexpected results, learning from,
    21–22
feelings
  intensity of meaning, changing, 154
  kinaesthetic senses, 187
Field of Dreams, NLP process
    examples, 296
fight or flight response, 130
financial interests
  conflict of values, 66
  health values and, 60
  toward values, 64

values and, 67
wheel of life demonstration, 43
first position, perceptual positions, 114
flexibility. *See* behavioural flexibility
forgiveness, 206
Frank Daniels Associates, contact
    information, 302
Frankl, Viktor (*Man's Search for*
    Meaning), 179
freedom
    toward values, 64
    values and, 67
Frida, NLP process examples, 296
friendships
    values, 77
    wheel of life demonstration, 43
From Frogs to Princes (John Grinder and
    Richard Bandler), 288
frustration, internal state, 71
fulfillment, values and, 66
fun
    as stress reliever, 16
    wheel of life demonstration, 43
function switch technique, conflict
    resolution, 220
future, time lines, 207
fuzzy images, visual submodalities, 157

• *G* •

galeophobia, 58
Gattaca, NLP process examples, 296
Gelb, Michael, 293
generalisations
    from bad memories, 80
    beliefs and, 75
    cultural, 230
    Meta Model patterns, 228, 230–232
    Milton Model patterns, 240
    presuppositions and, 18
generosity and kindness, good
    communication techniques, 81
genuine interests, rapport-building
    techniques, 106

Gestalt Psychology (Fritz Perls), 11
gestures, rapport-building techniques,
    106, 109
global conflicts, 221
global preferences, metaprograms,
    128–129
goals
    adjusting, 41
    commitments, 44
    contextualised, 39
    dream diaries, 44–45
    ecology checks, 40–41
    first steps toward, 41
    long-term, 44
    personal goals, wheel of life, 42–43
    positive, well-formed outcomes, 37
    self-initiated, 38–39
    short-term, 44
    writing down, 44–45
grammar, transformational, 227
greetings, rapport, 102
Grinder, John
    communication management, 72
    From Frogs to Princes, 288
groupthink, defined, 247
guilt, away from value, 64
gustatory senses
    anchors, 143
    deep love strategy, 192
    discussed, 23
    gustatory words, 91

• *H* •

habits
    cigarette smoking, 38, 214
    ecology checks, 40
    eliminating, using swish technique,
        154, 156
    nail-biting, 164
Hall, Edward T (*The Dance of Life*), 197
Hall, L Michael (*The User's Manual for the*
    Brain), 287

hand movements, as physical anchor, 139–140
happiness
  health values and, 60
  toward value, 64
  values, 63, 77
health values
  beliefs and, 60
  discussed, 77
  financial interests and, 60
  happiness and, 60
  maintaining, 283–284
  negative behaviours and, 38
  public speaking, anxiety, 149–151
  toward values, 64
hierarchy of conflicts, 212–213
honesty, values, 77
honourable intentions,
    communication, 22
humour, in story telling, 259
hypnosis
  defined, 245
  discussed, 238
  fear of, 245
  Milton Model, 238–242
  relaxation techniques, 246–248
  unconscious mind control, 244–245
  vagueness, 242–244
  views on, 244

• *I* •

identification
  conflicts, discussed, 212
  conflicts, root of problems, identifying,
    214–215
  logical levels of change, 178–179
  metaprograms, 133–134
imagination
  lateral thinking, 221
  story telling, 250
imprint period of life, creation of
    values, 65

inconsiderate behaviours, 25
indirect metaphors, 257–258
influencing people
  question-asking, 265
  strategies for, 194–195
Influencing with Integrity (Geine Z
    Laborde), 288
information switch technique, conflict
    resolution, 220
inquisitive mindset, self development,
    277–278
inspiration, successful performance, 29
integrity
  manipulation versus, 12
  rapport-building techniques, 107
intense anchors, 140
intensity
  kinaesthetic submodalities, 158
  of meaning, changing, 154–155
intention, rapport-building
    techniques, 106
intergroup conflicts, 221
internal preferences, metaprograms,
    126–127
internal representation, 73
internal response, communication, 70–71
internal state, internal response, 70–71
international conflicts, 221
International NLP Trainers Association,
    contact information, 302
International Teaching Seminars (ITS),
    contact information, 302
Internet communication, rapport in, 110
interpersonal conflicts, 220
interviews, question-asking techniques,
    271–273
in-time diagrams, time lines, 200–201
intragroup conflicts, 220
intrapersonal conflicts, 220
introductions, story telling, 260
introvert tendencies, metaprograms,
    76–77
intuition, unconscious mind control, 51

isometric metaphors, 257–258
ITS (International Teaching Seminars),
    contact information, 302

• *J* •

James, Tad (*Presenting Magically*), 289
Janes, Bob, contact information, 304
Jernbanevej 1, contact information, 305
job interviews, question-asking
    techniques, 271–273
John Seymour Associates, contact
    information, 302
journals, story telling, 258–259
judgments, deletion patterns, 228, 240
Jung, Carl (*Psychological Types*), 119

• *K* •

kinaesthetic senses
    anchors, 143
    deep love strategy, 192
    discussed, 23
    feelings, 187
    kinaesthetic words, 91
    submodalities, 158
kindness and generosity, good
    communication techniques, 81
Kline, Nancy (*Time to Think*), 266
Korzybski (*Science and Sanity*), 18

• *L* •

Laborde, Geine Z (*Influencing with
    Integrity*), 288
language
    body language, 94–97
    chunking, 244
    deep structure of, 225
    logical levels of change and, 180
    Milton Model patterns, 239–240
    patterns, metaprograms and, 119–120

preferences, listening and, 90
rapport-building techniques, 111
surface structure of, 225
lateral thinking techniques, conflict
    resolution, 221
laughter, as stress reliever, 16
leadership goals, logical levels of
    change, 171
learning, from unexpected results, 21
left brain processes
    right brain processes versus, 51
    story telling, 250
left-handed people, eye accessing cues,
    95
legacies, fulfilling, 36
letters, rapport in, 110
life-changing experiences, 161
limiting decisions, 80
linguistics, defined, 10
listening
    language preferences, 90
    question-asking and, 267
    without hearing, 86
locations
    auditory submodalities, 157
    kinaesthetic submodalities, 158
    time lines, 204–205
    visual submodalities, 156
logic, conscious mind control, 51
logical levels of change
    behaviours, 173–175
    beliefs, 176–178
    capabilities, 175–176
    conflicts, 212
    congruence, 169
    considerations, 169
    environment, 172–173
    identity, 178–179
    language and, 180
    neurological levels, 168
    overview, 168–169
    positive energy forces, 167–168
    purpose, 179–180
    requirements for, 172

logical levels of change *(continued)*
  resources, compiling, 171
  step-by-step guidance, 170–171
  team building techniques, 180–181
  uses of, 171–172
  values, 176–178
logical words, digital processing, 92
loneliness, away from values, 64
long-term goal setting, 44
looking without seeing, 86
love
  deep love strategy, 192–194
  toward values, 64

• *M* •

The Magic of Metaphor (Nick Owen), 255, 289
Manage Yourself, Manage Your Life (Ian McDermott and Ian Shircore), 288
manipulation
  beliefs, 61
  integrity versus, 12
  memory control, 31–33
  values, 66
Man's Search for Meaning (Viktor Frankl), 179
matching and mirroring, rapport-building techniques, 108–109
mathematics, conscious mind control, 51
The Matrix, NLP process examples, 296
McDermott, Ian (*Manage Yourself, Manage Your Life*), 288
meaning, intensity of, changing, 154–155
means values, 64–65
meditation, unconscious mind control, 52–53
meetings, meta-mirror exercise, 115
memories
  association, 32
  changing, through mind-control, 159
  dissociation, 32
  distortion and generalisation from, 80

manipulating, 31–33
negative beliefs, changing, 162
negative emotions, releasing through therapy, 124
negative emotions, unresolved, 52
organization structure, 198
repressed, 52–53
root cause, 198
short-term, conscious mind control, 50–51
storing, unconscious mind control, 51
traumatic, 59
Meta Model, experience and language links
  deletion patterns, 228–229
  discussed, 226
  distortion patterns, 228, 232–234
  generalisation patterns, 228, 230–232
  Milton Model versus, 238–242
  transformational grammar, 227
  when to use, 234–235
meta-mirror development (Robert Dilts), 115–116
metaphors
  direct, 257–258
  indirect, 257–258
  isometric, 257
  story telling and, 254–255
  as therapeutic communication, 255–257
metaprograms
  away from tendencies, 122–124
  behaviours and, 120
  combinations of, 132–133
  decision-making strategies and, 120
  defined, 117
  detail preferences, 128–129
  difference preferences, 130–132
  discussed, 75
  external preferences, 126–127
  extrovert/introvert tendencies, 76–77
  global preferences, 128–129
  history, 119
  identification, 133–134

internal preferences, 126–127
language patterns and, 119–120
list of, 118
options preferences, 125–126
proactive tendencies, 120–122
procedures preferences, 125–126
reactive tendencies, 120–122
sameness preferences, 130–132
sameness with difference preferences, 130–132
toward tendencies, 122–124
Michael Gelb Web site, 293
Miller, George (Seven Plus or Minus Two theory), 72–75
Milton Model (Milton H Erickson), 238–242
mind control, unconscious
  conflicts within self, resolving, 216
  conscious mind versus, 50–51
  discipline, 11
  discussed, 49
  hypnosis, 244–245
  meditation and relaxation activities, 52
  memories, changing, 159
  morality issues, 53–54
  negative and repressed memories, 52–53
  positive thoughts, 52
mind reading, distortion patterns, 228, 240
mind-body connection, 27–28
misinterpretation, distortion, 74
mismatching, rapport and, 111–112
modalities, representational systems, 86, 185
modeling period of life, creation of values, 65
morality issues, unconscious mind control, 53–54
motivation
  story telling as, 251–253
  values, 63
movement
  kinaesthetic submodalities, 158

visual submodalities, 157
movies, NLP process examples, 295–298
multi-sensory experiences, 86
multi-tasking, 72
music, as emotional state alteration, 145–147
Myers-Briggs Type Indicator personality type tool, 119

• *N* •

nail-biting habits, 164
name, addressing questions by, rapport, 111
National Institute of Mental Health, 27
negative anchors
  changing, 148–149
  discussed, 140
negative behaviours, health values and, 38
negative beliefs, changing, 162
negative emotions
  abuse, 204
  anger, 205
  divorce, 204
  phobias, 204
  releasing through time lines, 203–206
  trauma, 204
negative memories
  releasing through therapy, 124
  unresolved, 52
negotiations
  rapport-building techniques, 112
  win-win solutions, 279–280
Neill, Michael, contact information, 304
Neuro-linguistic Programming. *See* NLP
neurological levels, logical levels, 168
neurological system, communication processes, 10
Neuro-Semantics Web site, 293
neurotransmitters, mind-body connection, 27–28
neutral state, desensitisation, 148
neutral words, 91

NLP Center Denmark, contact information, 305
NLP Comprehensive, contact information, 304
NLP (Neuro-linguistic Programming)
  communication model, 14–15, 70–72
  defined, 9–11
  future of, 11
  history of, 11
  pillars of, 12–14
nominalisations, deletion patterns, 228, 233, 240
non-sensory words, 91
normal feedback, 21
nouns, abstract, 233
novelty values, RAS, 54–55

• *O* •

obnoxious behaviours, 25
observation, heightening skills through, 140–141
obsessive-compulsive disorder, *As Good as it Gets* movie example, 295
olfactory senses
  anchors, 143
  deep love strategy, 192
  discussed, 23
  olfactory words, 91
online resources. *See* Web sites
options preferences, metaprograms, 125–126
otophobia, 58
outcome thinking
  checklist for, 309
  choices and, 13
  discussed, 12–13
  knowing what you want, 36–37
  lateral thinking techniques, conflict resolution, 221
  outcome frame approach, 35
  resources needed for, 24, 40
  success formula, 42

think before you speak, 81
values, conflict of, 66
well-formed outcomes, achieving, 37
out-of-character behaviours, 58
overriding values, 67
Owen, Nick (*The Magic of Metaphor*), 255, 289

• *P* •

pacing to lead, rapport-building techniques, 106
panic disorders, 57
parts intentions, conflicts, 214
patterns, breaking, 148
pauses, during question-asking, 266
peladophobia, 58
perception
  belief systems, 20, 33
  cultural differences, 19
  other people's, 60
  perceptual positions, rapport, 114
  senses and, 18–19
performance
  determination, 29
  excellence, 29
  logical levels of change, 171
Performance Partnership, contact information, 302
Perls, Fritz (*Gestalt Psychology*), 11
person switch technique, conflict resolution, 219
personal anchor charts, 142
personal appearance, conflict of values, 66
personal goals, wheel of life, 42–43
personal relationships, maintaining, 278
personality traits, time line effects, 200
personality type tools, Myers-Briggs Type Indicator, 119
perspectives, behavioural flexibility, 13
philophobia, 58

phobias
  dissociation, 59
  fast phobia cure, 58
  negative emotions, 204
  origins, 57–58
  stimulus, phobic responses to, 59
phobophobia, 58
phone conversations, rapport in,
    110–111
physical anchors, hand movements as,
    139–140
physical movement, breaking rapport,
    111
pictures
  associations, 155
  sight and, visual dimension, 87
points of view, understanding others,
    114–116
political and religious views, rapport-
    building techniques, 107
positive attitudes
  achieving, 15–16
  SMART model, 38
  toward change, 16
  unconscious mind control, 52
positive beliefs, empowerment, 163
positive energy forces, logical levels of
    change, 167–168
positive feedback, 23
positive goals, well-formed outcomes, 37
positive intent
  behaviours, 25–26
  secondary gain, 25–26
positive role models, 147
positive statements, question-asking, 266
Post Traumatic Stress Disorder (PTSD),
    56–57
poverty, away from values, 64
power
  of beliefs, 60–62
  values and, 66
  of words, 10

PPD Learning Ltd Web site, 303
predicates, 88
presentations, effective communication,
    280–281
Presenting Magically (David Shepard and
    Tad James), 289
pressure, kinaesthetic submodalities, 158
presuppositions
  assumptions, 29
  generalisations and, 18
  unfamiliar territory, 19
primary representation system
  critical submodalities, 160
  discussed, 23
proactive tendencies, metaprograms,
    120–122
problems
  heart of, identifying, 214–215
  problem solving techniques, 34–35
procedures preferences, metaprograms,
    125–126
procrastination, 130
professional environments, story telling
    in, 251–253
professional relationships,
    maintaining, 278
Psychological Types (Carl Jung), 119
PTSD (Post Traumatic Stress Disorder),
    56–57
public speaking, 149–151
publications
  Awaken the Giant Within (Anthony
    Robbins), 289
  Changing Belief Systems (Robert
    Dilts), 287
  Clinical Hypnotherapy (Milton H
    Erickson), 11
  Conjoint Family Therapy (Virginia
    Satir), 11
  Core Transformation (Connirae
    Andreas), 288
  The Dance of Life (Edward T Hall), 197

publications *(continued)*
  Encyclopedia of NLP and NLP New Coding (Robert Dilts and Judith DeLozier), 120
  From Frogs to Princes (John Grinder and Richard Bandler), 288
  Gestalt Psychology (Fritz Perls), 11
  Influencing with Integrity (Geine Z Laborde), 288
  The Magic of Metaphor (Nick Owen), 255, 289
  Manage Yourself, Manage Your Life (Ian McDermott and Ian Shircore), 288
  Man's Search for Meaning (Victor Frankl), 179
  Presenting Magically (David Shepard and Tad James), 289
  Psychological Types (Carl Jung), 119
  Science and Sanity (Korzybski), 18
  Time to Think (Nancy Kline), 266
  The User's Manual for the Brain (Bob G Bodenhamer and L Michael Hall), 287
  Words that Change Minds (Shelle Rose Charvet), 122, 289
purpose, logical levels of change, 179–180

• Q •

quality, kinaesthetic submodalities, 158
Quantum Leap, Inc Web site, 293
questions, asking
  belief sets, challenging, 270–271
  clear and concise questions, 236, 264–265
  decision making, 269–270
  effective listening, 267
  influencing people, 265
  job interviews, 271–273
  pauses during, 266
  positive statements, 266
  rapport-building techniques, 235
  within self, 273–274
  strategies, 264–267
  tag questions, 240–241
  triggers, 263
  voice sensitivity, 236
  what to ask, 267–268

• R •

racist behaviours, 26
rapport
  and word, when to use, 112–114
  breaking, 111–112
  building rapport through words, 90–92
  but word, when to use, 112–114
  in chats, 111
  communication wheel and, 106–107
  in conference calls, 110
  conversation starters, 106
  discussed, 101
  in diversity, 110
  in e-mail, 110
  eye-to-eye contact, 107
  facial expressions, 111
  in faxes, 110
  flexibility, 103
  greetings, 102
  importance of, 102–105
  in Internet communication, 110
  language styles, 111
  in letters, 110
  matching and mirroring, 108–109
  meta-mirror technique, 115–116
  mismatching and, 111–112
  in negotiations, 112, 280
  pacing to lead, 106
  perceptual positions, 114
  in phone conversations, 110–111
  points of view, understanding others, 114–116
  question asking, 235
  rapport-building techniques, 105–109

recognition, 102–103
as relationship builder, 12
sales relationships, 280
self-assessment form, 307–308
in small talk, 111
story telling, when to stop, 113
in transactions, 110
in video-conferencing, 110–111
in virtual communication, 110–111
voice volume, 111
whom to build rapport with,
        identifying, 103–104
in workplace, 110
RAS. *See* Reticular Activation System
Rasey, Chris, contact information, 304
reactive tendencies, metaprograms,
        120–122
Ready, Romilla, contact information, 301
Ready Solutions Ltd Web site, 301
Realisation at Stenhouse, contact
        information, 303
reality, VAK (visual, auditory, and
        kinaesthetic) senses, 86–90
recognition
    anchors, 142–143
    rapport, 102–103
reframing technique, conflict resolution,
        219–220
reinforced anchors, 140
relationships
    logical levels of change, 171
    personal and professional,
        maintaining, 278
    rapport-building techniques, 12
    wheel of life demonstration, 43
relaxation
    hypnosis, 246–248
    music, as therapy, 145–147
    unconscious mind control, 52
religion
    religious and political views, rapport-
        building techniques, 107
    religious beliefs, 60

repetitive behaviours, behavioural
        flexibility, 16
representational systems
    modalities, 185
    senses, 88
    strategies, 185
repressed memory, 52–53
resentment, internal state, 71
resourceful states, anchoring
        techniques, 139–140
resources
    compiling, logical levels of change, 171
    need for, identifying, 40
    outcome thinking, 24, 40
    rapport-building techniques, 106
    time management, 282
respect, rapport-building
        techniques, 107
response, to communication
    discussed, 22
    elicit response, anchors, 140–141
    elicit response, discussed, 69
    emotions about, 22
    fight or flight, 130
    internal response, 70–71
    phobias, 59
    sympathy, 41
    tolerance, 20
results, unexpected, learning from, 21
Reticular Activation System (RAS)
    discussed, 44
    novelty values, 54–55
    survival criteria, 54–55
    values and, 63
rhythm, auditory submodalities, 157
right brain processes
    left brain processes versus, 51
    story telling, 250
road rage, 186
Robbins, Anthony (*Awaken the Giant
        Within*), 289
Robbins Research International, contact
        information, 304

role models, as emotional state
    alteration, 147
root cause, memories, 198

• S •

sadness, away from values, 64
sales relationships, rapport, 280
sameness with difference preferences,
    metaprograms, 130–132
Satir, Virginia (*Conjoint Family
    Therapy*), 11
Science and Sanity (Korzybski), 18
science fiction, distortion, 232
second position, perceptual
    positions, 114
secondary gain
  ecology checks, 40–41
  positive intent, 25–26
security, values and, 66
SEE (Significant Emotional Event),
    198, 213
self-beliefs, 45
self-defeating behaviours, 216
self development, inquisitive mindset,
    277–278
self-employment, evidence procedure, 39
self-esteem, 33
self-initiated goals, 38–39
self-sabotage, 216
self-talk, internal processes, 70
senses
  anchoring techniques, 143
  auditory, anchors, 143
  auditory, deep love strategy, 192
  auditory, discussed, 23
  auditory, sound, 87
  auditory, submodalities, 157
  auditory, word association, 91
  awareness, 12
  deep love strategy, 192
  filtration process, 18

gustatory, anchors, 143
gustatory, deep love strategy, 192
gustatory, discussed, 23
gustatory, gustatory words, 91
kinaesthetic, anchors, 143
kinaesthetic, deep love strategy, 192
kinaesthetic, discussed, 23
kinaesthetic, feelings, 187
kinaesthetic, submodalities, 158
kinaesthetic, words, 91
modalities, 61
multi-sensory experiences, 86
olfactory, anchors, 143
olfactory, deep love strategy, 192
olfactory, discussed, 23
olfactory, words, 91
perception and, 18–19
power of words and, 10
primary representation system, 23
representation systems, 88
touch, emotional aspects of, 87
VAK (visual, auditory and kinaesthetic),
    86–90
visual, anchors, 143
visual, beliefs and, 33
visual, confirmation, 186
visual, deep love strategy, 192
visual, discussed, 23
visual, sights and pictures, 87
visual, submodalities, 156–157
visual, visual remembered position, eye
    accessing cues, 95
visual, words, 91
sensitive discussions, meta-mirror
    exercise, 115
sensory awareness, 12, 42
sensory-specific words and phrases, 91,
    93
Seven Plus or Minus Two theory (George
    Miller), 72–75
sexual content in negotiation, breaking
    rapport, 112

shape, kinaesthetic submodalities, 158
The Shawshank Redemption, NLP
  process examples, 297
Shepard, David (*Presenting Magically*),
  289
Shircore, Ian (*Manage Yourself, Manage
  Your Life*), 288
short-term goal setting, 44
short-term memory, conscious mind
  control, 50–51
sight and pictures, visual dimension, 87
Significant Emotional Event (SEE), 198,
  213
sites. *See* Web sites
size, visual submodalities, 157
skills, conflicts, 212
small talk, rapport in, 111
SMART (Specific, Measurable,
  Achievable, Realistic and Timed)
  model
  discussed, 37
  evidence procedure, 39
  goals, contextualised, 39
  goals, ecology checks, 40–41
  positive attitudes, 38
  resources, need for, 40
  self-initiated goals, 38–39
smoking. *See* cigarette smoking
socialisation period of life, creation of
  values, 65
sounds
  auditory dimension, 87
  auditory submodalities, 157
  sensory awareness, 12
spatial anchoring, 151
Specific, Measurable, Achievable
  Realistic and Timed model. *See*
  SMART model
spelling strategies, 195–196
spirituality, wheel of life
  demonstration, 43
S-R (Strategy-Response) model, 184
stage anchors, 149–151

Stand and Deliver, NLP process
  examples, 297
still images
  kinaesthetic submodalities, 158
  visual submodalities, 157
stimulus
  internal representations, 73
  phobic responses to, 59
  triggers, 142
story telling
  creativity, 250
  in family environment, 253–254
  humour in, 259
  imagination, 250
  introductions, examples of, 260
  journals for, 258–259
  left brain processes, 250
  metaphors, 254–255
  as motivation technique, 251–253
  in professional environments, 251–253
  for purposeful reasons, 251
  right brain processes, 250
  story loops, 260–261
  techniques, 259–260
  visualisations, 250
  when to stop, rapport-building
    techniques, 113
Straker, David, contact information, 302
strategies
  capabilities, acquiring new, 189–191
  decision-making strategies,
    metaprograms and, 120
  deep love, 192–194
  for influencing people, 194–195
  other peoples strategies, recognizing,
    187–188
  overview, 183
  question-asking, 264–267
  representational systems, 185
  spelling, 195–196
  S-R model, 184
  success, 196
  TOTE model, 184–187

Strategy-Response (S-R) model, 184
stress
  PTSD (Post Traumatic Stress Disorder),
    56–57
  stress relievers, laughter and fun as, 16
subjective experiences, 10
submodalities
  association, 154–155
  auditory, 157
  contrastive analysis, 154
  critical, 160–161
  defined, 153
  dissociation, 154–155
  examples of, 154
  kinaesthetic, 158
  life-changing experiences, 161
  meaning, intensity of, changing,
    154–155
  memories, changing through mind-
    control, 159
  positive beliefs, empowerment, 163
  visual, 156–157
  worksheet, 165–166
success
  coaching, 282–283
  determination, 29
  formula for, 42
  performance, excellence, 29
  strategies, 196
  values and, 66
Success Made Fun Web site, 304
Success Strategies, contact
    information, 292, 304
surface structure of language, 225
survival criteria, RAS, 54–55
swish technique, eliminating bad habits
    using, 164, 165
sympathy, as response technique, 41
Syque Web site, 302

• *T* •

tag questions, 240–241
talking to self, internal processes, 70

teaching, story telling and, 251
temperature, kinaesthetic
    submodalities, 158
tempo, auditory submodalities, 157
Test, Operate, Test, Exit (TOTE) model,
    184–187
texture, kinaesthetic submodalities, 158
therapeutic communication, metaphors
    as, 255–257
therapy, Time Line Therapy
  discussed, 65
  negative memories, releasing, 124
  online resources, 291
theta brain waves, 146
think before you speak. *See also*
    outcome thinking, 81
third position, perceptual positions, 114
thought processes, awareness, 86
The Three Faces of Eve, NLP process
    examples, 297
through-time diagrams, time lines,
    200–201
Time Line Therapy
  discussed, 65
  negative memories, releasing, 124
  online resources, 291
time lines
  anxiety, releasing, 207
  changing, 200–203
  childhood experiences, seeking, 207
  forgiveness, finding, 206
  future, creating better, 207
  in-time diagrams, 200–201
  locations, 204–205
  negative emotions, releasing, 203–206
  overview, 199
  personality traits, 200
  through-time diagrams, 200–201
time management, 282
time switch technique, conflict
    resolution, 219
Time to Think (Nancy Kline), 266
timely anchors, 140
tolerance, response, 20

tone of voice
  auditory submodalities, 157
  rapport-building techniques, 106, 109
TOTE (Test, Operate, Test, Exit) model,
    184–187
touch senses, emotional aspects as, 87
touching without feeling, 86
toward tendencies, values
  discussed, 64
  metaprograms, 122–124
trainers, competence, 284–285
trance. *See* hypnosis
transactions, rapport in, 110
transformational grammar, 227
translation, effective communication,
    92–94
trauma, negative emotions, 204
triggers, stimulus, 142
triskadekaphobia, 58
tunes, auditory submodalities, 157

• *U* •

unconscious mind control
  conflicts within self, resolving, 216
  conscious mind versus, 50–51
  discipline, 11
  discussed, 49
  hypnosis, 244–245
  meditation and relaxation activities,
    52–53
  morality issues, 53–54
  negative and repressed memories,
    52–53
  positive thoughts, 52
unexpected results, learning from, 21
unfamiliar territory, presuppositions, 19
unique anchors, 140
universal quantifiers
  deletion patterns, 228
  generalisation patterns, 240

The User's Manual for the Brain (Bob G
    Bodenhamer and L Michael
    Hall), 287

• *V* •

vagueness, hypnosis and, 242–244
VAK (visual, auditory, and kinaesthetic)
    senses, 86–90
values
  achievement and, 66–67
  adventure, 66
  away from tendencies, discussed, 64–65
  away from tendencies, metaprograms,
    122–124
  career and work ethics, 63
  changing, 66
  conflict of, 66–67, 212
  contextual, 78
  creation of, 65
  eliciting, 65–66
  ends values, 64–65
  family, 63
  financial interests, 67
  freedom, 67
  friendships, 77
  fulfillment and, 66
  happiness, 63, 77
  health, 77
  honesty, 77
  importance of, accessing, 78
  logical levels of change, 176–178
  means values, 64–65
  motivational, 63
  negative beliefs, changing, 162
  overriding, 67
  power and, 66
  RAS and, 63
  security, 66
  success and, 66
  toward value tendencies, 64–65
verbal communication, 24

verbal language, conscious mind control, 51
verbs, unspecified, deletion patterns, 228, 239
video-conferencing, rapport in, 110–111
virtual communication, rapport in, 110–111
visual, auditory and kinaesthetic (VAK) senses, 86–90
visual senses
  anchors, 143
  beliefs and, 33
  confirmation, 186
  deep love strategy, 192
  discussed, 23
  sights and pictures, 87
  submodalities, 156–157
  visual remembered position, eye accessing cues, 95
  visual words, 91
visual squash technique, conflict resolution, 217–218
visualisations, story telling, 250
voice
  pitch, auditory submodalities, 157
  sensitivity in, question asking, 236
  tone, auditory submodalities, 157
  tone, rapport-building techniques, 106, 109
volume auditory submodalities, 157

• W •

war victims, Post Traumatic Stress Disorder, 56
Web sites
  Accelerated Success, 303
  Advanced Neuro-Dynamics, 291, 304
  Anchor Point, 291
  ANLP (Association of NLP), 301
  Association for Neuro-Linguistic Programming, 292
  CANLP (Canadian Association of NLP), 304
  CountyMark House, 303
  Crown House Publishing, 292
  Customised Management Consultancy Group, 303
  Design Human Engineering, 292
  Encyclopedia of Systemic NLP and NLP New Coding, 293
  International NLP Trainers Association, 302
  ITS (International Teaching Seminars), 302
  Jernbanevej 1, 305
  Michael Gelb, 293
  Neuro-Semantics, 293
  NLP Center Denmark, 305
  NLP Comprehensive, 304
  PPD Learning Ltd, 303
  Quantum Leap, Inc, 293
  Ready Solutions Ltd, 301
  Success Made Fun, 304
  Success Strategies, 292, 304
  Syque, 302
weight loss, away and toward tendencies, 123
wheel of life, 42–43
words
  abstract nouns, 233
  and word, when to use, rapport, 112–114
  auditory, discussed, 91
  auditory, submodalities, 157
  building rapport through, 90–92
  but word, when to use, rapport, 112–114
  digital processing, 92
  gustatory, 91
  kinaesthetic, 91
  neutral, 91
  non-sensory, 91
  olfactory, 91
  power of, 10

sensory-specific, 91, 93
transformational grammar, 227
translators, 92–94
visual, 91
Words that Change Minds (Shelle Rose Charvet), 122, 289
work ethics and career, values, 63

workplace, rapport in, 110
worksheets, submodalities, 165–166

• *X* •

xyrophobia, 58

Notes

Notes

Notes

Notes

Notes

FOR DUMMIES®

The easy way to get more done and have more fun

UK EDITIONS

The easiest way to rent out your property for profit **Renting Out Your Property FOR DUMMIES®** Melanie Bien Robert Griswold *A Reference for the Rest of Us!* **0-7645-7016-1**	*A state-of-the-art guide for British diabetics* **Diabetes FOR DUMMIES®** Dr Sarah Jarvis, GP Alan L. Rubin, M.D. *A Reference for the Rest of Us!* **0-7645-7019-6**	*An easy book for a tough game* **Rugby Union FOR DUMMIES®** Nick Cain Greg Growden *A Reference for the Rest of Us!* **0-7645-7020-X**
An insider's guide to Formula One™ **Formula One Racing FOR DUMMIES®** Jonathan Noble Mark Hughes *A Reference for the Rest of Us!* *** 0-7645-7015-3**	*"My kind of history."* **British History FOR DUMMIES®** *A Reference for the Rest of Us!* *** 0-7645-7021-8**	*Understand the system and get the price you're after* **Buying and Selling a Home FOR DUMMIES®** Melanie Bien *A Reference for the Rest of Us!* **0-7645-7027-7** **Due August 2004**
The easy guide for UK investors **Investing FOR DUMMIES®** Tony Levene *A Reference for the Rest of Us!* **0-7645-7023-4**	*Show you know your business numbers – in any career* **Understanding Business Accounting FOR DUMMIES®** Colin Barrow *A Reference for the Rest of Us!* **0-7645-7025-0**	*Understand business basics and be your own boss* **Starting a Business FOR DUMMIES®** Colin Barrow *A Reference for the Rest of Us!* **0-7645-7018-8**

**Available in the UK at bookstores nationwide and online at
www.wileyeurope.com or call 0800 243407 to order direct**

 **WILEY**

* Also available in the United States at www.dummies.com

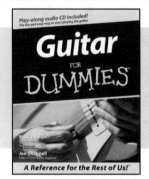

FOR DUMMIES®

The easy way to get more done and have more fun

COMPUTING & TECHNOLOGY

0-7645-0893-8

0-7645-4356-3

0-7645-1664-7

0-7645-4074-2

0-7645-0261-1

0-7645-4173-0

Also available:

Dreamweaver® MX 2004 For Dummies®
0-7645-4342-3

Microsoft Office 2003 For Windows For Dummies®
0-7645-3860-8

Windows XP All-in-One Desk Reference For Dummies®
0-7645-1548-9

Office XP For Dummies®
0-7645-0830-X

Excel 2003 For Windows For Dummies®
0-7645-3756-3

Macromedia® Flash™ MX 2004 For Dummies®
0-7645-4358-X

PHP and MySQL™ For Dummies® 2nd Edition
0-7645-5589-8

Word 2003 for Windows For Dummies®
0-7645-3982-5

Access 2003 For Windows For Dummies®
0-7645-3881-0

Creating Web Pages All-in-One Desk Reference For Dummies®, 2nd Edition
0-7645-4345-8

Networking For Dummies®, 6th Edition
0-7645-1677-9

HTML 4 For Dummies®, 4th Edition
0-7645-1995-6

Creating Web Pages For Dummies®, 6th Edition
0-7645-1643-4

Upgrading and Fixing PCs for Dummies®, 6th Edition
0-7645-1665-5

Photoshop® Elements 2 For Dummies®
0-7645-1675-2

Red Hat Linux Fedora For Dummies®
0-7645-4232-X

Microsoft Windows Me For Dummies®, Millennium Edition
0-7645-0735-4

Troubleshooting Your PC For Dummies®
0-7645-1669-8

Macs® For Dummies®, 8th Edition
0-7645-5656-8

Linux For Dummies, 5th Edition
0-7645-4310-5

VBA For Dummies®, 4th Edition
0-7645-3989-2

C# For Dummies®
0-7645-0814-8

Web Design For Dummies®
0-7645-0823-7

PMP Certification For Dummies®
0-7645-2451-8

AutoCAD® 2005 For Dummies®
0-7645-7138-9

Paint Shop Pro® 8 For Dummies®
0-7645-2440-2

Available in the UK at bookstores nationwide and online at www.wileyeurope.com or call 0800 243407 to order direct

Also available in the United States at www.dummies.com

5860

FOR DUMMIES®

The easy way to get more done and have more fun

TRAVEL

0-7645-3875-6   **0-7645-5478-6**   **0-7645-5455-7**

0-7645-5495-6   **0-7645-5451-4**   **0-7645-5477-8**

0-7645-5494-8   **0-7645-5453-0**   **0-7645-1979-4**

Also available:

Alaska For Dummies®
1st Edition
0-7645-1761-9

Hawaii For Dummies®
2nd Edition
0-7645-5438-7

Arizona For Dummies®
2nd Edition
0-7645-5484-0

California For Dummies®
2nd Edition
0-7645-5449-2

Boston For Dummies®
2nd Edition
0-7645-5491-3

New Orleans For Dummies®
2nd Edition
0-7645-5454-9

Las Vegas For Dummies®
2nd Edition
0-7645-5448-4

Los Angeles and Disneyland
For Dummies® 1st Edition
0-7645-6611-3

America's National Parks For
Dummies® 2nd Edition
0-7645-5493-X

San Francisco For Dummies®
2nd Edition
0-7645-5450-6

Europe For Dummies®
2nd Edition
0-7645-5456-5

Mexico's Beach Resorts For
Dummies® 2nd Edition
0-7645-5781-5

Honeymoon Vacations For
Dummies® 1st Edition
0-7645-6313-0

Bahamas For Dummies®
2nd Edition
0-7645-5442-5

Caribbean For Dummies®
2nd Edition
0-7645-5445-X

France For Dummies®
2nd Edition
0-7645-2542-5

Chicago For Dummies®
2nd Edition
0-7645-2541-7

Vancouver & Victoria For
Dummies® 2nd Edition
0-7645-3874-8

**Available in the UK at bookstores nationwide and online at
www.wileyeurope.com or call 0800 243407 to order direct**

Also available in the United States at www.dummies.com